THESE AREN'T MY PANTS!

The Dumbest and Dimmest From the Files
of *America's Dumbest Criminals*™

With new stories by

Daniel Butler and Alan Ray

Illustrations by Mike Harris

RUTLEDGE HILL PRESS®

Nashville, Tennessee

In loving memory of Douglas C. Jarnagin Jr.

Compilation and editing copyright © 1999 by Rutledge Hill Press®
Stories selected from *America's Dumbest Criminals* and *Wanted! Dumb or Alive* copyright © 1995, 1996 by
    The Entheos Group, L.L.C.
Stories selected from *The World's Dumbest Criminals* copyright © 1997 by Minor Miracle Enterprises, L.L.C.
Stories selected from *Crimes and MisDumbMeanors* copyright © 1998 by Daniel Butler, Alan Ray, and Larry Rose
Stories new to this book copyright © 1999 by Daniel Butler and Alan Ray

The authors have taken great caution to protect the true identity of persons depicted in this book. While the
crimes depicted are true, the names, gender, and races of the criminals depicted, and some details of the
crimes portrayed, may have been changed to safeguard those identities.

Published in Nashville, Tennessee, by Rutledge Hill Press®, Inc., 211 Seventh Avenue North, Nashville,
Tennessee 37219.

Distributed in Canada by H. B. Fenn & Company, Ltd., 34 Nixon Road, Bolton, Ontario L7E 1W2. Distributed
in Australia by The Five Mile Press Pty., Ltd., 22 Summit Road, Noble Park, Victoria 3174. Distributed in New
Zealand by Southern Publishers Group, 22 Burleigh Street, Grafton, Auckland. Distributed in the United
Kingdom by Verulam Publishing, Ltd., 152a Park Street Lane, Park Street, St. Albans, Hertfordshire AL2 2AU.

Typography by Roger A. DeLiso, Rutledge Hill Press®
Text design by Bateman Design

Library of Congress Cataloging-in-Publication Data
Butler, Daniel R., 1951–
     These aren't my pants: the dumbest and dimmest from the files of America's dumbest criminals / with
new stories by Daniel Butler and Alan Ray; illustrations by Mike Harris.
        p.   cm.
     ISBN 1-55853-772-4 (pbk.)
     1. Crime Humor.   2. Criminals Humor.   I. Ray, Alan.   II. Title.
PN6231.C73B88   1999
364.1'092'273—dc21   99-34842
[B]   CIP

Printed in the United States of America
1 2 3 4 5 6 7 8 9—04 03 02 01 00 99

Acknowledgments

To thank all the police officers throughout the world who so graciously gave us their time and stories would fill another book. Yet, there are some officers we have met over the years who have gone above and beyond the call of duty to help us in any way they could. Special thanks to Pete Peterson, Lynn Flanders, Captain Don Parker, Sergeant Dave Glover, Floyd Hyde, Sergeant Larry Mihlon, Gordon Martines, Captain Pete Biegleman, Shaun Chadwick, Chris Stuart, Special Agent Dan Laurila, and a bunch more that after four years, we just can't recall.

Thanks also to Larry Rose, Eric Hazelle, Randy and Spiff, Steve Skelton, Danny Ross, Little Snippy, Keith Destry, Eugenia Harris, Mike Towle, Larry Stone, Bryan Curtis, and many, many more that we met in passing.

And a most special thank-you to God, family, and friends.

Introduction

After years of visiting police stations, conducting interviews by the thousands, and writing four books, we probably don't need to preface this, our fifth book, with much of an introduction. But there are still some things that need to be told up front. For example, we've learned that every officer we've ever spoken with gets lied to on a daily basis. They've been told every story imaginable and some that aren't. From the guy who ran the red light and swore he was color blind, to the speeding woman who once told an officer that her brakes were going out, and she was hurrying home so she wouldn't have an accident. It all boils down to one thing: basic human nature. When people are caught doing something they know is wrong, they scramble to find an excuse for their actions rather than just admit and accept their guilt. It's something we all do.

Of all the excuses told to police on a regular basis, the overwhelming winner of the coveted "Most Told Lie in America" has to be "These aren't my pants."

The first time an officer told us that, we thought he was making a personal comment about his uniform. We just looked at him like he was crazy and asked, "What do you mean?"

"That's what they always say, 'These aren't my pants.'" We still didn't get it.

"Who says that?"

"Suspects, perps, you know, the criminals. They always say they are wearing somebody else's pants."

Now the cop was looking at us like *we* were crazy.

"Why would they say that?"

The officer sighed and explained the facts of life to us. "Look, whether you stop a guy in his car or on foot, you want to establish that he doesn't have a weapon. So one of the first things you do is have him assume the position and then you pat the guy down. I always ask a suspect, 'Do you have any guns, knives, or drugs on you tonight?' The suspect always says, 'No, officer' with this incredible innocence and disbelief. Like 'Who me? carry drugs or a weapon? Why, how dare you!'

"Then I pat him down, and I find a bag of crack, a Saturday night special, or a switchblade knife. When I ask him, 'What's this?' He tells me he's never seen it before. When I explain that it just came out of the pants he is wearing, without hesitating, he always says, 'These aren't my pants.'"

Now we're laughing in disbelief.

"Of course, I always have to ask, 'Well, whose pants are they?' And he always says he borrowed his brother's pants or his cousin's pants, and he had no idea there was all this illegal stuff in the pockets when he put on the pants."

After four years of asking the question, the same answer has come back thousands of times in police departments across the country and around the world. "These aren't my pants" is by far the most common and at the same time the most absurd lie that police officers hear, and they hear it literally every day.

Is there an international conspiracy afoot that incriminates innocent people with guilty borrowed pants? Highly unlikely. Do most people exchange pants with loved ones of exactly the same size? No one that we know does. Do criminals think that most cops just fell off the turnip truck and a really creative lie will totally befuddle them? Yes. Does this particularly stupid lie totally befuddle police officers? No. Never did and never will.

One guy even went further. The officer asked, "Do you have drugs or weapons on your person?"

"No, sir."

The officer patted the guy down and found a few packets of cocaine in the man's jacket. He showed it to the wearer of the jacket, and the guy was furious.

"This isn't my jacket. I borrowed it from my cousin. I can't believe that guy, leaving drugs in his jacket and lending it to me." The guy stripped off the jacket and threw it to the ground in disgust.

The officer continued with his pat down and found a few more packets of cocaine in both of the guy's shirt pockets. "And these would be a surprise to you, as well, I suppose?"

"Yes. I don't believe this. This isn't my shirt. It's my brother's. Gosh." He whipped off the shirt and threw it down.

The officer continued patting down the man's only remaining garment, his pants. You guessed it. The officer found a small pistol and several packets of cocaine.

"These aren't my pants either! They belong to my buddy. I can't believe that they would do this to me." Now the guy was on the street next to the patrol car left wearing only his boxer shorts—well, we're assuming they were *his* boxer shorts. The officer figured he'd better take the guy back to the station to search him any further.

So innocent people beware! Never borrow pants from a stranger, a friend, or a relative. You never know what they may have hidden in the pockets. You just can't trust a friend who would give you the shirt off his back or the pants off his backside.

So now settle in for some *real* humor. We present for your reading pleasure from the dumb criminal "Hall of Shame," the sour cream of the crop of *America's Dumbest Criminals* in *These Aren't My Pants!*

1. Why Didn't I Use Spellcheck?

A thirty-seven-year-old man in Kansas was convicted of forgery and after doing some of his time, was paroled early. When he broke the restrictions of his parole about four months later, he was right back where he started. That's when this guy made the fatal error of thinking that he was "good enough for government work."

The inmate charmed his way into some letterhead stationery from the chaplain and began work on his masterpiece. This was the *tour de force* of a somewhat dismal career. He spent hours at night practicing the governor's signature copied from a Christmas card he had received as a state employee. "May your days be cheery and white . . . Your Governor, Jimmy Thompson Jones." None of his days were cheery, and it never snowed indoors at the prison, but the forger had definitely nailed the guv's John Hancock.

When he presented his early release forms signed and sealed three months later, all his work paid off. He sailed through an uneventful discharge. Until a few weeks later when a secretary assigned to file his paperwork noticed that the governor was now spelling his title, "g-o-v-e-n-o-r." Prison officials were really embarrassed that they had been duped. Well, they were really only embarrassed for about two hours. That's how long it took to go by the forger's house and pick him up again.

2. Positive I.D.

Detective Chris Stewart of the Brunswick (Georgia) Police Department told one of our *America's Dumbest Criminals* field reporters about a robbery suspect he transported back to the scene of the crime for a positive identification:

"We had gotten a call informing us that a woman had had her purse stolen from a shopping complex," Stewart says. "A short time later, we saw a man who fit the description given to us by the victim. So we picked him up and took him back to the scene of the crime."

Stewart explained to the suspect that they were going to take him back to the scene and that when they arrived he was to exit the vehicle and face the victim for a positive I.D. The man in custody heard this when the detective radioed ahead to the officer with the victim. Stewart said he had a man in custody who fit her description of the robber and they would be arriving shortly.

When they arrived at the scene, the suspect did exactly as he had been told. He stepped from the car and looked up at the victim. And before anyone could say anything, he blurted out, "Yeah, that's her . . . that's the woman I robbed."

He has been given a new photo I.D. for his cooperation . . . and this one included a prison number.

3. The Great Train Robbery

(Switzerland)

Only one train makes its way up the steep Alpine slopes to the little storybook village of Wengen, and it's a tiny one, with just enough room in the passenger cars for one seat on either side of the aisle. The Wengen station is also tiny, just a single track and a miniscule platform.

But none of this mattered to the pair of thieves who took the last train up from the valley one evening near sunset. All they cared about was that the train would leave Wengen for the two villages above it on the mountain and then come right back down the mountain, stopping in Wengen just one hour later. That hour would give them just enough time.

Once off the train in Wengen, the dual dummkopfs headed directly for the village toy store. They waited patiently outside until the owner locked up and walked away, then they hurried to break in through a back window. Within ten minutes they were walking back toward the train station with two armloads of expensive model railroad sets.

They boarded the train and smiled broadly at the conductor, who congratulated them on their fine purchases. They laughed as he continued down the aisle into the next car; they had actually pulled it off! Their faces fell, however, when the train reached Interlochen in the valley below and they saw two police officers waiting for them. Their theft shouldn't have been discovered until morning. What had gone wrong?

The detail they had overlooked was a significant date in the toy-store owner's life—his wedding anniversary. He and his wife had boarded another car on the same train for an anniversary dinner in Interlochen. And when his friend, the conductor, offered congratulations on his big sale, he insisted he had sold no trains that day. That's when the conductor, who had watched the men get off empty-handed and reboard with armloads of trains, put two and two together and wired ahead for the police.

The next day's headlines gave appropriate if misleading credit: "Great Train Robbery Foiled by Quick-Thinking Conductor."

4. Stickin' to the Job

Here's the story of the man with the plan to get high and who stuck to his plan. In Baton Rouge, Loggins Taylor had just finished inhaling his last tube of glue. The tube was empty and so were his pockets (and, presumably, his head), but he was still flying with no desire to land. It was the middle of the night and he was desperate.

Idea! Less than three blocks away was the mother ship—a glue factory. Fifteen minutes later Taylor was climbing through a broken warehouse window.

Once inside, he was awestruck. There was more glue here than he'd ever imagined. There was white glue, brown glue, wood glue, metal glue, and airplane glue. His heart pounded. He ran over to a fifty-five-gallon drum of airplane glue and quickly pried the lid off. The fumes rushed out. With both hands on the rim of the barrel he lowered his face and inhaled deeply several times.

He got high.

He got sick.

As his knees buckled, he gripped the barrel tighter to keep from falling. Then he blacked out.

After countless hours, Taylor started coming to. He could hear voices. He opened his left eye. He could see feet, lots of feet. Why wouldn't his right eye open? Where was he and why couldn't he move?

"Just take it easy, pal. We're gonna get you out," came a voice from above.

A policeman, his face turned sideways, lowered himself into Glue Man's view.

"Do you know you pulled a barrel of glue over on yourself?"

"You're stuck to a warehouse floor!" the officer told him, trying hard not to laugh. "Do you know you pulled a barrel of glue over on yourself? You don't look so good."

Taylor couldn't raise his head. The right side of his face was glued tight to the floor, as were his body and both arms. Taylor's legs were crossed and glued to each other. He could hear scraping and picking sounds. And laughter.

It took more than three hours to peel Taylor from the floor. He was arrested, led away in handcuffs, and is now *stuck* in jail.

5. Roll Call for Criminals

Getting a sincere confession of guilt that is admissible in court is often difficult, but when it happens, the sense of satisfaction makes up for all the lean times.

One such case in the Southwest involved two men on trial for armed robbery and assault. You could hear a pin drop in the courtroom as the prosecutor questioned the victim, who, along with her husband, had been robbed at gunpoint. Her voice quavered, and she seemed terribly frightened. Noting this, the prosecutor raised his voice and turned his gaze away from the woman, hoping not to intimidate her any further.

"Are the two men who committed this horrible crime in the courtroom today?" he sternly asked.

At that, the two defendants raised their hands. The courtroom gallery and even the judge snickered. Noticing the two arms in the air, the prosecutor said, "Your honor, may the record show that the defendants raised their hands and have just confessed to the crime."

6. I'm a Criminal Trainee— Please Bear with Me

Job orientation is a time-consuming and difficult task for anyone, but especially for criminals and bank tellers. When a criminal trainee and a bank trainee cross paths, the results can be time-consuming and hilarious.

Two would-be bank robbers were completing their on-the-job training by pulling a bank heist in Virginia Beach, Virginia. They carefully followed step one: case the area and make sure there are no police officers around. Check.

Step two: Approach the bank in a normal manner, and mentally note your escape route. Check and check.

Step three: Put on a mask, remember the bag for the money, and enter the bank with confidence. Check. Check. Check.

Step four: Approach the first teller you see, and ask her to put all the money in the bag. Check.

This is our trainee-meets-trainee moment.

"I'm sorry, sir. This is not my window," the bank teller trainee responded. "I was just getting some more deposit slips for my window."

Uh-oh. This wasn't covered in the criminal trainee's training program.

"Well, uh, take me to your window and get the money from your window," one of the robbers intoned. (Aha, problem-solving skills are a must in a good criminal—give 'im two points.)

"I'm the drive-through teller today, sir, and this is only my third day," the courteous teller countered, still sticking to bank policy by the letter. "You'll have to drive through in a car." Good Trainee.

"Well, uh, can't you just open the door and take me back there?" Credit him with another few points.

"I can't, sir. I'm sorry. They haven't given me the code to open the doors yet." She's cooperating with the robber as best she can, which is bank policy. It's also bank procedure to hit the silent alarm, which she did as she spoke.

The criminal trainee mulled the situation over a bit and then started to run out of the bank, only to remember that he had left his backpack back on the counter. Subtract five points for leaving his personal belongings at the scene, but add ten points for remembering.

6

The criminal trainee jumps in the getaway car and the driver guns the motor. Remembering not to draw attention to themselves, they immediately slow down to the same speed as the traffic around them. Add five points.

Surrounded by squad cars and officers with guns drawn, the criminal trainees put their hands in the air and surrendered. Give these guys, oh, twenty-five points, er, years. The final tally from the judges: bank trainee, 100 points; criminal trainees, minus 45 points. No contest.

7. The Considerate Criminal

Working the front desk at a police station on a Saturday night is one of the most harrowing and maddening jobs imaginable. An officer can easily get behind in his duties when the phone is constantly ringing, prisoners are going in and out of the jail, paperwork is piling up, traumatized victims and witnesses are being herded through the hallways, and the miscellaneous weird people are wandering in. Bob Ferguson, an Indiana cop now retired, was working the desk on just such a night.

"A guy comes in around two o'clock in the morning and says, 'I'm wanted for robbery in Illinois, and I wanted to turn myself in,'" Ferguson says. "It just so happened that the desk I was working was located in Indiana. It was a crazy night, and there were a lot more pressing problems at hand than this guy. We were booking a rather violent guy on narcotics, and I had drunk teenagers throwing up in the lobby. Not to mention a prostitution sting that was processing about three hookers and five johns every ten minutes."

In the confusion, the officer blurted out, "That's all well and good, but I'm kind of busy. Either go to Illinois or come back at six." And at six o'clock on the dot, the man came back and turned himself in.

Bob Ferguson told the man how much he appreciated his punctuality " . . . then I politely booked him."

8. An Ice Guy

Officer Ernest Burt was executing a search warrant for an armed robber and going through the Birmingham, Alabama, house for the third time when he happened to look up and notice that a square of the false ceiling had been moved. Aha!

Right below the ceiling square was a large chest-style freezer, so Burt stepped up onto it to have a look up past the ceiling. Then he thought, *Wait a minute.* He stepped down off the freezer and opened the lid. Gotcha! The man he was looking for was sitting there with his arms wrapped around his legs, rocking back and forth. His skin had turned ashen, and his lips were blue.

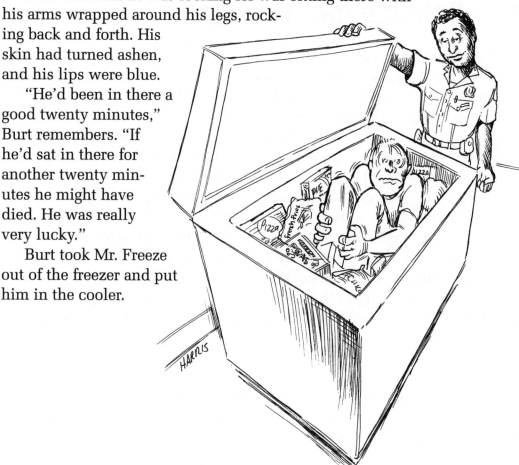

"He'd been in there a good twenty minutes," Burt remembers. "If he'd sat in there for another twenty minutes he might have died. He was really very lucky."

Burt took Mr. Freeze out of the freezer and put him in the cooler.

His skin had turned ashen, and his lips were blue.

9. Trading Places

A friend in need is a friend indeed. But one should be clear about what that need is before you decide to help out. As the guy in this story learned.

After posting bail on charges of shoplifting, two friends in Jonesboro, Arkansas, decided to call their buddy to come down and fetch them from jail. The friend didn't hesitate. Nor did he quite understand what they meant by, *Come down to the jail and get us*. Unaware that his pals had already posted bail and only needed a ride, their friend drove down to the jail at break-neck speed and steered his Jeep Cherokee right through the plate glass doors into the front lobby of the police station to help his buds. After crashing through the front doors, the man then jammed his car into reverse and peeled away from the station. He crashed his Jeep two blocks later and was quickly apprehended by pursuing police.

The two stunned shoplifters were allowed to go on home after police decided they had no idea that their wackazoid friend was going to take them so literally.

So the next time you ask a friend for help, be specific.

10. A Flare for Smuggling

(Puerto Rico)

It takes a pirate's heart and steady nerves to be a drug smuggler. Pepe Orlando had neither.

On his first job he had loaded a small airplane with so much pot that he flew only ten feet off the ground before crashing into the trees at the end of the homemade runway. All Orlando had to do this time, for his second job, was sit out in international waters and wait for the pickup boat to arrive.

Eight hours passed and there was no sign of them. He glanced at his watch—2:00 A.M. Where were they? In another four hours it would be daylight. Orlando didn't want to be sitting on the open ocean in a small boat with eight hundred pounds of marijuana on board. And it was getting foggy.

9

Around 4:30 A.M. visibility was still poor. On the edge of panic, he could make out the silhouette of a boat. It was passing back and forth, probably looking for him. He ran out onto deck.

"Hey! Hey, come back! Over here!" he yelled, jumping up and down and flapping his arms. Then he remembered—the flare gun! He ran to his tackle box, opened the lid, lifted out the tray, and grabbed the gun, which had been tangled up in a bunch of loose fishing gear.

As he ran toward the bow of the boat with gun in hand, Orlando stepped on a wad of fish line hanging from the gun. In that moment his arm was yanked down and, with his finger on the trigger, he fired a flare—right into the cabin. Soon, flames were racing from the cabin onto the deck and leaping ten feet high.

Well, the "pickup boat" by now had turned around and was racing back toward him with sirens blaring. What he had mistaken for his contact ship in the fog was actually the Coast Guard, patrolling international waters for smugglers like Orlando.

11. A Single Thread of Evidence

This story is about three stooges who managed to leave behind a string of evidence connecting them to the crime.

Los Angeles Sheriff's Deputy Charles Cortez responded to a silent alarm at a business on the south side. Cortez noticed broken glass in the alley directly below a window apparently used to gain entry. Shining his flashlight through the window, he could see the entire floor of the sewing shop. His sweeping light landed on an open door on the other side of the room. *Well, I know how they got in and I know how they got out,* he thought to himself. *Now, what'd they get?*

He crept down the alley and turned the corner, where the open door stood. Just then a backup unit pulled up.

"Think they're still in there?" an officer asked.

"No, they're long gone by now," Cortez responded, shining his light up and down the open door.

"The owner's on his way down to see what's missin'," the backup informed him.

Deputy Cortez smiled. "I know what's missin'. A sewing machine. One of those big industrial jobs."

"How do you know that?" the puzzled officer asked.

"Look down here."

Inside the circle of light lay a thread—a heavy duty industrial thread. Its loose end had hooked itself on the rough wooden floor. Officer Cortez began to follow the thread . . . out the door . . . down the alley . . . across the street . . . up another alley. Then through a backyard, up some steps, and under a door. He radioed for assistance.

With policemen surrounding the house, Cortez knocked on the door. It flew open just long enough for the occupant to slam it shut. Officers stormed the house, past the stolen sewing machine in the kitchen. The three men inside were arrested and charged with breaking and entering, burglary, and possession of stolen property.

Caught by a single thread of evidence. Some people can be sew dumb.

12. Drive Around, Please

J. D. Roberts has a colorful past. He has served as a member of the army's elite Delta Force and as a narcotics agent for the Drug Enforcement Agency. He has even worked security for some of Hollywood's top action-adventure celebrities. He now uses his expertise and experience as an instructor at the Federal Law Enforcement Training Center in Brunswick, Georgia. When we asked him if he had ever run into any dumb criminals, one incident immediately came to his mind.

One night Roberts was involved in a raid on a drug house that was doing a brisk business in marijuana sales. He and the other agents were dressed in black "battle" fatigues with "Narcotics Agent" stenciled on them. Local uniformed officers in marked police cruisers also took part in the raid.

Roberts and his team easily entered the house and apprehended the suspect. Several hundred pounds of marijuana were confiscated without incident. Within minutes, the officers were collecting evidence and finishing up at the scene.

As Roberts started out the front door, he noticed a pickup truck parked

The two customers headed back to their pickup, oblivious to the uniformed officers and the two marked police cruisers in the driveway.

behind one of the marked police cruisers in front of the house. Two long-haired individuals got out of the pickup and strolled past the police cruisers parked in the driveway, then walked up to Roberts and his partner.

"Hey man, he still selling pot?"

Roberts looked at his partner, then back at the guy. "Yeah, he is. Just go around and knock on the back door."

"Cool." The two men nodded and walked on.

Roberts watched in amazement as the two individuals sauntered around to the rear of the house. Roberts radioed the officers still inside the house that they had customers at the back door.

The uniformed officers inside quickly hid while one plainclothes detective answered the door. The new customers asked where the old owner was, and the officer explained that the owner had stepped out but that he could help them.

They requested a fifty-dollar bag of marijuana. The officer went to the next room, grabbed a handful from the four hundred pounds of pot they had just confiscated and stuffed it into a plastic bag. The two customers were ecstatic. They thanked the officer for his generosity.

Roberts and his partner were still in the driveway, still wearing the black battle fatigues with "Narcotics Agent" stenciled on their chests, when the two customers headed back to their pickup, oblivious to the uniformed officers and the two marked police cruisers in the driveway.

Finally, Roberts walked up to the two satisfied customers and arrested them. The agents reconfiscated the dope and impounded the pickup—just as another prospective customer pulled up.

Roberts decided this was too easy to ignore. "We moved the two cruisers and started putting the impounded vehicles in the back. We made about fourteen more sales and arrests that night. By the time we were through, the backyard was filled with cars. It was the darnedest impromptu sting I've ever seen."

13. Not Quite Clever Enough

A young man in Pensacola, Florida, was enterprising enough to "acquire" a woman's purse.

He was also clever enough to forge the woman's signature on a note saying: "It's my son's birthday, and I am too sick to get out of bed. Please let my son spend up to five hundred dollars. Thanks very much."

Our young entrepreneur went to a department store and purchased a lot of nice clothes and some really cool shoes. He signed the charge slip, gave the lady his *real* home phone number, and went merrily on his way.

The police were having a nice chat with his *real* mom by the time he got his packages home.

14. Don't You Hate It When That Happens?

It was, of course, another beautiful day in Hawaii, and just an ordinary morning at Honolulu's Ala Moana Shopping Center—until a shopper on a mission came hurtling into one of the mall's specialty shops. Grabbing six expensive leather handbags, he was gone almost before the clerk had time to blink. Now, while most sticky-fingered criminals are notoriously fast on their feet, this guy was creating a breeze, although it was his brakes he needed to be concerned about.

The clerk hit the alarm and guards were right behind the handbag snatcher as he bolted through the mall doors and sprinted toward his car in the parking lot. Just as the chase was warming up, however, it screeched to a halt. The guards were mystified when the dumb criminal stopped beside his car and began to weep.

They had to ask, "Why are you crying? Why didn't you try to drive away?"

Pointing inside the car, the thief tearfully explained, "I left my keys in the ignition and locked myself out."

15. Chauffeur Driven, with Locked-in Freshness

(Germany)

An armored car driver in Hamburg was making his usual round of pick-ups at the end of the day. Pleased that they were ahead of schedule, he whistled as he waited for his assistant to come back with the money bags from the last bank.

Suddenly, a lone gunman appeared. "Step aside, if you know what's good for you."

The driver complied. The gunman stepped into the vault of the armored car, his gun still trained on the driver. When he turned to face the stacks of cash, however, the driver slammed the heavy-gauge steel door shut. *Clank!*

When the assistant returned, the driver casually told him to ride up front, explaining, "I just need to drop something off." Within minutes they were at the police station, where the cops happily took custody of the uninvited cargo.

16. The Dirty Dozen

As the officer was walking out of the Mesa, Arizona, police station, toward his squad car, he was struck by a flying doughnut. Thinking it was another officer just having some fun, he continued toward the lot. Two steps later he was pelted by another doughnut and still another. The last two strikes were thrown with force and, as far as the officer was concerned, the fun was over.

As the officer turned to locate the source of the barrage, another doughnut landed at his feet. Then he spotted a man standing in the shadows holding a small box. "What's your problem?" the officer wanted to know. "Is it the cops or the doughnuts you don't like?"

"Both," the man said dryly, reaching for another missile. Before you could say "dunk a doughnut," the man was arrested, handcuffed, and led into the station.

Inside the booking room, the sergeant took one look at the doughnut-meister and said, "Weren't you released from here not twenty minutes ago?"

"Yeah, so what?" he said.

"So, what are you doin' back in here already?"

"Assault with a weapon on a police officer," the cop interjected.

"What kind of weapon?"

"Doughnuts!" the cop and Idiot said together.

The Sergeant peered into the box and then at the man. "They both look glazed to me," he said. "Okay, let's find a box for this guy." A box, that is, with three walls and a row of bars.

As best the officers could figure, after his release from jail some twenty minutes earlier, the man walked across the street to the doughnut shop, purchased a dozen glazed, walked back across the street, and began throwing them at the first cop he saw. The man was clearly a real (dough) nut case.

**"What's your problem?" the officer wanted to know.
"Is it the cops or the doughnuts you don't like?"**

17. "We Card Because We Care"

In the wee hours of the morning, a convenience store clerk can expect some pretty seedy customers, especially if the store offers a full line of domestic and imported brewskys. So it was no big deal when a young man pulled up to the Sack Rite All Nite Market in Detroit, Michigan, entered the store, and made a beeline to the beer cooler. When he set the two six packs on the counter, he didn't pull out his money or his I.D.—he pulled out a small pistol. He seemed awfully nervous when he said, "Give me the money, and I'm taking this beer."

The old hand behind the counter explained that the money slid into a locked safe on a timer. His entire cash drawer amounted to change for a twenty.

"Fine, give me what you got and . . . and a pack of smokes." The kid was not going to be denied. The old guy tossed $18.93 on the counter, but he was a law-abiding man, so he had to ask.

"I'll need some I.D. for the beer and the cigarettes." The kid reached for the cigarettes, but he was too late. The old man had grabbed the beer and now held the six packs and the cigarettes out of the kid's reach.

"I'm eighteen, you old coot! Give 'em to me." The kid was about to crack.

"Then show me some I.D. and I'll give them to you." The kid stuck the gun right in the old man's face and then pulled out his wallet. He gave the old man his license while he kept the pistol aimed at the old guy's head. The clerk studied the license and then handed it back with the cigarettes and beer. The kid ran out elated.

Of course, an hour later when the cops showed up at his house, he wasn't so elated. Maybe he shouldn't have let the old guy memorize his name and address? Maybe beer and cigarettes *are* really bad for you?

Surgeon General's New Warning: "Stealing cigarettes is more dangerous than smoking them. It can lead to an immediate loss of freedom, causing the death of your social life and any shot at a seat on the Supreme Court."

18. Sorry about That

Officer Dan Newman of the Las Vegas (Nevada) Police Department told America's Dumbest Criminals of an unintentionally funny event that occurred while he was involved in a routine narcotics operation.

"We raided the house of a known drug dealer, and the suspect, upon our entering, went running down a hallway toward the back of the home," Newman said. "Unbeknownst to us, the man was an amputee who usually wore a prosthesis. After a moment or two of hide-and-seek, my partner yelled out from the back of the house, 'Hey, I've got the suspect here in the back bedroom . . . and he's unarmed!' "

It wasn't until Newman and his partner entered the room and saw the prosthetic limb lying on the bed that they realized the true impact of the statement. Even the suspect laughed—but not for long. He was arrested for possession of a controlled substance with the intent of resale.

19. The Sad Saga of Bad Luck Brown

Don Parker of Pensacola also has a string of tales to tell about a dumb criminal who richly earned his nickname of Bad Luck Brown.

"We called him that because this guy had atrocious luck," Parker remembers. "Plus he wasn't all that bright. He was a small-time crook who spent more time in jail than he did out.

"I think the first time I met Bad Luck was in 1978 when I rolled in on a robbery call at a church on Sunday morning during the sermon. Bad Luck had robbed the collection plate. He made good on his escape and got away clean with all the cash, but he dropped his wallet. All we had to do was check his driver's license, then go by his house and pick him up."

But the dumbest crime Bad Luck Brown ever committed was one of his unluckiest, too.

There had been a string of motel robberies in the Pensacola area, and the police had received a tip on where the motel thieves were going to hit next. They always hit the motels around midnight, and the cops planned to be ready for them. Officers were stationed in the motel office and in parked cars around the parking lot. Parker was in the woods across the street with three other officers.

Just past midnight, an old, beat-up station wagon slowly passed the motel. It rattled up the road, turned around, and came back. The vehicle didn't fit the description of the motel robbers, and there was only one person in the car. But the motel thieves might have changed cars, or they might have just been casing the place. All the hidden officers watched it carefully.

The car turned around and came back for a third pass. Don Parker called his sergeant across the street on his walkie-talkie. "You think this might be our guys?"

"Nah, but he sure is interested in something."

The car stopped, a door opened, the driver leaned out and looked around cautiously. The sergeant wasn't taking any chances.

"All units stand by. We've got some activity out here, but I don't know what's going on."

Everybody watched as the mystery man stepped from the car.

"He's on the ground." The man walked around his vehicle and into the light of a street lamp. "He's on the street side of his car now. Okay, I can see him now . . . oh, no!'

Parker didn't like the tone of Sarge's voice. "What? What?"

Sarge radioed back, "It's Bad Luck Brown."

The man eased over to the patch of grass in front of the motel and finally stopped next to a lawn mower that someone had carelessly left out.

Sarge was almost laughing. "I don't believe it. He's stealing the lawn mower!"

Quickly and silently, Bad Luck Brown rolled the lawn mower to his station wagon, dropped the tailgate, and loaded the mower into his car.

"Move in." Sarge gave the command with a bit of resigned frustration in his voice.

The two unmarked cars in the parking lot pulled up to block the station wagon just as Bad Luck started it up. The officers hopped out with drawn guns and called him to freeze. Instead, Bad Luck jumped out and made a run for it. He dashed across the street into the woods—right where Parker was hiding.

"We almost scared him to death when we jumped out. But he was determined to get away this time, so he bolted to the left into the dense

But Bad Luck Brown's luck held true. Just as he was about to disappear, he tripped over one of the officers and sprained his ankle.

undergrowth. Now, a foot chase at night in the woods is the worst. You're running into trees and falling down into gullies. So I decided to try to scare him into stopping.

"'Halt, or I'll shoot!' I fired my gun into the ground. Unfortunately, this didn't have the effect I had hoped for. All the officers hit the ground, but Bad Luck just sped up. It looked like he was going to get away clean."

But Bad Luck Brown's luck held true. Just as he was about to disappear, he tripped over one of the officers and sprained his ankle.

"We never did see the motel thieves that night," Parker says. "But once again, it was our privilege to book Bad Luck Brown. He never ceased to amaze us."

20. Another Run of Bad Luck Brown

Yet another story about the notorious Bad Luck Brown from Pensacola, Florida, involves a time when this dumb criminal's bad luck *almost* changed.

One sunny afternoon Bad Luck Brown entered a busy liquor store with the intent of robbing it. Once he got into the store, however, there were too many people around for a real stickup, so he switched to Plan B. Fishing in his pocket for a piece of paper, Bad Luck scrawled a note to the cashier demanding money.

The cashier read the note and quickly handed over all the money in the drawer. In a flash, Bad Luck was out the door and gone. He seemed to have pulled off his robbery with flawless precision.

Except for one thing.

When the police arrived on the scene, they found the holdup note used in the robbery. When they turned it over, they knew exactly who to go after and where to find him.

Bad Luck Brown had written the note on the back of a letter he had received from his probation officer—complete with his name and address. When police tracked him down at home, they were able to inform him that his streak of bad luck was still intact.

21. Not My Brother-in-Law-to-Be's Keeper

(Canada)

If and when you plan to pull off a burglary, be sure to keep track of where your relatives are. There's nothing more embarrassing than running into members of your own family while you're committing a crime—unless it's running into your future in-laws while you're in the act of stealing their neighbor's stuff.

George McMillan was sitting in his Toronto apartment, watching TV and minding his own business, when a familiar face walked by his back door. George thought idly that the passerby looked a lot like his sister's boyfriend. Then the guy strolled back by, pulling a ten-speed bicycle, and George was sure: It was his brother-in-law-to-be, all right.

George assumed he was simply borrowing a bike from a friend—until the neighbor started yelling. Then George realized he had just witnessed a crime, and he knew exactly who the criminal was!

"I'll get your bike back," George told the frantic neighbor. He knew exactly where to go. Sure enough, the dummy-in-law-to-be was at home readjusting the seat of his newly acquired bicycle. With loot and culprit in tow, George returned to his apartment, where his neighbor and the Mounties met him. The thief went from possible in-law to outlaw.

22. There Will Be an Additional Charge

One time while processing new prisoners at the downtown Birmingham, Alabama, jail, Capt. Arnetta Nunn was frisking a large woman for drugs and weapons when she touched what felt like a gun handle in the woman's girdle.

"What's that?" Nunn asked.

"That's a gun," the woman casually said. "But don't tell anybody I've got it."

"Don't tell anybody? Ma'am, I'm a police officer. I *have* to tell somebody."

Luckily, the woman was just dumb and not crazy.

"Are you right- or left-handed?" Nunn asked.

"I'm right-handed," the woman said.

"All right, then, with your left hand, reach into your girdle. Using your thumb and index finger, very slowly remove the gun from your pants."

In the next moment the officer was holding a fully loaded .38-caliber revolver. To go with the woman's original charges, she was charged with trying to smuggle a weapon into a correctional facility.

Captain Nunn recounts, " 'Don't tell anybody'? Why do I get all the fools?"

DUMB CRIMINAL QUIZ NO. 53

How well do you know the dumb criminal mind?

A man was sentenced to ninety days in jail for disorderly conduct, a fairly minor offense that carried a fairly minor sentence. While he was in jail did he . . .

a) take a matchbook correspondence course in VCR repair?

b) whittle a replica of the White House to scale out of soap?

c) invent a straw that you could eat chili with?

d) plot and execute a difficult escape?

Answers (a), (b), or (c) could all be rationalized as a good use of his time, but a criminal in Rhode Island chose (d). For eighty-eight laborious days he toiled over his plans, and then he finally accomplished his feat. On the next-to-last day of his ninety-day sentence, he made good his escape—for about five minutes. He was then re-arrested and sentenced to eighteen months.

23. Aliens Stole My Brain!

Years ago the police in the Boston area were having a scanning problem. Specifically, police scanners were in the wrong hands. When the bad guys can listen to everything the good guys say, serving warrants, raiding drug houses, and catching crooks in the act becomes that much harder.

These officers took a cue from Orson Welles and his famous *War of the Worlds* radio broadcast. Only theirs went out over a "police only" frequency.

The dispatchers sent out an alert of a "massive alien invasion over the South Downs." They described huge spaceships and warned of possible annihilation for mankind. Actually, the officers were parked in their cars watching an empty field. Within moments, though, that empty field was filled with strange creatures.

When the police flipped on their headlights, they gasped. Before them were drug dealers, petty crooks, and otherwise law-abiding citizens who were illegally monitoring police communications on restricted frequencies. The cops confiscated drugs, made arrests, got people with outstanding warrants, and gave a stern lecture on the use of scanning equipment. But they all had one chance to "phone home" from the station downtown.

24. Grind This, Pal

(Italy)

Organ grinders with trained monkeys are a fixture of literature, art, and opera. There never were a large number of people practicing the profession—today there are almost none. But in Brindisi, a young man recently took up the craft, much to the delight of the children and tourists. He added great local color to the town square.

At night, however, the organ grinder and his monkey had another life. The organ grinder would force his hairy companion to dive into mailboxes and bring out handfuls of envelopes. The trick also worked with bank night depositories and bags of money.

Local police were stumped. In each case, there was no forced entry, no sign of entry at all. No fingerprints and no clues. The organ grinder was getting rich, but the monkey was getting ticked.

The monkey had had enough. When the organ grinder sent the monkey through a vent in a restaurant to raid the cash register, the monkey saw his chance. The organ grinder waited below the vent for what seemed like forever. Still no monkey. Finally, the little monkey appeared in the vent to a torrent of epithets from his master. One little hand held out a wad of cash, then the other little hand produced a hand gun he had found behind the cash drawer. *Blam!* The little monkey nailed his master in the arm and skittered away.

The organ grinder tried to convince the police that he had stopped the robber and struggled with him to get the money and a nasty flesh wound. That's when the monkey returned with the gun. The organ grinder screamed and tried to run, sure that the monkey would finish him off. But the police disarmed the little fella. The organ grinder is still doing time grinding rocks instead of tunes, and the monkey works in school outreach as the police force's mascot.

The monkey had had enough.

25

25. Parting Is Such Street Sorrow

Lieutenant Mary Meyers of the Akron, Ohio, Police Department sat in the parking lot directly across the street from the all-night gas station/market. An increasing number of "drive-offs" had been reported at this location lately, and it was felt that the presence of a marked unit in the area would deter such crime. For your average criminal, a squad car across the street from your target would probably send up a red flag. But when you're one of America's dumbest . . . well, that's why he's in this book.

Officer Meyers watched as the man with the rusty old Lincoln nervously looked around while returning the nozzle to the gas pump. A quick glance over each shoulder (he should have looked across the street), and he jumped into his car and peeled out of the station. Meyers whipped out after him. She lit him up with the blue lights and hit the siren. The chase was on.

About a mile down the road the suspect took a hard right onto what Officer Meyers described as "an old hard dirt road with a surface like a washboard." She was having a lot of trouble seeing because of all the dust being kicked up by the suspect's car. Her patrol car was taking quite a beating on that rickety, old road so she began to slow down considerably—it wasn't worth compromising her safety or the public's over a stolen tank of gas. The suspect's vehicle was far enough ahead of her now on smooth pavement, so it appeared he may just get away with it. And he might have *if* he hadn't decided to take another hard right turn. A fatal decision. A near 90-degree turn at sixty miles an hour. It was more G's than the old Lincoln could withstand. The tires broke loose in mid-turn and, on two wheels now, the car slid sideways off the road, ripping across a back yard that lay about six feet below the lane. Still doing around fifty, the Lincoln straightened out, shot straight across the yard, rocketed up the other bank, and crash-landed in the middle of the street. Upon impact, the car broke into two separate pieces. The rust and dust were still settling as Officer Meyers arrived on the scene. She exited her patrol car and through tears of almost uncontrollable laughter, promptly arrested the dazed, albeit, uninjured driver still sitting in the front half of his car.

"I really had a hard time keeping my composure," Officer Meyers told us. "Every time I looked at that old rust bucket sitting there in two pieces . . . I just cracked up!" She added that when the tow truck driver arrived, he had to radio for a second tow truck to pick up the back half.

So for about ten bucks worth of gas, the man was charged with failure to pay, felony evasion, and reckless driving. All told, the fines reached about $2,000, and the man spent a nice little stretch in jail. Not to mention the cost of his car.

I wonder if the driver ever realized that in actuality he ended up paying about $200 a gallon for the same gas that was too high to pay a dollar for? Just think, he could've used that two grand to build that two-car garage he's gonna need when he gets his *Lincolns* back.

26. Stealing Home!

It was the early 1990s and baseball would never again be played in the old Comiskey Park in Chicago. Cheering crowds believed they had seen the last play at the historic stadium. Not long afterward, however, two dumb but nostalgic baseball fans decided to try one last half-inning on their own.

The two men climbed onto the field at night with the intention of stealing the old home plate for a souvenir. Silently, they crept over the field with their shovels, peering nervously over their shoulders, jumping at the slightest sound, but determined to obtain their prize. What a collectible!

But surely they paused for just a moment to contemplate, to look up at the silent, shadowy stands and hear the cheers once more. They must have gazed down at that old plate, envisioning all the runs that had been scored from that spot, all the great batters who had stood there, all the great pitchers who had hurled the ball toward home.

They paused for just a moment to wonder how they were going to get away with their crime now that two security guards were running toward them on the field.

There was a frantic rundown play between third and home before the two thieves were captured for the unofficial final out at the old Comiskey Park.

27. Honesty Is the Best Policy

(Belgium)

A man suspected of robbing a jewelry store in Liège was arrested, booked, and arraigned for trial, all the while protesting that he was innocent.

Finally, his day in court arrived, and the man had a chance to prove his claim. To everyone's astonishment, he produced an ironclad alibi, which the police later confirmed:

"Your honor, I could not have robbed that jewelry store because at *that* time on *that* day, I was breaking into a school across town."

You know what happened next. Police arrested him for breaking into the school.

28. He Got a Charge out of It

The General Services Administration (GSA) has its own criminal investigators to handle reports of crimes in federal buildings. One afternoon they received a report that a man was attempting to steal an air conditioner from outside one of the federal buildings in Atlanta. GSA investigators hurried to the scene, but as it turned out they could have taken their time—because they were dealing with a dumb criminal.

This particular genius was using a huge meat cleaver to cut through the various hoses, pipes, and other lines connected to the air conditioner. The cleaver was metal. All metal. No wooden or plastic handles on this baby. It was 100 percent metallic, and it was doing a good job cutting the copper pipe and rubber hoses. Of course, air conditioners run on electricity, and the heavy cleaver did a good job of cutting the electrical lines as well. It also did a good job of conducting the electricity from the electrical lines into the would-be thief, who lit up like a Christmas tree.

When the GSA investigators arrived, they found the dazed and slightly singed suspect lying on the ground, his eyes still rolling around in his head. He offered no resistance, but he made it clear he wanted nothing more to do with that air conditioner.

The heavy cleaver did a good job of cutting the electrical lines as well.

29. My Name's Steve, and I'll Be Your Dealer Today

Giving one more glance around the crowded bar, Agent Johnson (who's still working undercover in the South somewhere and shall therefore remain otherwise nameless) yawned and sighed. He was working undercover narcotics and had wanted to bust a certain known dealer that night. But the dealer had never appeared. Whatever the reason, the whole evening had been a colossal waste of time.

The agent was about to pay his tab and go home when a man slid onto a stool next to him and struck up a conversation. Johnson began to suspect that this man might also have connections to the drug culture.

"Hey, man," he asked his new acquaintance, "you know where I can buy some reefer?"

The man said evenly, "As a matter of fact, I do." After a few more minutes' conversation, Agent Johnson understood that the man was referring to himself.

By now Johnson was wondering, *How am I going to find out who this guy is?* He had to have a name in order to serve a warrant. And he had to serve a warrant, because to arrest the man on the spot would jeopardize the entire operation and blow his cover as well.

The new suspect didn't feel comfortable selling drugs in the bar, so they strolled outside into the parking lot. The man led Johnson to his car. The agent was still racking his brain, trying to think of a way to learn the dealer's name.

Then the dealer himself solved the problem.

"Listen, man, it's nothing personal," he said. "But I don't know who you are. I mean, you could be a cop for all I know. So can I see your driver's license?"

With a rush of relief, the agent pulled out a phony driver's license that he used for undercover work. And then he said, "Hey, I don't know who you are either. Can I see *your* driver's license?"

"Sure," the dealer replied.

The agent looked at his license, memorized the information, and made the buy. About a week later, the dealer was treated with a personalized warrant for his arrest signed by his new friend, Johnson.

30. You Snooze, You Lose

Detective Dennis Larsen tells us about a pair of high achievers who were fired from their jobs at a Las Vegas, Nevada, car rental agency. Disgruntled, they plotted to rob the manager. They knew the exact time and bank at which the manager made a nightly deposit. So they hatched a plan whereby one of them would lie in wait with a gun and the other would cruise the area on getaway standby.

The first conspirator (we'll call him Heckle) dropped his partner (Jeckle) at the bank about thirty minutes before the manager was due. Jeckle donned a ski mask and took his place behind a Dumpster with a commanding view of the night depository. Heckle set about inconspicuously driving around the block at three miles an hour.

Jeckle waited. Heckle drove. Jeckle got drowsy. Heckle drove. Jeckle fell asleep. The manager made his deposit. Heckle drove. Jeckle slept. Heckle drove.

Police responded to a report of a man sleeping in a ski mask behind a Dumpster and a car out of gas nearby.

31. The Half-Naked Truth

On a cold winter's night in rural Illinois, the brainier folks snuggled under warm covers. One dummy, an armed robber, thought it would be a perfect night to "make some money" at an out-of-the-way tavern with few customers but plenty of cash on hand.

The robber drove out into the cold night, parked his vehicle alongside the tavern, grabbed his shotgun, pulled on a ski mask, and boldly strolled into the tavern. Three minutes later, his business was done.

Moments later, after the bartender had called police, a man walked in wearing only underwear, sat down at the bar, and ordered a cup of coffee. When the state police arrived, the bartender mentioned that the half-naked man looked like the robber. The officer looked over at him. Even if the cool guy was innocent, the officer was curious why anyone would be running around almost naked in twenty-degree weather.

"I lost my clothes playing poker and came here to drown my sorrows."

"Aliens abducted me and probed me with strange surgical devices."

"A gang jumped me to get my trendy team jacket and expensive sneakers."

The officer patiently waded his way through the stories before the man finally confessed: "The robbery went just like I planned it. Nobody got hurt and nobody could identify me, and then I got back to my car. That's when I realized I had locked the car and left the keys in the ignition."

"But how did you lose your clothes?"

The naked numbnut figured if he started down the road, the police would spot him and question him. But maybe if he deposited his clothes, weapon, and stolen loot in the dumpster near his "getaway" car, he might get away unnoticed. The police found the dummy's clothes, shotgun, and cash right where he said they'd be.

"I lost my clothes playing poker and came here to drown my sorrows."

32. Taken for a Ride

Let's take a minute and flash back to the good ol' seventies.

Working undercover narcotics back then was a little more informal than it is today. A "flower child" mentality still prevailed in certain segments of the drug scene. This allowed for spontaneous and often funny moments.

At Purdue University, three undercover narcotics agents had been assigned to look for possible links to the drug culture. While cruising near the campus late one summer afternoon, they came upon a bearded hitchhiker with sun-bleached, shoulder-length hair. Peace signs adorned his Levi jacket and his army surplus backpack. Not having anything really pressing at the moment, the officers pulled over their Volkswagen van and offered the man a lift.

"Far out, man," he said, climbing in.

Soon the three of them were chatting with their new passenger as he babbled on about Nixon, Vietnam, and how much fun it would be to get high. Before long he had pulled out a fat marijuana cigarette.

"If you guys want to score really big," he offered, "I know just the place."

This was too easy. The agents eagerly agreed to take the man wherever he wanted to go. He'd make the buy, and they'd make the bust.

No one was home at the first house they tried. Their luck didn't get any better until the passenger remembered a dealer in another town. Would they drive the extra fifty miles to get the drugs?

"Sure, why not?" they said. After all, they were just out looking for a good time. Then, on a lark, they decided to pick up a friend of theirs, the crime analyst for their narcotics unit.

Now Roger, the analyst, didn't fit in with the rest of the group, who were all clad in leather jackets and sporting long hair and beards. Roger was clean-shaven, with a short, military-style haircut, and wore a tie and glasses. The passenger didn't seem to notice. He continued his friendly banter as he gave directions.

Before long the merry band of five was on its way in search of drugs, which the hitchhiker was readily able to supply. Finally, after a day of wandering from house to house, increasing their illegal stash at each stop, it was time for all good things to come to an end. Telling their newfound friend that they had some place they wanted to take him, the agents decided to wrap up the evening and drove him to the police station.

"This will be your new home for a while," the agents said to the passenger, who by this time was somewhat stoned and obviously flabbergasted. All he could do was shake his head as they explained they were police officers and that he was under arrest.

33. Hi, I'm Working My Way through Prison

Chief Ray Kaminskas of the Crystal River Police Department in Florida believes that every day in some way opportunity knocks, but it's up to you to answer the door. One of his officers took this saying to heart and found that the chief couldn't have been more right.

A local drug dealer decided to borrow a selling tradition from the folks at Amway and Avon and pedal his wares door-to-door. Like any vacuum salesman or Fuller Brush man, the dealer wasn't making a whole lot of sales with his new technique, but he was making a lot of new friends. His salesman's spiel must have gone something like this:

"Hi, I'm Tom Smith, and I'm working my way through prison. If you buy an ounce of pot from me today, you will put me over my two-pound quota and I'll qualify for a felony! Today and today only, as a bonus for helping me reach my goal, I'll throw in rolling papers and a disposable lighter at absolutely no extra charge to you!"

The wandering Johnny Potseed made his last sales call of the evening at the home of an off-duty Crystal River police officer. The chief's words rang in his ears as the doper laid on the hard sell. The cop definitely made the door-to-door doper's day—by giving him a free pair of metal bracelets and confiscating all the product and samples that the kid was carrying. It turns out the doper had done well with magazine subscriptions as a child and just figured the same approach would work with a controlled substance.

34. Debriefing

Bank robbing is one of those high-pressure professions. Stress certainly is part of the job—and one, we presume, that is not covered in the group medical plan.

Not all bank robbers are up to the task. Take the case of the Charlotte, North Carolina, bank robber, fleeing from the scene of his crime. In a brilliant flash of inspiration, he stripped to his underwear, figuring there was no way he could be identified by specific articles of clothing. Next, of course, he would stuff the large bundle of heisted greenbacks down the front of his underwear.

His plan seemingly worked. No one came forward to identify the robber. Someone, however, *did* call the police and point him out as the "sweaty man wearing nothing but strangely bulging underwear." The officers report that after the man was "debriefed," the money was recovered.

35. The Age of Asparagus

Here's a man who confuses his legal rights with a popular musical group from the seventies.

One Friday night, Officer Jack Dedmon was booking a "hippie-looking" burglary suspect in Fresno, California. The space cadet was cooperative until Officer Dedmon attempted to fingerprint him.

"*I know my rights, man!*" he protested loudly. "*I don't have to let you take my fingerprints!*"

Okay, the guy wasn't the sharpest knife in the drawer, but he did have to be printed.

"*I know my rights and I don't have to!*" he shouted.

Dedmon was puzzled. "Why won't you let me take your fingerprints?"

"*Because my mama told me I didn't have to, and I'm standin' on the fifth dimension!*"

Obviously.

36. Plastic Dummy

A Cincinnati woman was waiting in an ATM line when a young man grabbed her purse and ran away. As he ran, however, he dropped a VISA card.

The officer responding to the call thought the card was probably stolen, but he ran a check on it anyway. Lo and behold, VISA said the card had not been reported stolen and supplied a photo from surveillance-cam footage of the last man who had used the card. His appearance matched the description given by the victim perfectly, right down to the clothes he was wearing.

The officer was astonished, but the dumb criminal wasn't. "I was wondering when you'd come for me," he told his arresting officers when they showed up at his door.

37. The Running of the Fools

(Spain)

Pamplona is famous for its Running of the Bulls, an annual festival in which wild herds of people run through the streets of town chased by charging bulls. Now, thanks to a couple of dumb criminals, Spain adds to that distinguished event "the Running of the Fools."

Enrico Cortez and his brother Miguel were thieves with a plan to rob a merchant who had been collecting money for a sick child. Knowing the store would be closed for the festivities, the Cortezes figured they would break in during the festivities and escape by stepping out into the street and blending in with the milling crowd. What could be easier?

Everything was going exactly as planned. They quickly entered the targeted shop and found the locked metal box containing the cash. Then came the unexpected sound of rattling keys at the front door. With no time to think and nowhere to hide, the brothers grabbed the money box and ran. And run they did—out the back door, onto the street, and directly into the path of a crowd of frantically screaming people.

"El Toro! El Toro is coming!" came the collective shouts. Too late. The

two wild-eyed brothers were mowed down by running hordes of people. Twenty seconds later, the bruised and confused Miguel watched his big brother Enrico rise unsteadily to his feet, only to be hooked by the seat of his pants on the horns of a very enraged bull. He was tossed about fifteen feet into the air where he spun in awkward gyrations. Gravity pulled him back down headfirst on the unforgiving cobblestone, just in time for the second wave of runners following the bull to trample him again.

After the dust settled, the heartless pair were scraped up and turned over to the police. As for the trampled money box, it had miraculously landed in the doorway of the merchant who had been collecting for the child.

As you can see, the pain in Spain falls mainly on the brain.

"El Toro! El Toro is coming!" came the collective shouts. Too late.

38. It Seemed Like a Good Idea at the Time

When William S. Meyers was with the Anne Arundel County Police Department in Maryland, he heard about a couple of less-than-intellectual giants who decided they would rob an automatic teller machine.

Of course, our crooks knew they couldn't just walk up to a machine, point a gun at it, and demand money. They knew ATMs are protected by alarms and surveillance cameras: any attempt to break into the machine would likely result in a whole bunch of cops showing up. But they were going to avoid all that because they had a foolproof plan. They would steal the entire machine.

The scheme was simplicity itself. Late at night they would attach a chain to the ATM, then fasten the chain to the back bumper of their pickup. When everything was secure, they would hit the gas, jerk the machine right out of the wall, and be gone long before the cops arrived on the scene.

They picked a dark and rainy Friday night when the streets were deserted and the ATM was likely to have a fresh supply of money for the weekend. They quietly wrapped the chain around the machine, then tied it securely to the back bumper of their truck. The driver pushed the pedal to the floor, and the pickup shot forward.

Because the ATM appeared to be mounted securely, the would-be thieves had used a heavy chain to make sure it would stand the strain. Unfortunately for them, they had not used a heavy-duty pickup. When the chain snapped taut, it ripped the back bumper right off.

With alarm bells ringing, sirens yelping, and strobe lights flashing, the panic-stricken crooks didn't even slow down, and soon they were far away. Although shaken by the experience, they were happy to escape and even laughed at the thought of the cops arriving to find them long gone.

What they didn't realize was that when the rear bumper was torn off the license plate went with it. It didn't take long for the responding officers to obtain a registration, along with names and addresses. Within the hour, they were adding two more dumb criminals to the large selection already housed in the county jail.

39. The World's Fastest Cop

It was a typical cold night outside Fairbanks, Alaska, when Officer Mike Smith noticed a car's headlights peering out from a roadside snowbank—a fairly routine sight in Alaska in the winter. Smith lit a flare and started down to give assistance. Then he realized that the inebriated driver had no idea he was wedged into an embankment. He must have thought he was in a heck of a blizzard because he was staring intently at the snow ahead, driving for all he was worth. His foot was on the gas, and the rear tires were spinning as the car slid slightly from side to side.

Smith couldn't resist: He positioned himself just behind the driver's side window and began to run in place. He rapped on the glass with his flashlight.

The driver did a perfect double take and sped up; so did Smith. Sprinting in place, Smith again tapped the window. This time the driver relented and "stopped" his car.

When the driver's case came before the magistrate, the judge asked, "Are you guilty as charged?"

The man looked forlornly at the judge and said, "I must be, your honor. The officer chased me down on foot!"

40. The Light at the End of the Tennie

Just outside Lawrence, Kansas, police were called to an all-night market that had just been robbed. A male Caucasian had brandished a weapon and demanded money from a store employee. After stuffing the money into his pants pocket, he fled down the street.

Units in the area responded quickly to the alarm. Within moments, two officers on patrol had spotted a man running behind some houses in a nearby neighborhood. Certain that they had the right man, they gave chase on foot.

But the suspect wasn't really worried. It was dark, he was a very fast runner, and he knew the neighborhood like the back of his hand. He was sure he would have no trouble eluding the cops.

It didn't take long for the fleet-footed suspect to leave the first pair of

The pursuing officers had just followed the lights.

officers behind, but he was surprised when more officers quickly joined in the chase. Each time the thief would elude one officer, he would be spotted by another. The crook couldn't understand it; he was using his best moves.

At last there were too many officers on the scene who apparently could see quite well in the dark. Our suspect looked frustrated and surprised when he was finally captured.

But he was even more surprised and frustrated once the police told him how they knew where he was all the time. He really hadn't been hard to follow at all, thanks to advanced technology.

The pursuing officers had just followed the lights. Not the infared lights used for night vision, but the red lights on the heels of the suspect's high-tech tennis shoes—the ones that blinked on and off every time his feet hit the ground.

41. Psychic Inability

This short little story happened in Modesto, California.

Donovan Jackson was in big trouble. He had been arrested and charged with two counts of selling drugs. A class-A felony. Federal prosecutors decided they would offer him a plea bargain. That is to say, if Jackson would cooperate with authorities and give them the names of the others involved in the suspected drug ring, he would receive a maximum sentence of only two years in prison.

After listening to their offer, Jackson said he needed to make a phone call to get some professional advice. That was understandable considering he was facing heavy jail time if he refused. So he made the call. But he didn't call his attorney as one might suspect in such a situation: he called his *psychic*! The psychic told him not to worry, there was no way he was going to spend a day in prison. So he turned down the Fed's offer.

I suppose even Nostradamus had his off days. As it turns out, his decision and his psychic were both terrible. Jackson was convicted of the charges in federal court and now faces ten years in prison.

The next call he makes will be collect.

42. Gotta Match?

Capt. Mike Coppage, one of our Birmingham, Alabama, police acquaintances, told America's Dumbest Criminals of a strange domestic violence call that came in from a frantic woman. It seems she and her husband had been having quite a bit of trouble lately, and things had escalated to the point that her husband was now threatening to kill himself and her.

Police units and a S.W.A.T. team were immediately dispatched to the address, where they heard shouts and threats coming from inside the house. "I'll do it! Don't think I won't . . . 'cause I will. I'll kill myself!" Obviously, things were really getting out of control in there. When the police negotiator got the man on the phone, Coppage's crew realized just how bad it was.

"I'm gonna kill myself," the man threatened. "I've doused myself and the house with gasoline, and I'm gonna set myself on fire right now."

"Hey, we can work this out, Ronnie," the negotiator told him. "Come on outside. Let's talk about it."

"There ain't nothin' left to talk about, man. It's over."

Then the man set the phone down. There was an eerie silence.

Captain Coppage looked at the negotiator. He nodded his head. It was time to send in the S.W.A.T. team. The captain was about to give the signal to storm the house when suddenly the man was back on the line.

"Hey, y'all still there?" the man asked.

"Yeah, we're here."

"You got any matches?"

"Matches? You want matches?"

"Yeah, matches. You know, the kind you light? I can't find any in here."

"Let me look," the quick-thinking negotiator told him. "Yeah, I've got a book of 'em right here, Ronnie, but you're going to have to come out here and get them. I can't come in there."

"All right," Ronnie said. "I'll be right out."

True to his word, the man walked outside, where he was quickly apprehended.

43. D.O.B.

Officer Glen Biggs of the Knoxville (Tennessee) Police Department had a close encounter of the dumb criminal kind when he was booking a suspect on a narcotics violation. A simple transcript of the interrogation tells it all:

    Biggs: "What is your D.O.B.?"

    Dumb Criminal: "What's a D.O.B., man?"

    Biggs: "When's your birthday?"

    Dumb Criminal: "May 5th."

    Biggs: "What year?"

    Dumb Criminal: "Every year, man."

DUMB CRIMINAL QUIZ NO. 10,321

How well do you know the dumb criminal mind?

In Indianapolis, Indiana, Bobby Swope broke into his neighbor's house and stole a gun. Was he caught because . . .

a) He was arrested for DUI and the weapon found under the seat was traced to the rightful owner?

b) The gun didn't work, so he broke back into the house to return it?

c) The phony gun dealer he tried to sell it to was an undercover cop?

The correct answer is (b). B-lieve it or not, when Swope discovered that the weapon didn't work, he broke back into the house to return it. That's when he was caught by the police!

---

44. cixelsyD revirD eraweB

(England)

A traffic officer patrolling just outside of Chester spotted a car going well over the posted speed limit. He tailed the car for more than a mile—long enough to clock its exact speed. The driver never slowed down, until the officer pulled him over. Then he seemed genuinely bewildered.

"Didn't you know you were doing fifty-two in a twenty-five speed zone?" the officer asked.

"Oh, no, sir," he answered. "I respectfully disagree. I was doing fifty-two in a fifty-two-mile-per-hour zone."

The officer finally established that this gentleman suffered from dyslexia. He was genuinely reading the speed limit backward and obeying it to the letter. The officer let the driver go with a warning and a bit of advice: When in doubt about the speed limit, always choose the lower number if you have a tendency to reverse the digits!

45. Knife Girls Finish Last

After pumping ten dollars' worth of gas, Susan Shriver of Mattoon, Wisconsin, pulled her car up by the front door of the all-night gas station and market. Once inside, she went over to the cooler and picked up two cases of cold beer. She hefted them onto the counter.

"That'll be twenty-eight dollars and eight cents," the clerk informed her.

The woman dug around in her purse for a moment, then told him that she'd left her money in the car. The clerk watched as she rummaged around in her front seat. A few seconds later she emerged with a ski mask on her head (not over her face, *on her head*) and re-entered the store. She pulled the ski mask down over her face and whipped out a knife.

"I'm takin' this beer!" she exclaimed, "and don't try to stop me or I'll cut you up!"

The clerk, realizing that the women's straw didn't go all the way to the bottom of her glass, asked, "Are you gonna pay for the gas?"

She was stunned. "Say what? I'm stealin' the beer. Why would I pay for the gas?"

While Shriver was carrying the beer out to the car, the clerk hit the hot line button under the counter that dials 911. When the woman came back for the second case of beer, she noticed a collection jar on the counter. She lifted up her ski mask and peered inside. Without hesitation she grabbed the jar, set it on top of the second case of beer, got into her car, and pulled away. A pretty good haul—darned near forty dollars worth of stuff!

Well, she barely made it out of the parking lot before she was surrounded by the local cops. She was arrested and charged with felony armed robbery. Forty dollars might not seem like much, but when you spread it out over five years, it's even less.

"I'm takin' this beer!" she exclaimed, "and don't try to stop me or I'll cut you up!"

46. Out of the Frying Pan, into the Line of Fire

It was a moonless, balmy Pensacola, Florida, night, and there he was—a criminal fleeing on foot and feeling pretty good about his chances of making the next street and therefore slipping into the anonymous darkness.

Suddenly, behind him, came the screech of tires and the unmistakable flash of a police cruiser's lights. What to do? He knew the neighborhood well, having cased most of the houses during his career.

The next house on the left, he thought. *It's just that little old lady living alone. I'll bust in there. She won't be hard to deal with. After the heat's off, I'll help myself to her jewelry box and get out.*

He ran to the front porch and heaved himself against the front door. No luck. Again he rammed the door with his shoulder. Again it didn't budge. A step back, a swift kick, and the door finally flew open. He slipped inside the door and closed it.

Did they see me? If they did, I'll just take the old bag hostage.

From the darkened hallway came the distinctive sound of a twelve-gauge, pump-action shotgun being readied for use. A southern lady's delicate voice rose quite calmly from the shadows: "You might have better luck with those policemen outside, young man. If you move anywhere but out that door, I'll just have to blow your head off."

The patrolmen who had seen the idiot burglar-to-be enter the house reported that his exit was much faster and that he seemed rather relieved to see three policemen there to save him.

47. Door-to-Door Crime Buster

An officer in Savannah developed a bold but simple approach to drug busts. This uniformed patrolman would walk up to a known drug house or party and knock on the door. The occupant would answer the door with almost the same greeting every time. In fact, the similarity of the incidents was astounding. Each person reacted in almost the same manner every time the officer tried this very direct approach to crime busting. It went something like this:

Dumb Criminal opens door. "Uh . . . hello, officer. Is the music too loud? Did someone complain?"

"Nah, I just wanted to buy a bag of dope."

"Huh?"

"Do you have a bag of dope I can buy?"

"Well . . . but you're a cop."

"So? Can't I buy a bag of dope?"

"But . . . "

"Hey, I'm cool, okay?"

"Cool. Wait right here."

A minute later, the dumb (and about-to-be arrested) criminal would be selling the uniformed officer a bag of dope.

The bold officer made so many arrests this way that he was promoted to detective in record time. Almost all of his arrests were pleaded out without a trial because the criminals didn't want to admit in court they had sold drugs to a uniformed cop at their own apartment.

48. Beeper-to-Beeper Love

People are very attached to their beepers, especially when such devices are suddenly—and illegally—detached from their person.

A young professional in a small New York town was robbed and, among other things, the thief got his beeper. This was no cheapo beeper; this was the deluxe, voicemail-get-the-news-sports-messages-take-out-the-garbage type of beepers that run upwards of forty bucks a month. After two beeperless days of cold turkey, the yuppie called the cops with a plan.

The cops played along. The victim had his sister call the beeper and leave a message for the dumbo: "I really enjoyed meeting you, and I sure hope you're going to call me. My number is 555-7897. This is Rhonda. Call me, cutie." She led him on by saying that if he called in the next half hour, they could meet and have a grand time.

Sure enough, the dummy took the bait and called "Rhonda" back. With the officers calling the shots, she arranged a meeting on a nearby street corner. The thief described what he'd be wearing and hinted he would have a special surprise for her.

Four patrol cars lay in wait with six officers on foot when the taxi approached the corner. Hopping out of the cab was the man wearing the khakis and blue shirt the thief had described over the phone. Before he could introduce himself, the cops had him down, kissing the sidewalk instead of Rhonda.

As it turned out, the stolen beeper was the least of the bungler's problems. His "surprise" was a pound of marijuana in the back seat of the cab, which proves, once again, that with brains, a little creativity, and the right bait, you can catch any dumb criminal, any time.

49. Just His Bad Puck

(England)

"Wear a mask" is a basic rule of crime. A dumb criminal should remember to check that his or her mask has eyeholes. A really dumb criminal should also make sure that the eyeholes are in the right place.

Such was *not* the case at a holdup in a small village in Kent. Dumb criminal Mack Brown had a mask, all right. And it did have eyeholes. Unfortunately for him, the eyeholes had been cut an inch to the left and a half-inch below the actual eyes in his head. Lacking the foresight to try on his mask ahead of time, Mack didn't realize he was in the dark until he started to enter the store he was about to rob.

Stepping blindly through the door, Mack fumbled with one hand to line up his eyeholes while he searched for his knife with the other. Seeing all this, the shop owner didn't wait for explanations. He picked up his hockey stick and smacked Mack right in the ear with a slapshot that sent Mack skittering across the floor into the waiting hands of a constable, who happened to be shopping in the store at the time.

Mack was charged with attempted armed robbery and received four years. The shop owner was charged with high sticking and received two minutes in the penalty box.

**He picked up his hockey stick and smacked Mack right
in the ear with a slapshot**

49

50. Purloined Pizza Producer Popped by Pictures

In Ashland City, Tennessee, there was a popular pizzeria run by three generations of a local Italian family. When their huge pizza ovens were stolen one night, the pizzas stopped rolling out and the sudden pizza drought became a local catastrophe. Police were baffled. There were no clues. It was obviously a professional job. The family that ran the business was distraught. In one night, they had lost their jobs and the family business.

To improve their mood, the grandfather of the clan piled the whole family into his van and went across the border to a new pizzeria that had just opened in Kentucky. As soon as Grandpa saw the new pizzeria's ovens, he knew they were his stolen ovens. The owner of the new pizzeria protested that he had just purchased the ovens and that they were brand new. Grandpa called the cops and, when they arrived, the new pizzeria owner produced a receipt for the very expensive ovens. The police seemed satisfied that these were not the stolen ovens until Grandpa pointed something out.

The stainless steel ovens still had three refrigerator magnets stuck on them, featuring pictures of Grandpa's favorite grandchildren.

51. Jumpin' Jack Flasher

Just outside Little Rock, Arkansas, a known "flasher" was at it again. Jumpin' Jack, as he was called by the local police, would often get naked and do calisthenics at his apartment window across the street from the local bank. Not only were his exercise habits offensive to the people who worked in the bank; local merchants also complained that Jack's jumping was bad for business.

Now, Jack was bold and a little demented, but he wasn't stupid. He would always hide his face in some way or pull the blinds halfway so that he could only be seen from the waist down. These precautions made it more difficult for him to be identified (especially in light of the fact that the police don't hold naked lineups).

After receiving a number of complaints one day, the Little Rock Police Department sent over one of its best officers to investigate. As the detective knocked on Jack's door, he thought about how hard it was to prove cases like Jack's. Without a positive I.D., such situations quickly degenerate to "my word against yours." Our detective decided to take a different approach.

"All right, Jack, who have you got hiding in there with you?"

"I don't have anyone hiding in here!" Jack yelled angrily from behind the door.

"The girls over at the bank tell it differently. They say they saw someone sneaking in here a little earlier today."

Jack opened the door. "They're crazy," he said. "There hasn't been anyone in my apartment all day long except me. See for yourself."

The officer did. He saw it all, from Jack's head down to his toes. Jumpin' Jack was finally arrested for indecent exposure.

52. Beats the Hell out of Me

Marshal Larry Hawkins of Little Rock has his own story about Jumpin' Jack Flasher.

"I had a run-in with Jack myself once," Hawkins told one of our *America's Dumbest Criminals* writers. "One day I was patrolling the downtown area when this skinny little guy stops my car. It was Jumpin' Jack. From the looks of him, he'd been worked over pretty good by somebody who wasn't messin' around. His left eye had a huge mouse under it, his lip was split open, and his face was all red, with a couple of knots on his head as well. He just looked like hell."

"What happened to you?" Hawkins asked.

"I've been beat up," Jack mumbled through clenched jaws.

"I'll say you have. Who beat you up, Jack?"

"This woman down at the Laundromat," he confessed in obvious pain and embarrassment.

"A woman? A woman did this to you?"

Hawkins thought maybe Jack had mixed it up with his girlfriend or something. So he put Jack in the back seat of the squad car and drove to the Laundromat. Through the storefront windows, the men could see several women inside cleaning clothes.

"Jack, which one was it that beat you up?"

"I don't know," he muttered. "I didn't see her face."

"Wait a minute . . . let me get this straight. A woman in there beat you up, and you don't know which one did it?"

"I told you, I didn't see her face."

"All right. You wait here while I go in and try to find out what happened." So Hawkins walked into the place. One of the women addressed Hawkins, "Officer, we are so glad you're here. A man came in here about ten minutes ago, pulled his shirt up over his head, and then dropped his pants."

"He wasn't wearing any underwear, either!" added another woman.

"So what happened then?" Hawkins asked, smiling.

One of the women continued: "Then the man said, 'Hey girls, does this remind you of anything?' And Connie said, 'Yeah, it does—it looks like a penis, only smaller!' Then she reached out and grabbed him by the hair under his tee shirt and commenced to knock the hell out of him."

"Yeah," the officer admitted. "That much is obvious."

"His arms were up over his head in that shirt," the informant went on, "and he couldn't do nothin'. It was over in about thirty seconds." Then she added with some satisfaction, "You don't mess with Connie!"

She was right about that, too, Hawkins thought as he looked at a substantial woman in the corner nonchalantly folding some sheets. *I certainly wouldn't mess with Connie!*

Hawkins got back in the squad car and told Jack he was under arrest for exposing his privates in public.

"Well, what about that woman in there? Aren't you gonna do anything about her beatin' me up like this?"

"I thought you told me that you didn't see who did it," the officer said. "But if you want to go back in there and see if you can figure out who it was, I'll just wait here for you, Jack."

"Uhhh . . . no . . . that's okay. Let's just get out of here," Jack said. He kept staring through the window at Connie, who was still folding clothes.

"Fine with me, Jack," Hawkins said. "Let's go."

53. Brown-Bagging It

At about noon on a sultry North Carolina summer day, homicide investigator Darryl Price tells us, hundreds of motorists observed a man walking along a busy six-lane highway wearing a brown paper bag over his head, creating a hazard as he stumbled in front of traffic. Motorists used their car phones to alert police.

The man eventually entered a bank and began to shout. Several tense seconds went by. Someone finally asked, "I'm sorry, what did you say?" With no mouthhole, the bag-it bandit could not be understood.

Apparently very nervous, the man constantly turned his head, trying to watch everyone in the room. However, his bag did not turn with his head, so most of his time was spent realigning his eyeholes and, of course, repeating himself.

Money in hand, the robber stumbled blindly into six lanes of lunchtime traffic, narrowly avoiding being run down. He was quickly bagged by police.

He stumbled in front of traffic. Motorists used their car phones to alert police.

54. No, Honest!

An undercover officer infiltrating a California high school had been busy becoming cool enough to do business with the local schoolyard dealers. He knew he had it made the day a certain young man eased down beside him in the cafeteria.

"I heard you were looking for some dope."

"You heard right. What do you have?"

But the young man was suspicious. "You aren't a narc, are you?"

How many times had the young narc heard this question? For a change, he thought he'd try the truth.

"I sure am. I just finished with the police academy, and the drug task force asked me to come here."

The kid stared intently. Then he burst out laughing as he reached into his pocket for something to sell the truthful—but still undercover—officer, who had just told the nerd his departmental history.

Some dummies just never believe the truth.

55. A Lifer Turned Do-It-Yourselfer

Out of Cambridge, Massachusetts, comes the tale of the inmate who had been found guilty of a capital crime, escaped the death penalty, and received a life sentence, although he could not escape "the electric throne."

Inmates with televisions are required to wear headphones while watching the tube so as not to disturb the other inmates. The headphones had to be approved by the prison staff and meet safety requirements. Unfortunately, Laurence Baker, forty-seven, had other ideas. Brainy Baker made his own headphones and was using them without permission one night. He was watching *When Toilets Attack!* in his cell with his nifty homemade headphones on, seated on his deluxe prison toilet. Now, if you've ever seen a prison toilet, you know they are made entirely of stainless steel. Just take our word for it.

Engrossed in the show and still wearing his homemade headphones (which he had wired directly into the back of his television set), Baker was reaching for a necessary toilet accessory when his headphones gave him a little jolt of electricity. Larry jumped, the headphones slipped, and kerplunked into the toilet water. And voila!

Larry had just invented the first combination electric chair-toilet with a personal THX sound system built right in. We believe the late Mr. Baker is the only person who has actually tried this revolutionary device.

56. Is That You?

(England)

A pair of teenaged criminals in Liverpool had a good thing going. One would slowly cruise the block in his car while the other broke into a parked car. Their orchestration was such that the driver of the getaway car would ease around a corner just about the time his buddy was ready to hop back in holding a new radio, CD player, or cell phone. Within five minutes they would have the loot fenced for cash and be back on the street, hundreds of pounds richer.

Although aware of the incidents, police were finding this case hard to crack. There were no witnesses, no prints, and no clues, and none of the fences would talk. The only thing left to do was to step up patrols of the area.

One night two undercover officers were cruising a neighborhood at a crawl, checking out a parked car, when the back door of *their* car opened. In hopped a teen with a radio in hand.

"Hit it!" the youth implored. *"Go!"*

The officers looked at each other incredulously, stifled a laugh, and obeyed. They whipped around the block, cuffed their new passenger, and stopped the sedan that was honking its horn loudly. They had caught both perpetrators in the act. But how?

It turns out that the nearsighted point man had forgotten his glasses that night and mistaken the slow-moving officers' car for his accomplice's vehicle.

So the old fish story is true: Sometimes the fish really *do* jump into the boat.

57. Will the Last Person to Steal the Truck Please Turn off the Lights?

It had been snowing in Birmingham, Alabama, for a couple of days—a rare experience for that southern city. Officer Eric Griffin and his partner were patrolling near the railroad tracks by the switching station. It was pretty well deserted except for a couple of railroad workers sitting in a utility truck.

"They must've been doing some kind of maintenance work, because the two yellow bi-lights on the top of the truck were on," Griffin says.

The officers drove past the men and proceeded to the end of the road, where they then turned around. As they were heading back they came upon the two workers, now on foot. But there was no sign of the truck.

"They just stole my truck!" one of the men shouted.

"Who stole your truck?" the officers asked.

"Two men. We were checking for loose rails, and when I looked up there were these two guys gettin' into the truck, and they just took off! It's a blue Chevy pickup with the yellow lights on top. They hit the main road and went east toward town."

The two officers dropped the two men off at the brakeman's shack and rolled. As they got into town, they passed a housing project on their right.

"There they are!" Griffin's partner suddenly yelled. Griffin looked over. Sure enough, there was the truck, with the yellow bi-lights still flashing away. The officers turned into the projects and had to make several twists and turns in order to get over to where they'd seen the lights. When they got there, the truck was gone. But then Griffin's partner spotted it again. "There they go, the next street over!"

As the officers turned at the next street, the truck passed directly in front of them. The bi-lights were still flashing. One of the men was kicking frantically on the dash and holding a fistful of wires. He still hadn't found the off switch. Finally, with the help of another unit, Griffin and company were able to trap the vehicle and make the arrest.

"As we were taking the passenger out of the truck, I couldn't help myself," Griffin recalls. "I reached in and turned off the lights."

**One of the men was kicking frantically on the dash
and holding a fistful of wires.**

58. On the Inside Lookin' Out

Gumbo country. Effie, Louisiana. They've got their share of dumb criminals just like the rest of us, and here's proof.

One guy sat in the getaway truck a block away as his buddy cut a hole in the roof of the local drug store and jumped to the floor. This should go pretty smoothly. An old store, no security alarms, and plenty of free drugs inside. The man was in heaven. In just a few minutes, he'd filled the pillowcase he bought with all the drugs he could carry. Time to go. Oops. There was a padlock on the back door. But, no problem. He'd just go out the front door. Ooh . . . bars on the front door. Hmmm. Now what? He couldn't go out the back as planned, and he couldn't use plan B, the front door. The hole he'd cut in the roof was about fifteen feet over his head. So he did what any law-abiding citizen would do in an emergency—he called the police. The police, in turn, called the drugstore owner and asked him to come down and let the burglar out.

When the cop car passed by the pickup truck on the way to the drug store, the man standing next to the truck flipped his cigarette away and scrambled behind the wheel with a look of sheer terror on his face. Very suspicious. When a second unit rolled up, the man was trying to start the truck, but was having about as much luck as his partner had. The truck wouldn't start. Both men were arrested and charged with burglary.

This caper was doomed from jump street. He couldn't have gotten away, which he didn't . . . even if he could've gotten out . . . which he couldn't. Huh?

59. Love Thy Neighbor

The weary, disheveled woman tossed and turned in her bed. It was two in the morning, and the trucks at the nearby warehouse were grinding their gears, braking loudly, and making that maddening "Beep! Beep! Beep!" sound that a postal truck makes when in reverse gear.

What is so important that you have to truck it in the middle of the night? she wondered.

Finally, the unwilling insomniac could stand no more. She called the police and complained about the noise.

A quick check downtown revealed that the warehouse was leased to a toy import company. That set the officers to wondering. Christmas was still many months away. Why would a toy company be working round the clock to ship Chinese dolls and robots that spew smoke?

Ten minutes later, the two officers who had been sent to follow up on the disturbing-the-peace complaint pulled their cruiser up behind the working docks. When they stepped out of their vehicle, the men on the loading dock scattered and disappeared into the night.

The officers figured they must have a burglary in progress and called for backup. Three of the men were quickly apprehended in the neighborhood, but they turned out to be the rightful occupants of the warehouse.

So why had they fled?

Well, they weren't burglars, but they were guilty of a bit more than disturbing the peace. The police searched the warehouse and ended up seizing twenty-two tons of cocaine, with a street value of more than six billion dollars.

It was the biggest drug raid in U.S. history, and it carries a lesson for all would-be dumb criminals: If you're going to mess with Uncle Sam, make sure you don't wake up the neighbors!

60. An Irish Tale

(Ireland)

Now, mind you, this is an unconfirmed bit of what might be blarney from an off-duty local officer, but we'll report it all the same because it just might be true—even if only in the Republic of Ireland.

The officer in question was making his way down a narrow road between Waterville and Kenmare when he observed a car driving erratically. In a moment he had caught up to the car and popped on his lights. One quick blast of the siren brought the car jerkily to the side of the road. The officer made note of the license plate and cautiously stepped out to approach the vehicle.

Meanwhile, the car's two occupants were discussing strategy. Both were well inebriated, but the passenger had a plan.

"Take the label off the whiskey bottle and put it on your forehead and don't say a word," he said, "I'll do all the talking."

The driver was so gone that he obeyed immediately. The passenger disposed of the bottle, and the driver turned to face the officer with a "Bushmill's" label on his forehead. The officer inspected this spectacle for a moment, then asked with a grin, "Now, you two gentlemen wouldn't have been drinking tonight, would you?"

The passenger quickly replied with a bit of a slur, "No, sir. No indeed, sirrrrr. We were at our Alcoholics Anonymous meeting. As you can see, my friend is on the patch." Without saying a word, the driver pointed to the label on his forehead and nodded.

As we said, only in Ireland.

61. Where There's a Will, There's a Spray

This story of woe begins and ends in Harvey, Louisiana. A teenage girl approached a man loading his van with boxes for delivery. As he started to get into the van, the young girl walked up to him and demanded the keys to the van. The man refused. The juvenile whipped out a knife.

"Now gimme the keys!" she demanded. The driver tossed her the keys. The youngster hopped in, started the van, and sat there for several minutes. Apparently unable to drive a stick shift, the frustrated teen exited the van and ran off. The driver called the cops.

A few blocks from the scene of her original attempt, she again tries to hijack a vehicle. This time it's an exterminator's truck. She swiped at the man with her knife and grabbed for the keys. The man jumped back, and with the wand attached to a canister of bug spray, fought off her first attempt to cut him.

She was relentless. Again and again she attempted to get to him with her knife, and each time her thrusts were parried by the exterminator. Fencing for his life, the man opted for chemical warfare. He began pumping up the pressure on his tank with his left hand. *"Take that!"* he cried, unleashing a pressurized stream of pesticide into the deranged girl's face.

Coughing and sputtering and half-blinded by the spray, the girl gave up and ran off. Now he called the cops.

Needless to say, the police were on the lookout for a young girl carrying a knife and reeking of bug spray. Moments later a patrol officer spotted the girl. He gave her chase on foot and was about to apprehend her when she suddenly turned and tried to slash him. More chemical warfare. Coughing and gagging again, this time from pepper spray, the girl was subdued and arrested.

The disturbed girl was booked on two counts of attempted carjacking, five counts of assault, and one count of resisting arrest by flight. *Whew*!

The man opted for chemical warfare. . . ."Take that!" he cried.

62. The Fall to Grace

Sgt. Johnny Cooley was running radar on the interstate outside Birmingham, Alabama, one night when he witnessed a bona fide traffic miracle.

The street was slick from a rain that had just ended, and the pace of traffic was again picking up. An eighteen-wheeler came barreling around a curve, when a car suddenly switched lanes directly into the truck's path. The truck driver hit the brakes and began to hydroplane across the lanes, out of control. The cab of the truck hit the railing at full speed and the trailer followed, disappearing over the edge of an overpass.

Cooley knew there was a basketball court below, and chances were real good that a pickup game was in progress. Cooley quickly radioed in for paramedics and backup. When he got to the twisted, crushed semi, his worst fears surfaced, although it appeared that the basketball players had escaped: they were all busy looting the trailer of its beer and wine haul. When they saw Cooley, they made a fast break toward the shadows.

Sergeant Cooley sighed as he stepped out of his cruiser for the worst part of his job—visually confirming the traffic fatality. He stepped up on what was left of the cab's running board and peered into a small opening that used to be the driver's side window. He gritted his teeth and swallowed hard. But when he looked in, he couldn't believe his eyes. There was a woman lying comfortably stretched out on the seat, reading a book.

"Ma'am? Are you okay?"

The woman calmly closed her book and smiled, "Oh, I'm fine, thank you."

Cooley could not believe that she had survived the crash, much less the sixty-five-foot drop.

"Were you driving the rig, ma'am?"

She smiled again, "Yes, sir, but I had some help."

"Help? You mean another driver? Where is he? The paramedics are here."

"My copilot's right here," she said, holding up the Bible she had been reading. "God."

Granted, the only dummies in this story were the free-loading basketballers, but it's a story that just had to be told.

63. Party Pooper

(Canada)

Whoever first pointed out that "love hurts" probably spoke from painful romantic experience—but nothing close to that felt by an ardent but especially foolish young criminal in Vancouver.

It began the evening one of the city's nicer restaurants threw its annual Christmas party. The event was closed to the public, but this particular young man managed to make it in uninvited. He was sweet on a young woman who was attending the party and he wanted to see her. It turned out, however, that she did *not* want to see him. An argument ensued between the two, and several guests came to the young woman's defense.

The uninvited guest was politely asked to leave. He responded less politely by throwing a punch, and the "discussion" moved outside into an alley. There the fisticuffs suddenly ceased when the gate-crashing Romeo pulled a .357 Magnum and threatened the whole crowd with it.

You do not argue with a .357 Magnum, especially when it's being held by a very shaky, very upset young man in love, who just got shot down in flames. The crowd slowly backed away without saying a word.

Romeo thought he was in control of the situation now, so he got a little cocky. He began to tell the whole group what he thought of them and of the girl who had just jilted him. After a stream of very unkind remarks, he apparently decided that he had given the crowd a piece of his mind and could put away his "piece." Like a cool Canadian "Dirty Harry," he jammed the huge pistol into the waistband of his pants, and "*Kaboom*!"

The emergency surgeons worked hard, but they could not undo all the damage that had been done by Romeo's cool move.

Needless to say, that was the last bullet he would ever get to fire.

64. Pride Goeth Before the Brain

An officer in Nashville, Tennessee, responded to a burglar alarm at a convenience store. Within moments his K-9 partner had located the perpetrator, but the officer could not figure out how the man got into the store. When he asked, the culprit led him to a small missing windowpane. The officer could not believe the man could get through such a small opening, but brainus minimus insisted that he had. The more the officer protested, the more the crook insisted that he was "that good."
Finally the break-in artist insisted that if the officer didn't believe him, he should take a look at the restaurant three blocks away. "I broke in there earlier tonight . . . through an even smaller windowpane!"

65. Bound for the Cooler

One bright spring morning in Lafayette, Louisiana, Louis Albright had the bright idea of robbing a branch of a local bank. Louis had an even more brilliant idea for a low-cost, low-fat, completely disposable disguise. He would cover his entire head with whipped cream.

A few trial runs indicated his idea would work beautifully. The foamy "mask" sprayed on quickly and was easily wiped off. It completely covered any distinguishing marks, even his hair color. And it tasted wonderful, to boot.

Congratulating himself on his innovative idea, the human hot-fudge sundae walked into the bank and approached the teller. Unfortunately, the employees' response to his delicious disguise was just the opposite of what he wanted. The giggles were discreet at first, but when he said, "Put all your money in the sack," the giggles dissolved into open laughter.

By this time the whipped cream was getting warm and beginning to slide. And the teller had long ago punched the silent alarm. Before you could say "banana split," the police arrived. The rapidly melting bank robber was quickly arrested and refrigerated downtown.

By this time the whipped cream was getting warm and beginning to slide. And the teller had long ago punched the silent alarm.

66. Jail Bird

The guy in Woodbury, Minnesota, was a good thief. He'd broken into a pen housing at least a dozen homing pigeons and had stolen every one.

All had gone smoothly until he sold the birds to a "fence" on the black market. The buyer of the stolen goods was very upset the next day when he discovered that all the pigeons had flown the coop. The homing pigeons had returned to their rightful owner.

Acting on an anonymous tip (wonder who that might've been), the police arrested the young "bird brain."

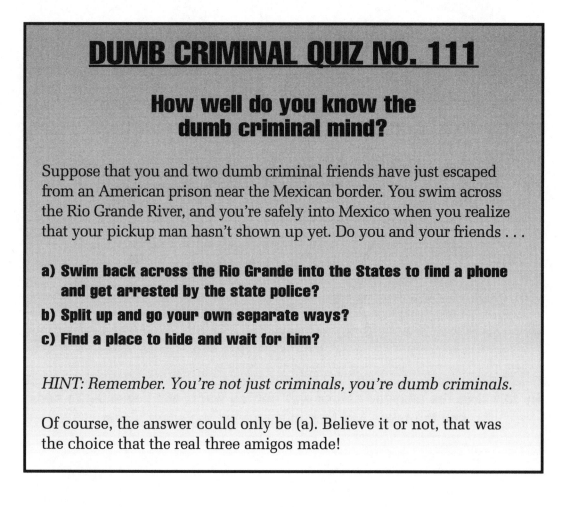

DUMB CRIMINAL QUIZ NO. 111

How well do you know the dumb criminal mind?

Suppose that you and two dumb criminal friends have just escaped from an American prison near the Mexican border. You swim across the Rio Grande River, and you're safely into Mexico when you realize that your pickup man hasn't shown up yet. Do you and your friends . . .

a) **Swim back across the Rio Grande into the States to find a phone and get arrested by the state police?**

b) **Split up and go your own separate ways?**

c) **Find a place to hide and wait for him?**

HINT: Remember. You're not just criminals, you're dumb criminals.

Of course, the answer could only be (a). Believe it or not, that was the choice that the real three amigos made!

67. Steals and Deals

From Altoona, Pennsylvania, comes this tale of a dumb car thief who becomes an even dumber car salesman.

Karen Ruohs awoke to find that her car had been stolen sometime during the night. She immediately telephoned the police. Along with a description of her vehicle and its contents, she mentioned to the detective that her car also had a mobile phone. The officer asked if he might have the number.

After filling out the report, the detective got an idea. He phoned the mobile number and a man answered. "Yeah," the officer stated, "I'm calling about the ad in the paper for a car for sale. That's just the car I'm looking for and I've got the cash." Thinking he had hit pay dirt, the man agreed to meet with the prospective buyer. The thief let him know right away that he was willing to make him a great deal on it. They agreed on a meeting place and a time. He knew this could be a very lucrative deal for him. Steal a car, ride around for a while, and then sell it for more cash than he could get from the pennies on the dollar that the chop shops paid.

Well, the ending to this story is pretty predictable, but we've got to finish it. The man showed up at the designated spot and was arrested and charged with car theft.

The next *cell* phone he talks on will be from jail.

68. The Name Game

Officer Ed Leach of Birmingham, Alabama, likes to tell the tale of two brothers, Jack and Joe, who greatly resembled each other in both physical appearance and their less-than-brilliant behavior.

Jack and Joe were often getting into trouble of one sort or another, only to weasel their way out of sticky situations by switching identities. If one got nabbed for doing something wrong, the innocent one would use the other's name to get out of trouble. The ploy usually worked, until Officer Leach decided to turn the tables while trying to issue an outstanding warrant on Jack.

On patrol one afternoon, Leach spotted Joe at a stoplight and pulled him over, hoping to get some information on Jack's whereabouts. It so happened that Leach knew Jack and Joe well enough to tell the two apart, even from a distance.

After Leach had stepped out of his car to speak to Joe, he happened to spot Jack nearby, walking across the street. Although Leach and Jack made eye contact, Jack just kept on walking as though nothing was wrong. Time for a little reverse psychology.

"I was on to their little game of mistaken identities, so I thought I'd give them a taste of their own medicine," Leach remembers. "I knew if I called out his real name, Jack would start running. So I didn't. Instead, I called out the name of his brother—who was standing beside me.

" 'Hey, Joe!' I yelled. 'Come over here and talk to me, would ya?' "

Now Jack, fooled into thinking that Officer Leach thought *he* was Joe, walked right up to Leach, who then grabbed the real jerk, er, Jack, by the shirt.

"You're under arrest, *Jack*," Leach said.

"Hey . . . but I thought that you thought . . . that I was. . . . Damn! Man, that's not right."

Jack knew he'd been had, and he didn't like it one bit. He had fallen for his own game.

69. Rocket Man

When one intentionally breaks the law and gets caught, he automatically becomes a dumb criminal. Even the smart ones.

Palmer Destry was brilliant. He worked at a jet propulsion lab in Pasadena, California. His was a high-paying job that earned him respect among his peers and a hefty salary to boot. But when five o'clock rolled around, Destry would begin his second job in another laboratory—in the basement of his exclusive high-dollar suburban home. Here, he wasn't formulating advanced rocket science. He was manufacturing the highly addictive and very illegal methamphetamine, otherwise known as crystal meth.

Destry took pride in his work. With his background in chemical engineering, he was convinced that his product was the finest money could buy. He was so enamored with his talent and the product he produced, he documented his genius. With a super-8 video camera mounted on a tripod, he created his own "infomercial." As writer, director, and star of the show, our egghead took us through his illegal lab step-by-step. He was ever so thorough in describing it.

Just as it is with all good things, all bad things must come to an end. Acting on a tip from a credible police informant, narcotics agents were able to obtain a search warrant, which they served early one morning on the unsuspecting Mr. Smug. Along with a mountain of evidence seized at his home, the video infomercial was confiscated as well.

At the trial, Destry's home movie proved to be the fatal nail in the proverbial coffin for our Captain Vidiot. He was found guilty on all charges and sent to prison for a long, long, time.

As one of the testifying officers put it, "This was one case where the drug dealer really was a rocket scientist!"

As writer, director, and star of the show, our egghead took us through his illegal lab step-by-step.

70. Self-Portrait of a Dumb Criminal

(New Zealand)

Here's the story of an armed robbery that took place at a family-owned food store in western New Zealand. The clerk on duty that night was twenty-two-year-old Danny Wilson. When the police arrived, Wilson told them that a lone gunman had entered the store around 11:30 that evening and had asked to use the rest room.

"I pointed to the door in the back," Wilson said, "and he went in. He stayed in there for about five minutes and when he came out, he was holding a gun. *'Give me all the money now!'* he shouted. Thinkin' I was gonna be shot at any moment, I did as he said."

When Wilson finished telling his story again, one of the officers said to him, "You've told what happened twice now and you've not mentioned a mask or disguise. Did you get a pretty good look at him, then?"

"I guess so."

"So, he wasn't wearing a mask of any sort?"

"No, he wasn't wearing no mask or nothin'."

"Officer Petersen, would you grab a sketch pad and come talk to this young man please?"

The young clerk began to fidget. He looked uneasy.

Officer Petersen took him aside and began asking him questions about the robber.

"I want you to look at some basic face shapes on these cards and tell me which one most fits the robber. Was it round like this one or more narrow?"

"It was thinner, like this one."

"Okay. Now, what can you tell me about the shape of his nose?"

The officer began to sketch as the clerk described in detail the eyes, the type of hair, and the color, even down to the bump on the bridge of his nose. The kid was fascinated as he watched the artist at work. Once in a while he would recall some small detail you wouldn't expect a person with a gun pointed at him to notice.

Twenty minutes later they had a complete composite. Officer Peterson looked at the finished sketch. With a puzzled look, he excused himself and went over to the sergeant in charge. They both looked at the drawing and then mumbled to each other. The clerk began scratching himself. The two officers approached him.

"You have an excellent eye for detail, son."

"That was quite a description that you gave to Officer Petersen," added the sergeant.

"Yeah, he's real good."

"Put your hands behind your back. You're under arrest for the robbery of this store."

Unbelievable. The fool was unable to describe any other face, save his own! He confessed that he was the robber. When the arresting officer asked him why, he responded, "I was just being honest!"

71. Camera Hog

An officer in Indiana told us of a very photogenic crook who insisted on arranging his own close-ups. This criminal specialized in safecracking. He was highly skilled, extremely thorough, and—at the same time—incredibly dumb.

Our safecracking star had targeted a small local business that kept more than seven thousand dollars in cash in a safe. There were no alarms, and the safe was an older model, relatively easy to crack. But when the criminal arrived at "work," he discovered a couple of video surveillance cameras in the building.

That wouldn't do. After all, nobody likes to work with someone watching over his shoulder, right? So our resourceful crook set about making his workplace more comfortable. He found a ladder, climbed up with his screwdriver, and proceeded to take the lens off each camera.

Now, the big problem with most video surveillance is that you really can't get close enough for a really good picture of the criminal's face. The quality is not that good, and the perpetrators are usually too far away for the ceiling-mounted cameras to capture a good image. But our star safecracker took care of that problem for the local police. While he diligently worked with his screwdriver right in front of the camera, he also provided the officers with the best close-up they'd ever seen—right down to the smallest wrinkle and mole. Meanwhile, the camera across the room was providing a full-length view of him working on the first camera.

The video was picture-perfect, and the safecracker was quickly apprehended.

Smile—you're a dumb criminal!

72. If at First You Don't Succeed . . .

Perseverance and determination are frequently the marks of successful people. But we emphasize *frequently,* meaning *not always.* Former Baltimore, Maryland, police officer Frank Walmer remembers a determined burglar who persevered until he managed to get himself arrested.

Walmer and his partner were dispatched to a burglary in progress in a residential neighborhood. "We arrived and contacted the woman who had called," Walmer said. "She told us that someone had been trying to break through her basement door and that he was still at it. As we stood in the living room, we could plainly hear all sorts of thumping and bumping coming from the basement."

The woman led the two officers down the stairs and showed them the door in question.

"It was just as she described," Walmer said. "Someone was on the other side of the door, methodically kicking it in. The bottom panel was beginning to give way. In a moment or two a hand reached through, but the hole wasn't big enough yet."

More kicking gradually widened the hole while the officers looked on. When the opening was large enough, a head popped through.

"My partner and I were standing on either side of the door," Walmer says, "but the guy never looked around. He twisted and wiggled and, with a great deal of effort, finally managed to squeeze through the hole he had made. Breathing hard, he stood up, dusted himself off, and suddenly realized he was looking down two gun barrels.

"At that point," says Officer Walmer, "we felt we had a pretty strong case."

He twisted and wiggled and, with a great deal of effort, finally managed
to squeeze through the hole he had made.

73. A Really Big Bust

At first, the customs officer thought the drug-sniffing dog was barking up the wrong tree. Or, rather, sniffing up the wrong tourist.

As the 475-pound man waddled through customs, the dog began to pay him close attention, sniffing suspiciously at the man's huge stomach. Annoyed, the man told the dog to "shoo." No luck.

The customs officer was a bit reluctant to approach the man, since he really didn't fit the profile of a smuggler, and his personal effects had already been examined. But the dog was relentless. Over and over it pointed its nose toward the tourist and kept sniffing and whining and sniffing. It was almost as though the dog itself was puzzled.

The officer finally conceded that something was awry.

"I'm sorry, sir," he told the rotund tourist. "I'm afraid you're going to have to accompany me to a dressing room for a strip search."

It was a task that neither man was looking forward to. But it had to be done.

Once inside the room, the tourist was ordered to disrobe, and a complete body search was initiated. It was then that a plastic bag containing eleven ounces of a white powdery substance was discovered—discreetly hidden amid the many folds of the man's tremendous stomach!

The substance proved to be cocaine.

The drug dog was vindicated.

74. My Karma Ran over My Dogma

(Syria)

The mindless mugger-to-be was Habib Rasham, who stood quietly in the darkened alley as he watched his approaching prey. Watching and waiting was nothing new to our foreign felon. With a large stick in hand, he would hide until his unsuspecting victim walked past, then step up quietly behind him, strike him over the head, and steal the victim's money.

Tonight was no exception. As Rasham stood in the darkness against the wall, a man passed within five feet of him. Out of the darkness he crept up behind the man and dealt him a sharp rap on the back of his head. The victim dropped facedown into the alley way.

Quickly, Rasham rifled through the man's pockets. In the back pocket he found a wallet. Just as the victim began to stir back to consciousness, two men entered the alley and shouted at Rasham, who took off running. In a flash he was down the alley, onto the street, and ambling along, trying to blend in with other pedestrians.

As Rasham walked along, he pulled out the stolen wallet and began removing the contents. First the money, then the identification. Suddenly, he stopped. *It couldn't be.* The color drained from his face. Not only did he know his victim, he *lived* with him. Rasham's karma had finally caught up with him. *He had just mugged his own father!* He sprinted back to the alley. No one was there. He looked down the street. Aha, there he was! As Rasham approached his father, the two men who had seen him shouted, *"That's him!"* Still holding his father's wallet, Rasham was immediately set upon by an angry crowd.

This Rasham family minireunion was not a pretty sight. Rasham was thoroughly trounced, probably disowned, and definitely arrested!

75. The One-Armed Orangutan

The ownership of exotic pets often seems to lead to frantic calls of one sort or another to police. One began as a routine burglary call. When Officer Ronnie Allen of Oklahoma City, Oklahoma, arrived at the apartment, he was greeted by an elderly gentleman. Senior citizens are all too often easy prey for burglars and other criminals, so Allen was feeling bad for the guy while he began the routine process of listing the stolen items. Then the old gent made a startling statement.

"But what I'm really worried about is my one-armed orangutan. He can get downright nasty when he's not fed."

"Your what, sir?"

"My one-armed orangutan. He's only about four-foot-six, but apes are unusually strong for their size, especially a one-armed ape. His left arm is as strong as three men's arms."

"You had a one-armed orangutan here?"

"Till he got stolen or ran off. He was here when I left. One of these burgers was for him. He'll be angry that he didn't get his burger."

At this point, Allen didn't know if the old guy was confused, pulling his leg, or the genuine owner of a missing one-armed orangutan. It's not something you want to call in without being really sure of what you're saying. But the old guy's story was confirmed when Allen heard a disturbance call from an apartment nearby. It seems a group of larcenous individuals were sitting around taking inventory of the items they had just stolen from the old man's apartment. The burglars were also inhaling toxic paint fumes to "cop a cheap buzz."

Unfortunately for them, the cracked crooks had forced a certain one-armed orangutan, who just happened to be hanging out with them, to sniff the paint, too. The drugged-out ape had gone berserk and was wreaking havoc in the apartment. The police had to get the old man to talk the orangutan out so that the burglars could give themselves up to police without being torn apart.

76. Wrong Side of the Tracks

No officer likes to get a call involving a train accident. They are usually the bloodiest and most disgusting scenes imaginable.

One evening Marshal Larry Hawkins of Little Rock got a call that a pedestrian had been hit by a train. Expecting the worst, Hawkins reported to the scene. He arrived to find a crowd of spectators craning their necks to get a better look. The marshal elbowed his way through the crowd and saw the victim—standing up talking to someone and brushing off the dirt on his pants.

Here's the story Hawkins unraveled: The man and his wife were at Johnson's Tavern, which is right next to the railroad tracks. They both got drunk, and then they got into an argument. He said to her, "The hell with you, I'm walking home." The railroad track went right past his house, so he decided he was going to walk the tracks home.

Meanwhile, a southbound train was on its way. And somewhere between the tavern and home, the train and the drunk man managed to meet.

The conductors and the engineers all saw a man go down, and they were sure the train went over him. They assumed he had been killed. But somehow after the train had managed to stop, the dumb, drunk, and incredibly lucky criminal was still alive.

To this day, no one is sure exactly how it happened. The train might have knocked the man down, or he might have passed out on the tracks. But the important thing is that he was lying *between* the two rails when the train went over him.

Said Hawkins, "Now, there's always stuff hanging down under a train, like air hoses and stuff, and those things did clip him and roll him around. He was bruised, scratched, and cut, and his clothes were torn. But he was all right. He was up and walking around— still drunk and scared out of his mind. I took him in for his own protection and arrested him for public intoxication."

But the important thing is that he was lying between the two rails when the train went over him.

77. Every Day Has Its Dog

Insurance fraud is big business these days. Insurance companies pay out millions of dollars in false claims each year, which in turn drives up the cost for legitimate claimants. Some dishonest people do get away with it once in a while. But for the greedmeister in this next story, once was not enough. Not nearly enough. He was on to a good thing, and he wasn't about to give it up.

Douglas Owen Gantry of Greensboro, North Carolina, sobbed as he spoke to his insurance company. Yes, it was tragic. His favorite dog Lucky and seven other of his beloved dogs had been struck and killed by a fleeing motorist. "Wait a minute here, Mr. Gantry," the stunned agent gasped. "You're claiming that *one* car struck and killed eight of your dogs at once?"

"I know it's hard to believe," he said. "It's sad but true. My insurance covers it, doesn't it?"

"Well . . . your policy is in effect . . . but let me check your records and I'll get back to you right away. And you say the dogs were all registered purebreds?"

"Yes sir. I paid over $5,000 for those dogs."

"I'll get back to you, Mr. Gantry."

The agent hung up the phone shaking his head. He had been born at night . . . but not last night. Eight dogs? All struck by the same car? All killed? You'd think at least *Lucky* would have made it. Too strange. So the new agent pulled up the file on our incredible Mr. Gantry and was stunned at what he found. In the last year alone, the man had filed claims for the loss of fifty-nine dogs! All of them run over by cars. Sixty-seven if you count the eight today.

After calling in his discovery to the claims department, the agent had another phone call to place. To the police. An investigation was launched and it was discovered that not only had the man been paid over $32,000 through fraudulent claims, but he had never even owned a dog. He was arrested and charged with filing false claims and theft by deception.

The embarrassed insurance company had little to say regarding the case, but I'm sure they would agree with us that it was a doggone crime.

78. We Haven't Been Properly Introduced

Late one night in a small town in the state of Washington, a woman heard a noise coming from a back bedroom. Her husband had run to the grocery, so she went into the hallway and said, "Bob, is that you?"

A young man stuck his head out of the bedroom door and said, "No, I'm Brian."

She screamed and ran to the phone to call the cops. Brian took off. Moments later the police responded, but as they approached the woman's house, they passed a car with a young man driving. Knowing the suspect's description and his first name, they pulled the young man over and asked, "Are you Brian?"

"Yes, sir."

The wheels of justice turn so much faster when the criminals introduce themselves politely.

79. Photo Finish

Officer Aaron Graham of Louisville, Kentucky, likes to tell this story of a crime with a photo finish. It began with a woman strolling through a park en route to a company picnic. Swinging from her shoulder was her trusty Polaroid camera, all loaded and ready to catch some candid shots of this wacky annual summer get-together. The sun was setting, and the sky was ablaze with color as a breeze cooled the evening air. It was one of those relaxing evenings when you can't help but let your guard down just a little.

Suddenly, she heard running footsteps. Someone jerked the woman's arm and grabbed the camera. A patrol officer responded to the woman's screams and set out on foot in pursuit of the young thieves. While he ran, he radioed in a physical description of the perpetrators and their general direction of flight.

Meanwhile, in a small wooded grove not a quarter of a mile away, the thieves were checking out the camera. But something was wrong. They took each other's pictures easily enough, but the film that emerged from the camera was black. Disgusted, they tossed the photos and headed for the pawnshop to see what they could get for the malfunctioning camera.

Several police units and several bicycle and horse-mounted officers were close behind, forming a perimeter as our foot patrol officer stumbled into the grove of trees. There, lying at his feet, were the quickly developing Polaroid photos of the culprits. The officer knew he must be less than a minute behind them because the developing process was just finishing.

The two boys were nabbed about a half-mile away as they photographed squirrels. But they were still having problems. They would shoot a photo, look at it, and toss it down, grumbling, "Darn camera doesn't work!"

The trail of photos they left behind worked better than a trail of bread crumbs.

80. Spring Is in the Air

(Hungary)

Look before you leap. Most of us have been familiar with this old adage since childhood. Some of us, as our international nitwit was soon to discover, would do well to heed those words of wisdom.

A robber was being chased through the streets of Budapest by the local constabulary when he ran upstairs to the second story of an abandoned apartment building. With the police only moments behind him, he ran from room to empty room desperately looking for a place to hide.

As he entered another gutted apartment, he closed the door behind him. He could hear the shouts and collective footsteps of the authorities sweeping down the hall and kicking open doors. He was trapped! He ran over to the window and looked down to the street—it was probably twenty-five feet at least, but he had no choice.

He ran back to the door of the apartment just as the police arrived and they began pounding. With his body pressed hard against the door, he tried to hold them back, but the door was giving way. With one long adrenaline-pumped scream, he bolted from the closed door to the open window and, without missing a step, leaped to the street below just as the police entered the room.

The good news was he landed on something soft;
the bad news, it was a trampoline.

Now on any other given day that little leap of faith might have gone unnoticed but not this day. How could he have known that a circus was in town, that their parade had turned the corner and was passing directly beneath him? The good news was he landed on something soft; the bad news, it was a trampoline.

The police entering the upper-floor room saw him disappear from sight as he left the window. Five seconds later they saw him reappear in midair, only this time he was upside down. The second time he appeared, he wasn't quite as high but he was spinning. He didn't appear a third time.

When the police reached the Flying Nut, he was lying in a heap on the sidewalk across the street from the apartment building. He had suffered a dislocated shoulder, along with several contusions and a concussion. He was arrested and taken to jail, reminding him that even criminals who soar must eventually return to earth.

His only visitor at the jail we were told, was the owner of the circus who offered him a good paying job if he could repeat the trick twice a night. Perhaps that's an offer he should have jumped at!

81. In the Mood

Trooper Robert Bell shared this story of true romance at a very tender age in the Southeast:

Bell was headed out to the interstate highway through a small town when he noticed a classic car whipping by at a high rate of speed. It was a '64 Buick in mint condition. Radar revealed the vehicle was traveling at fifty miles per hour—*over* the speed limit.

When Bell closed in on the Buick, the speeder acted as if he might force a chase, but then he abruptly pulled over. Bell approached the idling Buick carefully. When he got to the window, he saw that the driver was an elderly man who appeared to be quite agitated.

"Sir," the trooper said, "were you aware that you were doing eighty-five in a thirty-five-mile-per-hour zone?"

"Of course I know how fast I'm going," the driver snapped. "It's an emergency!"

Concerned, the officer asked, "Is it a medical emergency, sir? I can get you to a hospital."

The driver's face reddened. "No, I have to go now. It's an emergency!"

"What's the emergency, sir? Maybe I can help you."

The old gentleman just looked angrier than ever. "I can't tell you. You'll laugh at me."

Bell tried to reassure him. "I won't laugh at you, sir. But if you don't tell me what the emergency is, I'll have to write you a ticket."

The senior speedster finally relented. "You promise not to laugh—man to man?" He was very serious.

"No, sir," Bell said. "I promise."

"Well, son, I'm eighty-two years old, and I haven't had an erec-uh . . . well, I haven't been 'in the mood for love' for more than two years now. Well, I have an—uh, I'm in the mood right now, and I'm on my way to my girlfriend's house!"

Bell was stunned, but only for a moment. "I had never heard that excuse for speeding before and—man to man—well, I had to empathize just a little. So I gave him a police escort."

82. A Workman Blames His Tools

William Chase of Putnam, Connecticut, had an ironic tale to tell. It seems his sister and brother-in-law were asleep one summer's eve when a robber came rapping, gently tapping at their window-mounted air conditioner. Chase's brother-in-law is not a small person. When he confronted the burglar, they struggled in the hallway, but the thief managed to wrestle free and get out the back door.

He had gotten in through a window and left a bag on the front steps. Along with the tools in the satchel was the burglar's identification. The truly ironic part: the thief ended up doing time at the very same jail where Chase and his brother-in-law are both correctional officers.

83. Ouch, I've Arrested Myself

(Canada)

A man was stealing sheets of plywood from a building supply company in Saskatoon during the middle of the night. One by one, he hefted the heavy, awkward sheets of wood onto his truck.

He was working for almost an hour, when he stumbled and fell. When he tried to get up, he couldn't budge.

The poor guy had fallen face-first onto the stack of plywood while holding a sheet in front of him. When he fell, he smashed his fingertips under the plywood. Now all of his weight was on top of the plywood, pushing down on his fingers.

He couldn't get his hands out because he couldn't get off the plywood. And he couldn't get off the plywood because his fingers were stuck. He lay there all night until an employee found him the next morning.

84. As Innocent as a Baby

Retired police captain Don Parker of Pensacola, Florida, knows as well as anyone that mistakes are sometimes made when it comes to enforcing the law. That appeared to be the case in an apparent shoplifting incident. When the policeman arrived on the scene at the security office of a large department store, he saw a young mother with an infant in a stroller. The woman was crying her eyes out as two store security people looked on.

"But I keep telling you, I didn't do nothing," she wailed as tears streamed down her cheeks.

The police officer asked the head of store security to step outside to discuss the case in private. The woman was suspected of stealing several gold chains, but no evidence had been uncovered during a search of the woman and the diaper bag. "I know she's got them someplace," the security guard muttered. "I just have to find them."

Back inside, the woman was still weeping. "I ain't got nothing to hide," she said tearfully. "I just want to take my baby and go home." The baby was starting to whimper, and the woman bent down to kiss him. "Now don't you fuss, darlin'. We'll be going home soon."

She began repacking the diaper bag as the baby continued to whine, plucking at his diaper and squirming in the stroller. Suddenly, his hand went down into his diaper and came out clutching three gold chains. He flung them onto the floor and went back for more.

By the time it was over, nine expensive gold chains had been recovered. The mother watched in grim-faced silence as the chains were gathered up, but as soon as the officer started reading her Miranda rights to her, she exploded.

"I hope you're not thinking about arresting me," she spat out. The officer replied that this was exactly what he had in mind. She shook her head and pointed at the infant. "He's the one who stole the chains," she said huffily. "I didn't do anything!"

Suddenly, his hand went down into his diaper and came out clutching three gold chains.

85. No Way Olé

What is it about young males driving around in cars at night? Get a group of young guys in a car driving around for more than one hour, and the odds are real good that a dumb crime is about to occur. Such was the case in Leawood, Kansas, on a warm July night.

Spiff and two buddies were working up an appetite cruising around Leawood. Teenage boys are basically a bunch of intense appetites bound together with hormones. These boys were not bound tight enough, judging from their brilliant scam. They noticed a large potato chip delivery truck behind a store in a strip mall, and their munchies got the better of them.

"Let's break into the truck and get some snacks!" It was only a matter of time. They'd been cruising for over four hours so they were due for a dumb crime. Spiff was nominated to do the dirty work and do it, he did.

Spiff didn't use a rock or stick to break the truck's window. Instead he used his hand. The window broke and Spiff seriously gashed his forearm and began to bleed profusely. A major loss of blood never slows a teenage boy, though, and Spiff came out of the truck armed with beaucoup beef jerkies, bean dip, and chips. He also discovered the keys to the truck in the front seat.

Now breaking into the truck was dumb, but cutting his arm was dumber. So what could they do to top that? How 'bout driving the truck from the fairly hidden remote area where they found it to a well-lit low-crime area in plain view of passing traffic? Yep, as soon as they arrived at a location where they couldn't help but be spotted, the three amigos began transferring the truck's contents into their trunk. A police car arrived, as if on cue for this comedy of errors, and two of the boys bolted into the woods. Spiff was by this point too tired from loss of blood to run very far. Obviously the loss of blood was also affecting Spiff's imagination.

The policeman looked at bloody Spiff and asked a simple question: "So, what are you doing?"

"Thank God, you're here. These two guys carjacked me, officer. And . . . and then they forced me to break into that truck. I guess they saw you coming because they just ran off. I was about to go to a phone and call you guys."

The officer got Spiff to an emergency room for some first aid. Before he had been stitched up completely, his friends were in custody. They, of course, put all the blame on Spiff. Proving once again that two out of three teenage boys are no good, and the third one is probably an idiot. Hence, teenage boys should not be allowed to drive unchaperoned near trucks bearing food products. They just can't help themselves.

86. Pulling the Rug Out

In Peoria, Illinois, police were called to the scene of a home burglary. The perplexed homeowners reported that the house had indeed been burglarized, but that none of the normal things were missing. The television and VCR were still there, although each had been moved a little. A stereo system, jewelry, and even some cash all could be accounted for. It turned out that only one major item was missing—but it was a significant one. An entire houseful of new wall-to-wall carpet had been taken up and stolen.

The officers on the scene were as perplexed as the burglary victims. They really had no idea how to track a hot carpet. Scratching their heads, they headed outside into the newly fallen snow to look around.

But wait! What's this? In the yard, footprints showed on either side of a long, scraped trail leading out toward a nearby field. Either the carpet had been dragged in that direction, or a brontosaurus had just strolled by.

The officers followed the trail across the yard, through the field, and into another yard, where the trail ended at a neighbor's front door.

When the police entered the small home behind a larger main house, they found not a brontosaurus, but the stolen carpet on the floor—recut and laid to fit its new home. The young man who lived there insisted that he had purchased the rug, but the police showed him his own trail from the "carpet store." He was arrested and charged with the crime.

87. On a Kaiser Roll

(Germany)

Heinrich Wehrman of Bonn had one too many steins of the ol' meister brau that night. He'd arrived at the bar around seven that evening and had been drinking heavily ever since. It was now well after midnight, and the usually short drive home was taking forever.

Wehrman was having trouble keeping his eyes open and everything appeared blurry. He closed his eyes often and rubbed them, hoping to clear his vision. Suddenly, he felt the front wheels of his vehicle veer to the left. He opened his eyes quickly, but it was too late. He pulled hard to the right to avoid the three pedestrians now directly in his path, but there wasn't time. He heard screams and saw the look of sheer terror on their faces as he lost consciousness.

At Wehrman's trial, the judge was reluctant to send the crippled man to jail, but justice must be served.

"Mr. Wehrman, you've been found guilty of driving while intoxicated. You were so drunk that you struck three people with your vehicle. You were very lucky someone wasn't killed. Be that as it may, I have no choice but to sentence you to the maximum six days in jail. And in the future, should you find yourself in a similar condition, you are hereby ordered not to drive your motorized wheelchair!"

88. A Doper Who Came Up a Little Short

After stopping a speeding car driving erratically across the George Washington Bridge one night, Officer John Frank and his partner observed the driver squirming around in his seat as they cautiously approached the car.

They asked the driver to step to the rear of his vehicle. The driver did as he was told, but he looked awfully nervous about it. As he stepped out of the driver's side door, he didn't seemed to straighten up all the way. He walked slowly, hunched over, with his trousers pulled up. He was sticking out his belly as far as he could, apparently trying to hold his pants up. The officers were grinning by the time this geek got to the trunk of his car.

Before Frank and his partner could say a word, the suspect took a breath and his pants slid down. When the guy straightened up ever so slightly, a glass vial slipped out of his pants leg and dropped onto the pavement. The officers stared at the vial and then looked up to see the suspect staring straight ahead and whistling, as though nothing were out of the ordinary. Then another vial fell. And another and another, until fourteen glass vials lay on the pavement at the man's feet—all filled with crack cocaine.

The pusher in the leaky pants smiled meekly back at the officers.

"I forgot that I wore boxers today," the sheepish dude said.

Which goes to show that briefs can be quite legal and sure hold contraband better than boxer shorts do.

Then another vial fell. And another and another, until fourteen glass vials lay on the pavement at the man's feet.

89. Right Is Right

An especially brilliant criminal in a small Iowa town decided to rob a bank. He planned carefully, executed his plan, and got away with the money. But he was arrested the next day at a motel near the state line, only twenty or thirty miles away.

When asked why he had stopped so close to the scene of the crime, he explained that he was on parole and couldn't cross the state line without permission from his parole officer.

Oh.

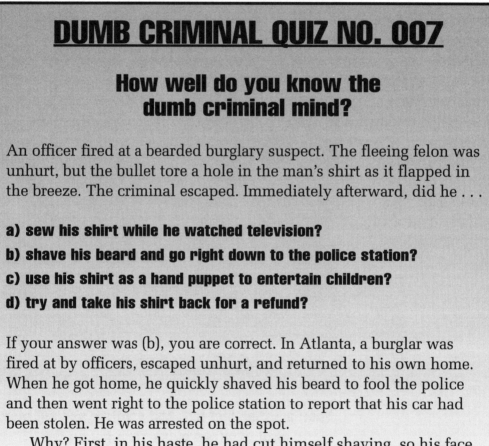

DUMB CRIMINAL QUIZ NO. 007

How well do you know the dumb criminal mind?

An officer fired at a bearded burglary suspect. The fleeing felon was unhurt, but the bullet tore a hole in the man's shirt as it flapped in the breeze. The criminal escaped. Immediately afterward, did he . . .

a) sew his shirt while he watched television?

b) shave his beard and go right down to the police station?

c) use his shirt as a hand puppet to entertain children?

d) try and take his shirt back for a refund?

If your answer was (b), you are correct. In Atlanta, a burglar was fired at by officers, escaped unhurt, and returned to his own home. When he got home, he quickly shaved his beard to fool the police and then went right to the police station to report that his car had been stolen. He was arrested on the spot.

Why? First, in his haste, he had cut himself shaving, so his face was a bloody mess. Oh, and he also forgot to change the shirt that had the bullet hole in it.

90. Another Crime of Passion

It's an age-old story of love, lust, and automobiles—with a new twist brought on by the current Age of Litigation.

A young couple became amorous in a car parked along their town's notorious Lover's Lane. They were in the throes of passion when another car pulled in slowly in front of them. The driver considerately turned off his lights. But then, trying to back up in the dark, the new arrival bumped into the lovers' car.

The couple sued the other motorist's insurance company for child support. The lovers claimed the fender bender outside the car caused another little accident inside the car. The bump from the untimely collision allegedly caused them both to momentarily "lose control"—and the result was an accidental pregnancy.

That's one for the record books—the first and only case (we hope) of a fender bender resulting in a "love child."

91. I Was Only Trying to Help . . . Myself

Officer Ernest Burt was once called to a break-in at a jewelry store in Birmingham, Alabama, during, appropriately, a terrible ice storm. Because few people were able to get around that night, the thieves figured the police wouldn't be able to, either. Wrong.

When Burt et al arrived at the scene, they saw that the front window had been knocked out of the store. Several people could be seen walking around inside the place. Burt and his fellow officers entered the store through the broken window and promptly arrested the six people inside.

"We had gone back into the store to try and find something with which to block up the window, when one of the officers turned to me and said, 'There's still somebody in here,' " Burt says. "I've been a police officer long enough to know that when another cop gets that feeling in his stomach, you pay attention to it. So we looked around some more and, sure enough, we found two more intruders. Then we found another one hiding in the back. That brought the grand total to nine. You've got to listen to those gut feelings."

All nine men arrested were carrying jewelry and watches in their pockets, and yet they still denied being in there to rob the place. Every one of them said he had just gone in to stop the others from taking anything and that he was only trying to help. Right.

"We heard them arguing among themselves later and discovered that the lookout man had gotten cold and gone inside to warm up," Burt says. Then he laughs, "We put them all on ice."

92. Insulated from Good Sense

A narcotics team had a house in Indiana surrounded. With warrants in hand, they entered the house and searched the premises. The man who was making most of the drug sales was nowhere to be found, but they knew he was in there somewhere. The house had been under surveillance for some time.

Finally, the search took the officers to the attic. The place looked deserted, just like the rest of the house. One officer then noticed the right cheek of a pair of blue jeans sticking out of a roll of fiberglass insulation. At this point, an officer armed with a shotgun loaded another round into the chamber of his gun, even though his gun was already loaded. He was counting on the ominous sound of a pump shotgun being loaded to bring the suspect out of hiding.

Suddenly, the fiberglass roll started shaking and moving around, and the suspect was hollering, "Don't shoot! Don't shoot! I'm coming out . . . I'm coming out!"

But it wasn't the loading of the shotgun that had prompted our friend to acknowledge his presence. Before the police knew it, their suspect was out of the roll and scratching himself all over. Every square inch of exposed skin was painfully red and inflamed from exposure to the fiberglass, and the suspect was so caught up in his scratching that he barely glanced at the cops. "I was ready to give up anyway," he mumbled.

That was one time a suspect was caught red-handed and red-faced . . . just itching to give himself up!

Suddenly, the fiberglass roll started shaking and moving around,
and the suspect was hollering, "Don't shoot! Don't shoot!
I'm coming out . . . I'm coming out!"

93. The Loan Bank Robber

When it was his turn in line, bank customer Johnny Neil Haynes didn't hesitate. He quickly approached the teller's window at a bank in Syracuse, New York, and set down the envelope he was holding. He produced a piece of paper from his pocket and, with the bank's pen, began to scribble. When he'd finished writing, he handed the note to the teller. *Give me all your $100 bills or else* the note read. The teller quickly complied, handing Haynes a bag of hundreds. In his haste to get away, he forgot to pick up the envelope he'd set down before he wrote the hold-up note. A crucial error.

When detectives arrived, they were given the envelope. A lucky break. Inside they found an application for a car loan that had been filled out by a Christine Haynes, complete with address and phone number. Johnny Haynes was arrested and charged with the robbery. Bank surveillance photos were used in conjunction with eyewitnesses to confirm him as the robber.

It wasn't disclosed whether the car loan ever went through.

94. The Bagman Cometh

Disguises often cause dumb criminals a lot of problems. Such was the case with the would-be robber who, according to Lt. John Hutchinson of Little Rock, Arkansas, was captured on surveillance camera video.

It seems our burglar had a carefully thought-out plan to rob an electronics store, but he forgot about his all-important disguise. So just before he entered the store, he grabbed a plastic bag and yanked it down over his head. Mind you, this was not a clear plastic bag, but the opaque garbage variety, and our suspect didn't take the time to cut out eyeholes.

Roll tape, and we see our antihero on surveillance video stumbling through the electronics store, falling over television sets and even tripping an alarm system on display. Finally, he falls to the floor, nearly suffocating on his plastic bag, and crawls to an exit.

But he's back minutes later, this time with two eyeholes cut out. This time he succeeds in grabbing more than sixteen hundred dollars' worth of electronic gear and getting away with all of it, scot-free.

Or so it seems.

After the police stopped laughing at the surveillance footage, they noticed that below the Bagman's clever disguise was a security guard's uniform complete with nametag. He was, they cleverly deduced, the mall security guard who was on duty at the time.

Sure enough, the security guard was setting up his new entertainment center at his apartment when the police arrived. Judging from this brilliant man's past history, we would not be surprised if he came back to rob the store again with a full-length, clear-plastic dry-cleaning bag to cover his uniform.

95. Armward and Upward

The man on the witness stand in New Orleans was in obvious pain. Moving his right arm ever so slightly caused him to wince. The attorney for the insurance company sat at one table. The man's attorney sat at the other.

The case was solid. The man had injured his arm six months earlier in a job-related accident. He was suing the insurance company of his former employer for permanent disability.

The injury wasn't disputed, but the permanency was. After a series of questions that his client answered perfectly, the man's lawyer had one final question. With the smug look of victory on his face, he asked the clincher, "How high can you raise your arm right now?"

Straining, the man slowly lifted his outstretched arm to shoulder level.

"Fine," his attorney nodded sympathetically. "And how far could you lift it before the accident?" Without hesitation, the man proudly shot the same arm straight above his head exclaiming, "This high!" He was still holding his arm up when the judge slammed down his gavel and announced, "Case dismissed!"

The arm works fine. Obviously it was the brain that sustained the real damage.

96. A Washout of a Robbery

(Germany)

Even in Germany the old saying, "People don't plan to fail; they fail to plan," holds true. But our research shows us that even the best-laid criminal plan still has a good chance of failing miserably. Take for example the Terrible Tunnelers of Hamburg. This dastardly duo plotted and planned their crime for months. They were going to execute the perfect bank robbery. No detail would be overlooked.

With intense study and crafty use of aliases and fake documents, the two had amassed a mountain of information for their heist, including the blueprints of the bank building and the surrounding buildings, a schematic of the alarm system, delivery and pick-up information from the armored car company, deposit and transfer schedules, and even some of the security codes from the bank itself.

These guys had done their homework, and the plan was flawless. They would dig into the basement of the bank from an adjoining building so as to avoid the alarm system. Then they would disable the security system from the inside and shuttle all the cash and the valuables from the safe deposit boxes through the tunnel to two getaway vehicles that would then head out in two different directions. It would be morning before the theft was discovered: By then they would be a full continent away.

Timing was everything, and the robbers' timing was perfect. The deposits were at their maximum. The vault was full. With the precision of a drill team, they began the theft that they had rehearsed countless times. Undetected, they slipped into the basement of the insurance company office next door to the bank and silently laid out their tools. Using high-powered drills wrapped in towels (to silence them), the sub-dynamic duo drilled holes in the basement wall at key spots, determined mathematically. Then the mastermind of the operation hefted a twenty-pound sledgehammer for the single well-placed blow that would crumble the wall and put them inside the bank.

The two genius robbers exchanged a smile, and then he swung. *Wham!* The wall cracked perfectly. Sections of plaster and wood gave way. Their chain reaction had begun. So far, so good.

So long.

Suddenly and shockingly, they were engulfed in a huge wall of water gushing from the gaping hole they had just put in the largest artery of the city's water main. In their detailed planning, the Terrible Tunnelers had neglected to check out the water company.

The moral of this story: Always call before you dig. The Terrible Tunnelers almost drowned in the deluge they had created, but the police arrived just in time to rescue them.

The moral of this story: Always call before you dig.

97. The Twenty-Eight Daze of February

Paul Marguiles, a Nashville police officer, gave *America's Dumbest Criminals* this story about a man with a short-term memory about long months:

On February 25, 1995, Marguiles and his partner stopped a car with a temporary license plate on it in a known drug-traffic area. In Tennessee a temporary tag, as it is known, is made of paper and carries a handwritten expiration date on it. Upon closer examination, they noticed that the tag had been altered from its original expiration date of 2-17-95.

"It did look quite convincing," Marguiles recalls. "The problem was that he had changed the date from 2-17-95 to 2-37-95. It doesn't take a math major to realize that there are only twenty-eight days in February, not thirty-seven."

A search of the vehicle yielded some crack cocaine and a small pipe used to smoke the drug. The car was confiscated, and the driver was arrested for simple possession of a controlled substance, alteration of an auto tag (which is a felony), and driving with a suspended license.

The driver was especially upset when he realized the crack was in the car.

"The car was pretty messy," Marguiles says, "and he apparently didn't realize the stuff was even there."

The only reason he had taken the car out in the first place, he told officers, was that he really needed to buy some drugs.

98. A G-Man-Style Takedown

Back in 1984, Chris Thomas was an FBI agent stationed in Washington, D.C., but engaged to a young woman who lived in New York City. Whenever Thomas got a night off and his fiancée could get away, she would hop on the shuttle and come down for a Saturday evening together.

On one such evening in the spring, the young couple decided to enjoy the night air with a walk among the cherry blossoms near the Capitol mall. Everything seemed perfect . . . until the two teenagers appeared with a pistol, demanding money. Thomas was furious, especially because these two young fools had broken the spell of the evening. Without really thinking, he reached into his jacket pocket and pulled out his badge in its leather holder, thrusting it in the boys' faces and screamed, *"FBI!"*

The two boys backed up a step. "It's cool, man. Everybody's cool." They never stopped stepping back as they lowered the pistol. "We didn't mean anything. We're cool." Then they ran off into the night.

Thomas and his fiancée had a good laugh and breathed a huge sigh of relief. But as soon as the boys ran off, Thomas realized he had grabbed his wallet, not his badge. While he was screaming *"FBI!"* the two boys had actually been staring at a photo of his fiancée. They must have thought he was crazy—and maybe he was. But Thomas still wasn't sorry for what he had done. In all his years of programming computers for the Bureau, he had always wanted to do that to a bad guy!

99. Coming Attractions

(Canada)

A small drugstore in southern British Columbia prided itself on providing personal service. The pharmacist knew all his customers by name and was familiar with their medical histories. So he wasn't surprised when a local troublemaker demanded that he fill an outdated prescription. He was well aware of Reggie's substance-abuse problem. What did surprise him, however, was Reggie's promise to return in half an hour to rob the drugstore.

The pharmacist alerted the local police, who scratched their heads, unable to remember another case in which a robber gave advance notice. Just in case, they stopped by to see if Reggie would keep his word.

Sure enough, Reggie arrived with a hunting knife, demanding money and drugs. A Mountie quickly intervened to disarm Reggie, who, as the pharmacist sympathetically pointed out, had been two minutes late to his own robbery.

100. Dumber Indemnity

Having just received an eviction notice from his landlady for nonpayment of rent, Henry came up with a brilliant idea that would allow him to, one, get revenge on his landlady and, two, grab some real cash! All he needed was a renter's insurance policy and a couple of cans of gas.

Henry bought an insurance policy with a benefit of ten thousand dollars. He then informed all his Pensacola, Florida, neighbors that he had to take a short trip out of town and would be back in a couple of days. No one would ever suspect!

He returned after dark, parked his car around the block, took two five-gallon gasoline cans from his trunk, and made his way stealthily through a wooded lot behind the house. Creeping to an open window, he poured in the ten gallons of gasoline. All he had to do now was let the gasoline soak in a bit, throw a match through the window, and saunter back to his car.

Unfortunately, gasoline does more than soak in; it fills any space with explosive fumes very quickly. Henry threw the match through the window and gave new meaning to the term "shotgun shack."

Brushing pieces of the house off himself, Henry limped to his car. Meanwhile, a quick-thinking neighbor who saw him had called 911. A patrolman, hearing the dispatcher's description of the car, quickly spotted Henry and pulled him over.

When the patrolman asked Henry to step out of his car, he was overpowered by the smell of pine. "Someone just set my house on fire, and I'm trying to catch him!" Henry told the officer. The officer, shining his flashlight into Henry's car, saw a can of pine air freshener on the seat.

"I see," the officer said. "What kind of car was he driving?"

As Henry continued his story, unfortunately, his pine cologne began to fade, giving way to the distinctive odor of gasoline.

On what must have been a long ride to the station, he asked the patrolman, "Do you think they'll still pay on my insurance policy?"

All he had to do now was let the gasoline soak in a bit.

101. Dumber than That Even

Detective Buddy Tidwell, now of Nashville, Tennessee, started out his career on the small police force of a quiet rural community.

One evening Buddy got a call from a neighbor describing one of the most unusual thefts in county history. It seems that Mr. McDonald had dropped off a truckload of hay about eighty miles away in the next county. Coming back, his truck had started to overheat, so McDonald had pulled over near a stream to give the forty-year-old Ford a cool drink from the creek. That's when three joyriding punks pulled up and decided to give Ol' McDonald a rough time.

"Hey, ol' man, nice ride," they hooted. "You must be one of them rich farmers with a million bucks stuffed in his mattress in an old sock, right?"

McDonald just shook his head and muttered under his breath, but he wasn't really in a position to fight off the three of them. So the punks took the old man's wallet and ran.

Going through the wallet, the punks discovered not only McDonald's hay money, but also the receipts for a VCR and a big-screen TV he had just purchased. The thugs decided to call the phone number they had also found in the wallet. McDonald answered. The punks said they knew where he lived and that they wanted his new TV and VCR. If McDonald didn't put all the new merchandise into a box on the lawn before nine that night, they said, they would come in and get him and his wife. The old farmer finally called the police. Buddy Tidwell took the call.

"The old guy was pretty scared, so we told him to get his family out of there and down to the station immediately," Tidwell says. "Then we rolled."

When the officers got to the house, they hid their cars. Buddy found the empty boxes for the TV and VCR still sitting in the garage. His partner helped him fill up the boxes with the first thing they could find in the garage—paving stones, lots of 'em. They quickly duct-taped the boxes up and slid them onto the lawn in front of the house. Then they took up positions in the bushes and waited.

Right on schedule, the punks pulled up, driving slowly with their headlights turned off. The three youths got out of the car, then tried to lift the biggest box of rocks.

"It probably weighed two hundred fifty pounds," Tidwell says, "but these boys managed to get it up and started to run, well, walk real fast with it."

The officers let the punks get pretty far along before they called out and identified themselves. They called for the fleeing thieves to stop, but the fools wouldn't. Instead, they changed direction and tried to jog into the woods with their heavy loot.

"We just kind of jogged behind them," Tidwell says. "We never got too close because we wanted them to carry that box as far as they could."

The criminals finally just wore out and collapsed, giving themselves up to Buddy and his partner. The officers couldn't wait to show them just what they had risked their lives to drag through the woods.

"At that point," remembers Buddy, "they definitely felt dumber than a box of rocks."

102. The Plot Thickens

Independence, Missouri, is a peaceful community with no great crime to report on any given day. That made this Tuesday morning rare indeed. Two Independence banks were robbed within fifteen minutes of each other. The police were just arriving at the first bank when the second alarm hit about two miles away. One of the responding officers thought he had a visual on the perpetrator, but lost him. He may or may not have been driving a new Chrysler LeBaron, which may or may not have been a rental.

There were no good clues. No legible prints. No I.D. from surveillance, just a close-up of a big hat, black sunglasses and a big brown coat. It could've been a woman—the robber never spoke. There was nothing to go on, really, other than the long shot tracing a LeBaron.

That's when the phone rang at police headquarters. It was the National Car Rental clerk checking on a stolen LeBaron reported by John K. Thompson. According to the clerk, Mr. Thompson left his keys behind by mistake and returned to find the LeBaron gone. The other line lit up while the sergeant was talking to the rental clerk. The other caller was John K. Thompson reporting a carjacking.

The perpetrator was calling in his getaway car as carjacked after he just told the rent-a-car company it was stolen from a parking lot with the keys in it. The police, of course, said they'd be right over. In subsequent questioning, Mr. Thompson lost his plot line several times, and finally confessed to the two bank robberies.

It would have been a difficult case. If the criminal hadn't called in, that is.

103. Accidental Confession

When Steve Hale was a law officer in Murray, Kentucky, back in the seventies, he received a call at two o'clock in the morning. A motorist reported a car weaving down the road.

Officer Hale found the vehicle within moments and popped on his lights. The car pulled over quickly, if somewhat awkwardly, onto the shoulder of the road. Hale approached the vehicle and explained to the driver he was about to receive a citation for reckless driving.

"I'm normally a really good driver, but I had a lot to drink. I'm really drunk," the guy admitted.

The man's confession certainly simplified things for Hale. All he had to do now was call for backup, go to a judge's house to get a warrant, and return to put the man under arrest.

When court time rolled around the next day, however, the motorist and his attorney had changed the tune. The motorist was willing to plead guilty to reckless driving, but he pled not guilty to driving under the influence. The judge pointed out to the motorist that Hale's report clearly stated the man had admitted being drunk when he was arrested.

Ah, but the motorist had a very good explanation for that. "Your honor, you can't hold that statement against me. When I said that, I was drunk, so it doesn't count."

Case closed.

104. A Dam Dumb Idea

In the great state of Tennessee three fools came up with a plan to make themselves rich. They were going to knock off the entire city of Nashville.

Our schemers needed a few supplies. Dynamite, for instance—lots of dynamite. Their warped plan was to blow up Percy Priest Dam approximately ten miles east of the city. This explosion, they believed, would pour millions of cubic feet of water onto the helpless city, transforming Nashville into a sort of country-and-western Atlantis. Then they would don their scuba gear, swim through the submerged city, and steal all the Rolexes, diamond rings, and money they could carry.

Bizarre, yes, but that was the plan. Our three aquatic airheads bought some dynamite, carried it to the dam, and succeeded in setting it off. The small explosion did little serious damage. The scheme wasn't even discovered until a short time later, when the explosive conspirators were captured and arrested.

This explosion, they believed, would pour millions of cubic feet of water onto the helpless city, transforming Nashville into a sort of country-and-western Atlantis.

105. Tinted and Towed

(Ireland)

Have you ever heard the wail of a home security-system alarm? They are loud and obnoxious, but the unfortunate truth is that they rarely prevent a break-in.

Such was the case in a wealthy suburb of Dublin a few years ago, where a woman heard that shriek of an alarm emanating from her neighbor's house. She ran to her front window and saw a German-made car with tinted windows speeding away. She immediately called the *gardai* (Celtic for *policeman*), and an officer took down a description of the car. Within moments, the vehicle was the object of a manhunt that seemed to include almost every cop in Ireland.

About a half-hour later, a detective returning from taking the homeowner's statement tried to pull into the police station parking lot, but a certain German-made car with tinted windows was blocking the driveway. *This was too easy,* he thought. Surely the burglar wouldn't just turn himself in. He was right.

Moments later, the bad guy came strolling out of the pawnshop across the street, whistling a happy tune and counting his money. He hopped into his car and turned the key. That's when the police closed in and apprehended him. Then they took him, oh, a good ten feet into the station for booking.

It turned out that the tinted windows were *so* dark that this particular dumb criminal couldn't see the police station sign glowing in the night, right above his parked car.

106. That Volunteer Spirit

Officer Paul Hickman and two other narcotics officers were searching a pair of crack dealers on a street corner in Charlotte, North Carolina. It was a bright, beautiful day. People were walking the sidewalks, taking in the air. It was the kind of afternoon when anything seemed possible.

As the officers were cuffing the crack dealers, a young man approached them and said, "Hey, do you want to search me?"

It seemed like a setup. No one would just come up out of the blue and offer to be searched if he had anything to hide. But one officer, perhaps enjoying the humor of the gesture, said, "All right" and proceeded to pat him down.

The officer found a bag of crack cocaine in the man's pocket.

"Oh, man," complained the volunteer, "I was just being polite! You weren't supposed to say yes!"

107. Don't Pull That One on Me

Although excuses for speeding are more numerous than pocket protectors at a slide-rule competition, this excuse just didn't add up. When an officer clocked a woman driving in excess of twenty miles per hour over the speed limit, he pulled her over.

He leaned into the driver's side window and observed the female driver of the car clutching painfully at her jaw. She mumbled to the officer. "I'b just cum from da dntest an wud goink homb ta git ma med-cine."

After about ten minutes of painfully slow translation, the officer finally deduced that the woman was speeding because she needed pain medication after a long session with her dentist. For some reason, the officer just wasn't buying her story.

"Maybe I better run a check on your license," the officer said, setting his bait. "I seem to remember a woman with this name who was wanted in an armed robbery."

The woman's eyes grew huge and indignant, and her mouth flew open. "Why, I have never been so insulted in all my life. How dare you accuse me of being a common—"

Then her hand flew to her mouth as she realized she had spoken very quickly and very articulately . . . and that the officer was not likely to overlook her very rapid emergence from the effects of the Novocain.

She was right.

The officer gave her a "tibket"!

108. Dope on a Rope

(Kenya)

Poaching endangered species is a particularly offensive crime. The incredible waste of killing a huge white rhino, then grinding its horn into powder for use as an aphrodisiac, is utterly insane.

Three village men in Kenya had set many traps in the game preserve. Now it was time to check the traps. But two of the poachers got cold feet. The government had recently increased patrols and was dealing severe sentences to poachers.

The third poacher stormed off into the jungle alone, cursing his compatriots. His partners had set most of the traps and they had the map. But on he went.

The poacher was trodding a well-worn path when suddenly he was flying through the air. His gun sailed out of his hands as his ankles were cinched in rope. The poacher was trapped in one of his partners' traps. Without a knife, he could not loosen the rope that bound him.

That's when he saw the rhino. The near-sighted rhino was barreling down on the hanging poacher, who somehow managed to swing just outside the rhino's path. The rhino did not give up, however: He turned and charged again. This went on for an hour until the rhino finally lost interest and left.

The poacher was hanging, limp on his rope, exhausted. That's when he saw the leopard in the tree above him. The leopard wanted to see more man antics, so he swatted at the rope and then he began to chew on it. The poacher was about fourteen feet off the ground, upside down and trying frantically to distract the leopard.

That's when he saw the giraffe. The giraffe mistook the poacher's hair for leaves and munched right down to the man's scalp.

The next morning, a game warden found the pitiful poacher, bleeding, cut, scratched, and bruised. The animals had passed a lovely evening of "turnabout is fair play." At least they didn't grind up the poacher's nose and sell it to a rhino as an aphrodisiac.

The near-sighted rhino was barreling down on the hanging poacher.

109. The Revolving Door of Justice

The Tarrant County Sheriff's Department in Fort Worth, Texas, is still laughing.

A known car thief had just been arrested for the umpteenth time. Having been through this drill before, he posted bond within two hours and walked out the front door, a free man. The jailers were stunned when police brought the same character in through the back door seventeen minutes later.

The Fort Worth officer told them this idiot had gone to the parking lot adjacent to the jail and was caught trying to steal another car. The professional bungler's excuse—he didn't have money for a cab. When crime statistics say a car is stolen every seventeen minutes, they don't mean by the same thief . . . or do they?

110. I Demand to Know Why I'm This Stupid

Who knows why we love talk shows? It's eavesdropping on a juicy bit of gossip, or it's live, let's-get-ready-to-rumble, in-your-face family counseling. Whatever your opinion, talk shows help catch criminals. Scientists have discovered that, for some strange reason, if you place a dumb criminal in front of a television camera, he will actually incriminate himself until you turn it off.

We offer this example for your scrutiny. This particular talk show was dealing with lovers who had broken up and still harbored a great deal of animosity toward one another. Ernest Johnson and Debra Looper filled the bill as guests. Debra was the instigator of the talk show visit when she responded to their request for people who would like to come on their show "I Demand To Know Why You Dumped Me!"

The two lovers had quarreled for months before and since their breakup. It was not pretty. It made great talk TV. In one of her angry diatribes, though, Debra went a little too far. It was the videotape of this segment that convicted her one month after the TV show appearance. A transcript for your perusal:

"I hate you! You no-good $#@!!#*. You deserve everything you get. Your waterbed and your car and your stereo—that's just the beginning. There won't be another woman in your life. Not while I'm around. I'm glad I wrecked your apartment. As soon as you buy new stuff, I'll do it again."

See, Ernest had filed charges when he discovered his waterbed punctured and his mirrors shattered. When he found his headlights smashed and sugar in his gas tank, he knew who'd done it. But it sure helps the judicial system crank into high gear when you tell the truth on national TV.

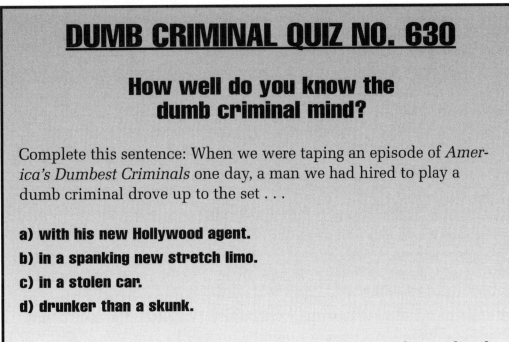

DUMB CRIMINAL QUIZ NO. 630

How well do you know the dumb criminal mind?

Complete this sentence: When we were taping an episode of *America's Dumbest Criminals* one day, a man we had hired to play a dumb criminal drove up to the set . . .

a) with his new Hollywood agent.

b) in a spanking new stretch limo.

c) in a stolen car.

d) drunker than a skunk.

The correct answer, believe it or not, is (c). Security police on hand noticed the smashed wing vent and ran the tag number. Stolen! The cops, however, sensitive to our tight production schedule, held off arresting the guy until after his scene was shot.

111. They're Gonna Get Ya

Detective Jerry Wiley of Birmingham, Alabama, has been involved in a lot of sting operations in his time, but none as outrageously successful as this one. It came about because his department was holding almost three thousand outstanding warrants for crimes ranging from parking violations to assault. Sending out warrant officers to track down each offender and serve each warrant would have taken thousands of man-hours and probably years. So the department decided that instead of going to the criminals, they would get the criminals to come to them.

Here's the sting setup: The police department put together a sports channel for the local cable system—on paper only. The letterhead and promotional brochure bore the phony sports channel's logo, WGGY, which, by the way, stood for "We're Gonna Get Ya." The president of WGGY was "J. L. Byrd," who sent out a letter to each offender explaining that he or she was "already a winner!" All the "winners" had to do was show up at a selected site at a certain time on the day of the drawing for an all-expenses-paid vacation to New Orleans.

The cops had no idea how many people would respond. Commercial direct-mail marketers consider a 10 percent response a huge success for promotions of this type. But on the day of the drawing, the police were stunned to see more than four hundred people already lined up waiting to claim their tickets and win the trip to New Orleans.

All the "winners" were asked to present a photo I.D. and informed that family members could not accompany them into the room where the drawing would be held. They would be processed in groups of twenty-five at a time. (The small groups were necessary to keep the crowd manageable and insure that no one would be injured.)

To keep the crowd entertained and involved as people were slowly being processed, Wiley took a video camera down the waiting line and interviewed the lucky "winners." He even asked some of them to do promos for the new sports channel. Looking right into the camera, dumb criminal after dumb criminal said, "WGGY got me. Did they get you yet?" Meanwhile, the people ahead of them were inside getting the surprise of their lives.

As each group sat down in the winners' room with their fingers crossed and their hopes high, President J. L. Byrd (actually, a detective from vice) stood behind the podium and explained the drawing. "We're about to give you your tickets and have the drawing for the trip to New Orleans. But first, we have one more surprise for you."

At that instant, the doors burst open with armed S.W.A.T. team officers surrounding the "winners," who immediately put up their hands in utter shock and disbelief. Since it was impossible to pat down the offenders for weapons, the appearance of the S.W.A.T. officers was so sudden that nobody even thought of responding.

The sting succeeded in taking more than four hundred criminals off the streets, collecting more than ten thousand dollars in fines, and saving the city thousands of dollars in door-to-door searches and warrant serving. Not a bad day's work.

Looking right into the camera, dumb criminal after dumb criminal said, "WGGY got me. Did they get you yet?"

112. Teacher's Pet

(Japan)

Women are assuming new roles in modern Japan. Men and women alike compete for the same jobs for the first time in the history of this great country. Some Japanese men, however, are not that excited about the gals' new presence in the work force.

"Not too excited" is too mild to describe the feelings of one man, Ito Tanaka, a teller in a downtown Tokyo bank. His supervisor had hired a very attractive, very young, very inexperienced trainee to work with him at his window. He was to mentor this new teller and acquaint her with the job. The teller resented her.

As he handled transactions, the veteran male teller totally ignored the trainee. The trainee occasionally asked questions, only to receive a short and sharp response. At lunch time, the teller was telling the young woman where she could eat and when she should be back to punch in, when he was interrupted by his supervisor.

"I'd like Ms. Li to keep the window open by herself and take a late lunch. You may run along." The teller was appalled. This was *his* window. That was *his* cash drawer. *His* customers came to *his* window.

Ms. Li managed fine with simple deposits and withdrawals during the first twenty minutes. She had paid close attention and, with little or no mentoring, she was doing quite well. At least until she was robbed.

The next man in line was wearing a ski mask and appeared to have a gun in his pocket. He demanded the money in a hushed, angry whisper.

"Open the drawer and look normal," he said. "I want all of the paper bills, including the ten-thousand-yen notes." The woman fumbled with the money, spilling yen all over the floor.

"*Pick it up!* The larger bills are on the left!"

She did her best to follow his instructions.

"Where are the ten-thousand-yen notes? Can't you remember anything, Ms. Li? I told you those are kept under the cash drawer."

Oops!

The bank officer and several tellers restrained the teller-robber, Mr. Tanaka, until police arrived.

113. Bare Truth

In a small town in Texas late on a Saturday afternoon, a small mom-and-pop store was robbed by a lone gunman. The prime suspect was quickly spotted. In fact, everybody in town spotted him. They didn't even need a detailed description. The fleeing felon was running down the street completely naked.

But Ted Jowers had a great alibi ready for the police officers who stopped him. "I like to get in touch with nature when I jog," he told them.

Somehow, though, Ted didn't seem like the nature type—or the jogging type, for that matter. The officers brought him in.

Ted finally broke down and confessed to the robbery. Then he explained to the police that he had stripped down to streak away after the robbery because he thought his clothes would make him more identifiable.

Ah, the ironic naked truth of the dumb criminal plan.

114. The Magic Answer Sheet

A man whom Officer Will O'Diear had stopped for driving under the influence in a southeastern city seemed quite anxious about what would happen to him next. During the course of his arrest, transportation to jail, and booking, he kept asking the same four questions: 1) "Why was I arrested?" 2) "What happened to my car?" 3) "How long will I be in jail?" and 4) "How much is this going to cost me?"

Each time he asked these questions, Officer O'Diear would answer them. Five minutes later, the drunk would forget and ask them all over again. All this was becoming very tiresome until O'Diear had an inspiration.

First, he wrote down the answers to the four questions on a piece of paper. Then he explained to the whining drunk that he was a magician. "I would be willing to share a special piece of magic with you if you'll promise to follow my instructions to the letter."

The drunk looked at the officer intently and nodded his head rapidly up and down. Then the officer held up his paper.

"This is a magic piece of paper. It has all the answers to life's most important questions on it. All you have to do is concentrate hard on your question, then open the paper, and the answer will be there. But you've got to have faith and not ask me or anyone else until you've asked the magic answer sheet." The drunk nodded solemnly and took the paper from the officer.

A few minutes later, O'Diear again heard those familiar words, "Hey, Officer, why . . . ?"

O'Diear just looked at the man. "Did you check with the magic answer sheet?"

The prisoner's eyes got very big, and he slipped the paper out of his sock. He carefully unfolded it as he closed his eyes tight, concentrating on his question. Then he slowly opened his eyes, peered at the sheet, and whooped with pleasure: "It works!"

115. The Cop Who Collared Too Much Criminal

New Jersey State Police pride themselves on fitness and speed, but sometimes creativity solves what muscle and sweat cannot.

One evening in a small New Jersey city a drug dealer led two officers on a very short foot chase. You see, this dealer weighed a hair over four hundred pounds. The sprint lasted about half a block. Sweating profusely, the out-of-shape hipster landed all four hundred pounds on the sidewalk. He would not move. Brilliant. The cops eyeballed the huge suspect. The problem with guys like this is that you can't find a good place to grab ahold. Dragging was out of the question.

Then a light bulb came on. The dealing dumbster had plopped down outside a building supply store where a man was moving lumber with a forklift. One officer waved the operator over and asked if he could heft the suspect into his squad car via forklift. "No problem. I got a scoop for fertilizer."

About this time, Jabba the Bubba decided to move on his own rather than getting forklifted out of freedom. He prefers to think of his time in the clinker as a trip to the spa.

Dragging was out of the question.

116. Arrest Record

The record for being arrested belongs to Tommy Johns of Brisbane, Australia. By 1985, Tommy had been arrested for drunkenness two thousand times, according to Brisbane police. His total number of arrests for public drunkenness at the time of his death in 1988 was "nearly three thousand."

Legend has it that when Tommy was cremated, it took three weeks to put out the fire.

117. Dumb and Semi-Stupid

Veteran female police officer Alson Dula told America's Dumbest Criminals this story about a man who, by any known standard, just has to be one of, well, one of America's dumbest criminals.

Officer Dula was on patrol in the lovely and historic town of Davidson, North Carolina, when she noticed that the man who just passed her had expired plates on his car. She hit the lights and with a quick blip of the siren pulled him over.

Dula ran the tag number. Not only were the tags expired, but they also didn't belong to the car. The man's driver's license had been revoked as well. She arrested him on those charges.

Exactly one month later to the day, the same man drove through town. Same car. Same tags. Same revoked license. Same officer. He was arrested on the same charges. He again went to jail, made bond, and was awaiting trial when one month later he decided to rob a department store.

He held a knife in his right hand and a newspaper in his left as he approached the counter, putting the newspaper in front of his face as he asked the clerk to hand over all the money in her drawer. She couldn't see his face, but then he had no way of noticing that the clerk was writing down the company name stitched on the blue work shirt the man was wearing, along with his name—which happened to be spelled out above his pocket. You know what comes next: He was found guilty of armed robbery and sentenced to prison.

One month later this guy broke out of jail at night and stole a Mack tractor-trailer truck, minus the trailer. Now he was a free man, so where did he go? Back to town, of course. The police spotted him in the stolen truck, and the chase was on. He was running from one county to another in that Mack truck and soon he had ten cop cars lined up behind him.

Eventually, he decided to drive by the trailer park where his mom lived. She was looking out her trailer window when she saw him go by, still honking the air horn with the squad cars in his wake. "Look, Ma, no brains!"

From there he drove over to the next county, where he and his wife lived in another trailer park. Doing about forty miles an hour, he drove the stolen Mack truck across his front yard and slammed the semi into the front door of his trailer. Then he jumped out of the truck and ran inside.

"Honey, I'm home!" She wasn't. His wife had been informed of his escape and had gone to stay in the neighbor's trailer, from where she watched the whole thing in numb horror.

Police were everywhere—local, state, and county. They surrounded the mobile home and cut off the power to his trailer. Approximately forty-five minutes later, our dumbbell cracked. He walked out of what was left of his trailer with his hands up and surrendered to the anxiously awaiting police. He is now serving his old and new sentences in the penitentiary.

118. That's a Spiceeeeeey "Meatball"!

(Italy)

A group of American college students on an archeological summer study program in Italy were having the time of their lives. During the day they dug and sifted through the fine Tuscan soil, uncovering Roman relics; at night they collapsed exhausted under the stars. Some evenings, though, they visited a restaurant in a nearby village to enjoy sumptuous seven-course dinners of pasta, fish, chicken, beef, and, of course, wine.

On one such evening, while the college kids were safely settled at Mama Dominici's restaurant, a drifter wandered into their dig. He helped himself to food, CD players, radios, and clothes, packed everything into a stolen backpack, and made off into the night. Actually, he stumbled into the night, falling several times in the moonless evening before giving up and deciding to wait for daylight.

The college kids returned to their camp too tired and tipsy to notice that they had been robbed; they all just crawled into their sleeping bags and started snoring. But the next morning one of the boys went for his toothbrush and realized his whole backpack was missing. He woke up his friends, and they were making an inventory of missing items when they heard a series of blood-curdling screams from nearby in the woods. They seemed to be coming from an animal in pain, and they would not stop.

The howling came closer and closer. Then they saw him. The drifter was stumbling into trees and bushes, clutching his throat, and screaming while flames shot out of his mouth! Yep, his mouth was on fire. He ran blindly into camp, collapsed to his knees, and plunged his whole head into the water bucket. His screams gurgled to a stop. Then he jerked his head up, gasped for air, and spat before plunging his head back under.

While some of the students attended to the fire-breathing drifter, two of the boys retraced his steps. Within moments they found the stolen backpack with the missing items. Lying together on the ground were a toothbrush, a pack of cigarettes, a toothpaste-like tube, and a lighter. When one boy picked up the tube, he solved the mystery.

Back in camp, they told the others what they assumed had happened. The drifter had awakened and rummaged through the backpack to find a toothbrush and what he thought was toothpaste. The tube actually contained Liquid Fire, a flammable paste used to start campfires. After giving his teeth a good brushing with it, the drifter had then decided to have his first smoke of the day—with dramatic and incendiary results.

Yep, his mouth was on fire.

119. Well . . . That Explains That

When police officers stopped a car belonging to Joe Katz of Atlanta, Georgia, they were surprised to find a .44 caliber revolver, one hundred bullets, eleven daggers, three switchblades, lock-picking tools, a lock puller, and a tear-gas gun. When the officers asked him to explain this arsenal, the man replied, "My hobby is shooting. I throw daggers and knives to amuse myself. I studied locksmithing, and I like to watch people cry."

120. What's the Number for 911?

Dumb criminals usually do their best to avoid arrest, but there are exceptions even to that rule. Charlie Hackett, chief of police in Kokomo, Indiana, remembers a criminal who decided the police were by far the lesser of the evils confronting him.

"There was a guy in town we'd had some problems with," Hackett recalls. "He was only about eighteen or nineteen years old, but he'd been arrested several times as a juvenile and was generally a troublemaker. And now he was wanted on a warrant for a burglary. So I was surprised when he called me on the phone at the station."

At the time, Hackett was a lieutenant working the detective division. His desk was in a large, busy room, and the room was so noisy he could hardly hear anything.

Hackett answered the phone and barely heard someone whispering, "Hello? Hello? Is this Lieutenant Hackett?"

The lieutenant put a hand over his other ear and shouted into the phone. "Could you speak up a little bit?"

"This is Joe Miller," whispered the voice on the other end.

"Joe, why are you being so quiet?" Lieutenant Hackett asked. Then he added, "We have a warrant for your arrest, you know."

"I know," Joe answered. "That's why I'm calling you . . . to turn myself in."

Over the phone, in the background, Hackett could hear a strange boom, boom, boom—like someone pounding on a door.

"C'mon Joe," he repeated, "speak up. I can't hear you."

"I can't talk very loud. I just wanted to turn myself in—come get me right away."

It turned out that an angry father and his son had caught Joe messing around with the man's daughter. Now they had Joe cornered in a room. One was at the front door, and one was at the back door. Turning himself in was just Joe's way of asking for police protection.

He figured—no doubt correctly—that almost any amount of jail time would be less painful than five minutes alone with that woman's father.

121. A Bad Hair Day

Officer Bill Cromie of the Oswego County (New York) Sheriff's Department has heard his share of excuses from traffic violators, but one in particular sticks in his mind.

On a warm summer afternoon he was working a traffic detail when he saw a car approaching at a pretty good clip.

"There was a young man driving, and I was struck by the fact that he was driving with his head hanging out the window like a cocker spaniel," Cromie said. "He was also doing sixty-five in a thirty according to my radar, but he stopped right away when I turned on my lights.

"I walked up to the driver's side and noticed that the man's hair was dripping wet. I asked him if there was some kind of medical emergency, but he said there wasn't."

It turned out the young man was on his way to his girlfriend's house and had just washed his hair. Unfortunately, his hair dryer was broken. "I just hate to go over there with wet hair," he said. "So I figured I would just stick my head out the window and let the wind do it for me. I guess I wasn't watching my speed."

Cromie said it was one of the most original excuses he had ever heard, so he let the young man off with a warning. As he was walking back to his patrol car, the now-happy man yelled his thanks, then added, "And I promise I'll get a new hair dryer."

122. All Thumbs

There are some days when nothing seems to go right—and this is truer of dumb criminals than it is of most of us.

Near Cleveland, Ohio, a lone gunman entered a cafe, pointed a gun at the waitress, and announced, "This is a robbery!" The waitress filled a paper bag with money as instructed, and the gunman escaped with the cash. But as the man ran across the parking lot the bag tore open, spilling bills and coins across the asphalt.

The hapless robber finally made it to his truck with a fistful of greenbacks, only to have his car key break off in the door. As if that wasn't bad enough, he shot himself in the foot with his revolver while struggling to open the locked door.

A few minutes later, he hobbled into a hospital emergency room. The police were notified and the footloose, clumsy, unlucky bandit was arrested.

The hapless robber finally made it to his truck with a fistful of greenbacks, only to have his car key break off in the door. As if that wasn't bad enough, he shot himself in the foot with his revolver while struggling to open the locked door.

123. Bedrock Blues

Sgt. Chip Simmons works undercover narcotics in a medium-sized city in the South. Like almost every other city in the United States, this particular city was known for having a few hot spots for drugs. The cops would do a sweep of those hot spots every few weeks or so, then the traffickers would get released and move a few blocks away to resume business. It was an ongoing cycle.

Sergeant Simmons was frustrated by this slow repetition of arrest, release, move on, and start up again. So he and his fellow officers would try to keep the trade in total chaos by staging frequent, sudden, and very visible "jump outs." Five or six plainclothes officers with badges and guns would target a hot spot for the evening, usually a nightclub parking lot, and, literally, jump out of an unmarked van to surprise the drug traffickers.

In the wee hours of a chilly morning, just about a half-hour before the legal closing time for taverns, Simmons and the van of officers eased in quietly to a space in a parking lot where twelve dealers were doing business. The dealers were already moving toward the van to sell dope to the new arrival when the back doors popped open and the Trojan van spewed out its load of narcotics officers. Dealers scattered, some falling to the pavement, some disappearing into the night, most finally surrendering.

Simmons collared one individual who was in possession of several "rocks" of crack cocaine but who didn't have any identification on him.

"What's your name?" Simmons asked.

"Tommy."

"Tommy what?"

"Tommy Smith, but most people call me Tiger."

"Tommy 'Tiger' Smith?"

"No, Thomas L. Smith."

The name games continued, and the officer got the distinct impression that this suspect was lying. Chip Simmons was the wrong man to choose for verbal sparring.

"Where do you live, Tiger?"

"Johnson Avenue," Tiger smugly replied.

"What number on Johnson Avenue?" Simmons asked, laying the bait.

"100 Johnson Avenue."

"The blue house?"

"Yeah, big blue house."

"And there's always a green car in the driveway?"

"That's my green car."

Simmons grinned from ear to ear. "Now I know you're lying."

Tiger was indignant. "I am not."

"I know you're lying, because I know who lives in that blue house. And it's not you; it's the Rubbles!"

Tiger's face went slack. He went back to rule number one of dumb crime: Deny, deny, deny!

"They do not!"

All the officers were now breaking into laughter as Simmons closed in for the kill.

"Yes, they do! Betty and Barney Rubble, good friends of mine, known 'em for years. They've always lived at 100 Johnson Avenue!"

Tiger was in a corner, but then a light went off in his empty little head.

"They don't live there now . . . because I bought the house from the Rubbles last month. That's who I bought the house from . . . the Rubbles! Betty and Barney!"

Later that night, Tiger's fingerprints revealed the dealer's real name. And guess what: it wasn't Fred Flintstone!

124. The Stooges Go North, Eh?

(Canada)

Canadian winters are long and hard, which is why the first warm days of spring find every Canadian fleeing the insanity of cabin fever for the great outdoors.

One such glorious spring day brought a group of five Windsor, Ontario, office workers outside for an ice cream bar during their lunch break. Enjoying the sun, they sat on benches in front of their building, which faced a bank branch office.

Quietly eating their ice cream and listening to the birds chirp, all five coworkers suddenly noticed a dilapidated car pulling up into the bank's driveway. They could clearly see three men in the car. The passenger in the front seat and the gentleman in the back seat quickly pulled ski masks over their heads, hefted handguns, and darted into the bank. The driver shifted the car into reverse and slowly backed up to right in front of the door, where he kept the car running. The five coworkers looked at each other in stunned silence. Before they could move, the two men who had entered the bank came running back out carrying money bags.

One masked man was almost to the car's back door when he stumbled. His hand clenched, his gun fired, and he shot himself in his left foot. The other masked man yelled *"Hit it!"* as he ran behind the car to get to the other back door. The driver obeyed and the car squealed off, *still in reverse,* flattening the second gunman. The driver slammed on the brakes just in time to be cut off by two police cruisers arriving on the scene.

As handcuffs came out and the arrests were made, the five coworkers sat with their mouths agape, staring at the slapstick scene that had taken less than two minutes to play itself out. In less than ten minutes ambulances had taken away the wounded would-be robbers, the police had returned the money to the bank, and break time was over.

125. Auto Suggestion

When police officers in a Louisiana city arrived at a vehicle accident call involving property damage, the driver was still on the scene, but not exactly "with it."

In a state of heavy inebriation, Montel Stenson told police that he had simply lost control of his European luxury car. During this momentary lapse, it seemed, he had wiped out an entire fence and slammed into a pole.

Officers on the scene were proceeding through their usual drunk-driver routines when Stenson suddenly went berserk. Running back to his automobile, he started it and began ramming one of the squad cars. Backing up and then hurtling forward, he continued to bash the police vehicle. He succeeded in pushing it up against a nearby garage before police were able to extract him.

What was the reason for this bizarre attack? Stenson told police that his European-made automobile had told him to kill the American-made car.

"I was just following orders," was Montel's truly dumb defense.

126. Have Gun, Will Travel

Many years ago, when Sheriff Loren Brand of Panhandle, Texas, was still a rookie, he encountered a dumb criminal who had to make a quick decision. Luckily for the quicker-thinking sheriff, it was the wrong one.

It all began one afternoon while Sheriff Brand walked his beat. As the officer was about to pass an open entrance to a building, he heard hurried footsteps coming down a flight of stairs to his right, with shouts of "*Stop! Thief!*" echoing above him. A man bolted out of the building and took off sprinting down the sidewalk. The young rookie gave chase.

In those days, Brand carried what he describes as "an old .38 revolver in a well-worn, hand-me-down swivel holster." At warp speed, he was closing the gap on the burglary suspect. All of a sudden, his revolver jumped from its holster and went skittering down the sidewalk in front of him. Unable to slow down, the officer accidentally kicked the weapon and sent it speeding toward the fleeing suspect, striking him in the back of his ankle.

The man turned, saw the weapon, and began to reach for it. In a no-nonsense voice, the heavily panting officer pointed his finger at the suspect and said, "Reach for that weapon and I'll shoot you!" The suspect stepped back from the loaded .38 and placed his hands over his head. Brand picked up his gun and placed the man under arrest.

Brand was thankful that the man was just as good a thinker as he was a burglar, or Brand might never have gotten the chance to tell us this story.

**The officer accidentally kicked the weapon and sent it speeding toward
the fleeing suspect, striking him in the back of his ankle.**

127. Looking at the World through Rose-Colored Glasses (And It Ain't Lookin' Too Rosy)

Special Agent Dan Laurila of the Minnesota Department of Public Safety, Alcohol and Gambling Enforcement Division, told us this story of three con artists with a plan to cheat a gambling casino using technology right out of an old James Bond movie.

The department received a tip that three men had approached one of the card dealers at a nearby casino and convinced him to switch a deck of their specially marked playing cards for one of the closely regulated casino decks. The backs of the new cards were marked with a special ink that was invisible to the naked eye. The numerical value of each card could only be seen by wearing a pair of special rose-colored glasses. Since their plan was to beat the blackjack table, it wasn't necessary to know the suit of the cards.

Agent Laurila prepared the casino's security cameras for their arrival. They zoomed right in on the three suspects the moment they entered the casino, closely watching their every move.

"We had dealt with these guys before." Agent Laurila told me. "They were the same ring known to work the casinos across the country on a regular basis. All their scams involved cheating the casinos. They would first 'buy' a dealer and, with his help, execute a broad range of deceptions: swapping casino decks for their own, getting paid more than they wagered, getting dealt winning hands. We've even got the dealers on video tape palming hundred dollar chips and passing them to some of the ring's members. They'd been at this game for a long time. They were pros."

Yeah, they were pros . . . but they were about to become cons. On the video tape you can see one of the men as he sits at the blackjack table, intently staring at the backs of the dealer's cards through his special rose-colored glasses. Something isn't right. It appears as if he is having trouble reading the cards. Maybe something to do with the low-level lighting. From time to time, he removes the glasses and wipes them clean, dons 'em again and strains to try and read the cards once more. Something's wrong, all right. After a few moments, one of his cohorts ambles up behind him. The man seated at the table shakes his head in frustration. He then gets up, removes his glasses and hands them to his partner who puts them on. But nooo . . . he can't see anything either. Just then a third man appears. They mumble to each other like they're not really talking, when suddenly the third man produces a pair of the same rose-colored glasses from inside his jacket. He nonchalantly puts his on . . . aaaaaannnd . . . no! He can't read em' either.

So with no way to read the cards, the men eventually give up on the glasses idea. But with all the other surveillance tape taken of the cheaters that night, Agent Laurila was able to get convictions on all three men and they were sent to prison.

Even though they were unsuccessful with the glasses, the three had no problem making a spectacle of themselves.

128. Will the Next Dumb Criminal Sign In, Please?

(England)

A Taunton, Somerset, shop allowed a certain citizens' group to leave a petition on the shop's front counter, primarily because the shop owner agreed with the group's agenda.

Some customers signed, others did not. Then one afternoon a pair of young men poking around inside the shop asked about the petition. A shop assistant explained that the petition sought better policing for Taunton. The two civic-minded citizens signed immediately. Then they held up the clerk at knifepoint.

When the police took the clerk's statement, they dismissed the petition names as phonies. One detective, however, stubbornly believed in the premise of never overestimating the power of the criminal mind. On a whim, he decided to stop by the address that the two young men had left on the petition.

Sure enough, they were home, and so was the stolen money. These young dumb criminals got what they asked for—better policing!

129. Through a Glass Dumbly

The Picture Window Flasher was notorious in Pensacola, Florida. He'd skulk around one of the numerous apartment buildings in town until he found a target he liked, then he'd expose himself through the window. Despite the fact that he left numerous fingerprints (and other smudges) on the windows, he had always managed to elude capture.

Detective Chuck Hughes, then a rookie, spotted Flasher one summer night behind an apartment complex. Hughes called for backup, and Flasher was soon apprehended. He was wearing nothing but a house key on a chain around his neck.

"Please take me by my house first," he begged as they were about to take him downtown. "I don't want to go to jail in the nude!"

The officers were kind enough to oblige him, and he was dumb enough to oblige them with another crime to charge. When they opened the front door to his house, they found a large mirror strewn with razor blades and a big pile of cocaine.

130. The Case of the Beer-Box Bandit

Most crooks who set out to rob a convenience store plan on some sort of disguise, such as a ski mask or even a nylon stocking, to hide their faces and avoid being recognized. But one bandit in East Tennessee wore none of the above. He created his disguise right there on the spot.

Retired officer David Hunter of the Knox County Sheriff's Department remarks that this criminal "had a plan, but his plan just wasn't too deep. He had forgotten to bring along a mask." But then he saw it—an empty cardboard beer box!

The robber entered the convenience store with gun in hand and the beer box over his head. He could just barely see out of the corner of it when he turned the empty case at an angle.

After smacking his knee on the door and knocking over several displays, the man finally managed to face the clerk and demand all the money. She put the money in his hand, and he stumbled and crashed his way out the door.

The man ran out and hurried to his getaway car, driven by his girlfriend. But she, too, seemed to have difficulty thinking clearly under pressure. When the bandit told her to turn right and head out of town, she turned left and was met by about fifteen sheriff's deputies. She almost literally ran into them. Although it was ten o'clock at night, she had neglected to turn on her headlights.

The clueless couple was captured, then released on bail. And about a week later the aspiring criminal hit on another brilliant plan: He would hit the very same market with the same disguise. The police would never expect it and this time, he'd do it right. Then people would remember him—that daring Beer-Box Bandit.

As it happens, the same clerk was working the night the bandit made his second attempt. She recognized him by his box; the door was locked and the sheriff's department was on its way before the bandit could even enter the store.

It's hard to get away with a box on your head . . . and this dumb criminal didn't. His career in crime was over. And yes, we still remember him— that incredible idiot, the Beer-Box Bandit.

The robber entered the convenience store with gun in hand and the beer box over his head. He could just barely see out of the corner of it when he turned the empty case at an angle.

133

131. Set Your Goals High

(Hong Kong)

Six young men attending college in Saskatoon were deeply envious of a wealthy classmate from Hong Kong. They were in awe of his possessions and resented his carefree attitude. He really was set for life; his parents would give him anything he wanted.

Boing! That's when the brilliant idea hit them. They would kidnap their wealthy Asian friend and hold him for ransom.

Their plan worked brilliantly. They waited until their classmate returned home on summer break and snatched him off a Hong Kong street. Who would suspect Canadian kidnappers in Hong Kong? Before he knew what hit him, the victim was whisked away to the airport, flown back to Canada, and shuttled across town to an apartment rented just for the occasion. Then he was forced to make the ransom call to his own mother.

What could he do but obey? The young man told his mom that he had been kidnapped and that his abductors were demanding a whopping fifteen thousand dollars. He told her the terms they demanded. He also told her where he was, who was holding him, and that she needed to call the Royal Canadian Mounted Police. But his kidnappers never knew about these additional instructions until much later because their prisoner was speaking to his mother in Cantonese.

They didn't understand a word, in fact, until the Mounties showed up and said, *"Freeze!"*

132. Stuck in Their Own Stupidity

A couple in Michigan ran a small convenience store near a lake—they did a booming business selling fishing supplies and cold drinks for fishermen's ice chests.

Once they got a call at two in the morning. The store's alarm had been tripped. When the police arrived, they found the front window of the store had been smashed and the store looted. The couple rolled back their surveillance camera tape and watched as the whole scene unfolded on this dumb criminal situation comedy.

It began when a car pulled up to the front door of their store, and two men hopped out. In full view of the cameras, one of the guys picked up a big rock and hefted it through the window. The Terrible Two stepped right into the store. Finding no money in the register, they grabbed some cigarettes and other essentials like beer and bait. While the two dummies scooped up several cartons of cigarettes, they looked right into the camera for a close-up on the surveillance camera. They disappeared as quickly as they had appeared and were nowhere to be found when police arrived at the scene. Until the next morning, that is.

The owner of the market was a little shocked when the crooks walked in the next morning. The two explained that their car was stuck. The owner went with them across the street while his wife called the cops.

It seems Slow and Slower had backed across the road after robbing the store. What they couldn't see in the dark of night was a boat ramp into the lake. Try as they might, they couldn't get their wheels out of the mud. So they walked home and waited for morning to retrieve their car. The market owner kept up the act by offering to call a tow truck, but before he could call, four squad cars and a police tow truck arrived and took care of them—for free.

133. The Wrong Guy

A man who had been involved in a hit-and-run . . . ran. He knew he was drunk, and he also knew that getting caught would mean a second conviction of driving under the influence. So he got out of his vehicle, stumbled to the next intersection, and flagged down a car at the stoplight.

"I've been in an 'accidentally,'" he drunkenly explained to the driver. "I need somebody to drive me home."

The driver of the car looked at him thoughtfully. "All right," he finally said. "Get in."

The intoxicated hitchhiker couldn't believe his luck. How often do you find such a willing accomplice on the first try? After just a few fumbles he got the car door open and climbed in beside his Good Samaritan.

But then the drunk man noticed something was wrong. True, his head was spinning. But he could swear that the driver had immediately made a U-turn and headed back in the direction of the accident.

"Hey, man, what are you doing?" he asked weakly.

The undercover cop reached under the seat and pulled out his identification and badge.

"Buddy," he said, "this just isn't your day."

134. The (Ex)-Terminator

Sgt. Perry Knowles got a call one night announcing that shots were being fired at one of the juke joints in Pensacola, Florida. Knowles was only moments from the little tavern, so he responded immediately and sped to the scene.

A few moments after arriving, he realized he was the first on the scene and that the shots were still ringing out. They seemed to be coming from inside. Knowles drew his gun and cautiously approached the front door. Inside, people were still dancing and shooting pool as though nothing out of the ordinary was going on. Another shot rang out. Without waiting for backup, Knowles dashed in, just as another shot sounded from the back of the club.

Gun drawn, Knowles hurried down a hallway and then crept around the corner, where he saw a man facing the other way with a pistol in hand, following the path of a huge cockroach. *Blam!* He blasted the cockroach with a close-range shot from a .38 and blew a big hole in the wall. After two more direct hits, the (ex)terminator broke open his cylinder to reload. That's when Sergeant Knowles jumped out from behind the corner.

"What in the world are you doing?" Knowles yelled while disarming the man.

"Shooting cockroaches!" the shooter said, apparently seeing nothing odd about his answer.

"Why?" Knowles asked.

"Well, we've tried everything else, and nothing has worked."

Blam! He blasted the cockroach with a close-range shot from a .38 and blew a big hole in the wall.

135. Who You Gonna Call?

An officer in Washington, D.C., answered the call about a car break-in along one of the main streets. He arrived at the scene to find the automobile in question, its trunk obviously jimmied, but no owner. Since the car was parked outside a bar, the officer stepped in to see if the car's owner was inside. He had to talk to several patrons before he finally found his man—who proved to be highly indignant.

"Well, it's about time. I called half an hour ago."

The officer pointed out that it had only been twelve minutes since his call and that he had been looking for the car owner for about five minutes. Then he asked the gentleman what exactly had been taken from his car.

"Ten thousand dollars in cash."

"Could you repeat that, sir?"

"Ten thousand dollars in cash, from my trunk."

The officer noted the amount and asked the man to show him the car. The owner stepped outside with the officer and directed him to the back of his car. The trunk's bent metal lid and twisted lock were telltale signs that a crowbar had been used to pry the trunk open.

"Would you open the trunk, sir?"

The owner didn't answer.

"Sir, would you open the trunk?"

"Why?" The owner looked seriously concerned about something.

"Well, sir, to file a report, I need to establish all the facts—such as the fact that the money isn't in the trunk now."

The car's owner thought for a moment, paced a bit, then asked the officer, "So if I open the trunk, you're just going to look for the money?"

"I need to establish that the money isn't in there. Yes, sir."

The car's owner thought a bit more and finally relented. He unlocked the trunk and stepped back. The officer's eyes landed immediately on a clear plastic bag containing approximately ten pounds of marijuana.

"Sir, you're under arrest for possession of a controlled substance."

"You can't do that! You said you were only looking for the money, and the money isn't there."

"Well, sir, the marijuana is in plain sight and, as an officer of the law, I cannot ignore evidence of a crime."

The man was furious. "Well, I suppose you're going to bust me for the cocaine under the front floor mat, too."

The officer couldn't believe his ears. "No, sir. I'll call a judge for a search warrant and then, if I find cocaine under the front floor mat, I'll bust you for that, too."

He did. The final count was ten pounds of marijuana, five grams of cocaine, one gallon of moonshine . . . and one very indignant dumb criminal, in custody.

Have a dumb day!

DUMB CRIMINAL QUIZ NO. 116

How well do you know the dumb criminal mind?

When released from prison on May 7, 1980, Paul Geidel had spent more consecutive years in a U.S. prison than any other convict in U.S. history. He was seventeen when he walked in. How old was he when he walked out?

a) 60 years old.

b) 77 years old.

c) 85 years old.

d) 93 years old.

e) 101 years old.

The answer is (c). Sentenced to prison for murder on September 5, 1911, Geidel walked out of the Fishkill Correctional Facility in Beacon, New York, a free man after having served sixty-eight years, eight months, and two days. He was eighty-five years old. Do you think his girlfriend waited for him?

136. Sheer Terror Is Extra

We've had many stories of drunks who passed out in running cars and never moved an inch, but this story from an officer who retired from the Peoria, Illinois, force has a Hitchcock twist.

Officer Steve Bryant observed a car parked along the roadside with its lights on. As he slowly approached, he heard the engine of the parked car running and was able to make out a head slumped forward on the steering wheel. The man appeared to be fine, just sleeping soundly. Officer Bryant pulled nose to nose in front of the sleeping motorist and left his patrol car running.

He approached the driver's side window and saw several empty beer cans on the floorboard. There didn't appear to be any signs of foul play. Officer Bryant rapped his flashlight on the roof of the car and watched as *Scream 3* unfolded before his eyes.

The drunk driver rose up, and when his eyes cleared the dashboard, he saw what he was sure was the patrol car ready to crash head-on into him. His scream could've been heard for a radius of over ten miles. He stomped on the brake pedal so hard, his foot nearly went through the floor of the car. He almost tore the steering wheel off trying to veer right and avoid certain and instant death. That's when he heard the officer's gales of laughter just outside his window. It was a lesson well-learned with a happy ending that is all too rare.

137. Write On!

"I've got another story for you," Detective Ted McDonald told us at a recent barbecue for *America's Dumbest Criminals* personnel in Brunswick, Georgia. "Adam Watson and I had to serve a warrant for cashing a stolen check on a man that lived here in Brunswick. I remember it because of the heat that day. It must have been a hundred. In fact, it was so hot that I saw two dogs fighting over a tree."

He smiled.

"As we arrived at the man's house and began to go up on the front porch, a dog starts barking. About this time a man comes from around the back of the house to see what the dog is barking at. It was us."

"Robert Norton?" the officers asked the man.

"Yeah, I'm Robert Norton. What can I do for you guys?"

"Mr. Norton, we have a warrant for your arrest for receiving and cashing a stolen check."

"Nah . . . you've got the wrong man." he said, shaking his head. "I never cashed a stolen check in my life. What makes you guys think I did something like that?"

"Well sir," Officer McDonald said, holding up the canceled check from the bank. "You forged the name the check was in on the front. But on the back, when you endorsed it, you signed your *real* name. And you provided the teller with your driver's license, complete with your current address."

"You weren't thinking too clearly at that moment, were you?" Watson asked.

"Let me see that check," the man said. He looked it over pretty good, front and back. Then he shook his head in disbelief and frustration.

"I'd never done anything like this before," he told the two detectives. "I guess when she asked me for my I.D. I just went into check-cashing mode. I can't believe I did that . . . pretty dumb, huh?"

"Pretty dumb," the officers echoed in unison. "Let's go."

138. Hot Dip Pursuit

(Australia)

An officer making his rounds behind the wheel in Sydney fell in behind a suspicious-looking car. The officer's interest had been aroused by the license plate that had been shoved haphazardly into the car's back window. A quick radio call revealed that the plate belonged to a different make and model of vehicle.

Just as the officer was flicking on his lights and siren, he realized he had been made. The door to the car flew open, and the driver took off on foot into a nearby neighborhood. By the time the officer had radioed his position and jumped out of his car to give chase, the suspect had a good fifty-foot head start.

It was the proliferation of backyard fences that enabled the officer to close the gap. With every yard, the suspect lost more of his lead. The suspect would scale one fence, tumble over to the other side, pull himself to his feet, and keep on truckin'. This went on for five backyard fences, with the officer gaining ground each time. He was almost within an arm's length when the suspect launched himself over a six-foot privacy fence. Then came the splash—and the screams.

Peering over the top of the fence, the officer started laughing as he watched his prey flailing helplessly in the beautifully landscaped swimming pool.

Now, a nice, cool dip might sound refreshing after a bit of hot pursuit, but there was one problem: Our dumb criminal couldn't swim. Instead of enjoying his dunking, he was gurgling, "Save me, please. Officer, help!"

Who says there's never a cop around when you need one?

But there was one problem:
Our dumb criminal couldn't swim.

142

139. Reach out and Touch Someone

Wanted for several dozen burglaries, East Coast fugitive Lester Willet had been eluding capture for several weeks. Although he had been seen in various bars, he always managed to be gone by the time the cops arrived. Friendly and outgoing, he had plenty of friends quick to tip him off each time the long arm of the law reached out to snag him.

But Lester Willet had a weakness, and her name was Charlene. A cocktail waitress at Taylor's Place, Charlene was a heavily made-up, gum-chewing, buxom beauty. Sadly, Willet's was an unrequited love, because Charlene adamantly refused to go out with him.

The investigator pursuing Willet learned about his infatuation with Charlene from one of his informants. He further learned that Charlene had this particular night off and that Willet had been calling her steadily from Taylor's pay phone, trying to talk her into going out with him.

Seized by a sudden flash of inspiration, the investigator decided to have someone call Taylor's, impersonate Charlene's voice, and ask to speak to Willet. Once Willet got on the phone, it would be a simple matter to swoop down and capture him. It was a good idea, although finding a convincing female voice was going to be difficult. Then someone suggested Dan Bulger.

Bulger was a brash communications dispatcher who also happened to be a wonderful mimic. He was on duty at the time, so the investigator sought him out and explained the plan. The capture team would wait a block or so from Taylor's as Dan, using his best female voice, called the bar, identified himself as Charlene, and asked for Willet. When Willet picked up the phone, the team would be notified by one of the other dispatchers and then make their move.

Their scheme worked perfectly. The pay phone was close to the main door, and when the team came around the corner there was Willet, the phone jammed against one ear and his hand pressed against the other. "Baby, you know I'm crazy about you!" he yelled into the phone. "You go out with me and you won't regret it, I promise."

So intent was he on the conversation that he didn't notice he was now surrounded by uniforms. He had a big smile on his face and was nodding his head. "Room nineteen at the Sunset Motel. Right."

The investigator stepped forward and tapped him on the shoulder. Willet looked up, and the smile disappeared. "Uh, I got to go, baby," he said. He hung up and shook his head. "Well, I hope you guys are happy. I was fixing to meet one of the finest-looking women I have ever seen, and she was even going to pay for the room."

It was just a short trip back to the jail, but Willet complained about his bad luck the whole way. Just to rub it in, the investigator had Dan come over from the radio room. Willet was being fingerprinted when Dan stepped to the door and, using his Charlene voice, said, "Honey, I told you to meet me at the Sunset Motel."

Willet spun around so fast he almost knocked over the fingerprint stand. Dan gave him a big smile. "But I've changed my mind, sugar. You pay for the room."

140. It's Later than You Think

Detective Jerry Wiley of Birmingham, Alabama, offers this story of stupidity concerning a man who entered a convenience store and told the young female cashier to back away from the register.

"Don't hit that button under there, either," he told her.

"How do you know what that button is?" she asked.

"Honey, I've been robbin' these here little stores since before you were born, that's how I know. I robbed my first one at the tender age of eleven."

The man took the money from the drawer, casually counted it, and stuffed it into his pocket. He then winked at the young girl as he opened the door to leave and said, "You'd have to get up pretty early in the morning to catch old Bo Ramsey!"

When the police arrived, the cashier described the man and repeated what he had said. They ran his name through the computer and got a copy of his driver's license, with picture I.D., which they showed the clerk.

"Yep, that's him. That's the pro."

141. I'll Be Right Back

(Bermuda)

Bermuda is not a big place. If you're a local and you pull a job in Bermuda, the odds are someone will know it's you. Yet, a local still decided to take his shot at the perfect crime.

First, he scouted the bank. A tape from the surveillance camera clearly shows him eyeballing the security devices, walking around the bank in a very colorful, very conspicuous shirt with a number on it. The tape shows the same man, in the same shirt, re-enter the bank wearing a ski mask.

The victims, witnesses, and bystanders all had the same story.

"Joe just robbed the bank."

Two officers went to Joe's house and picked him up. Everything is slower and simpler on an island, even crime.

142. Drag Race

It was another routine day on patrol at a shopping mall. Officer Dusty Cutler had just grabbed a quick lunch and returned to her squad car when she saw a blond woman sprint out the mall entrance and into the parking lot.

"She was an attractive woman," Cutler remembers. "She wore a nice print dress, high heels . . . and she was very tall."

But why was she running? Seconds later Cutler got an answer when two men ran out the door and pursued the woman across the parking lot.

At first, Cutler thought the two men were harassing the woman. Then they got closer, and she heard them shouting, "Stop her! She robbed us!"

Cutler later learned that the woman had shoplifted women's clothing from a store in the mall and then assaulted one of the managers. The two men chasing her through the busy parking lot were the store's other manager and a salesclerk.

As the suspect ran in front of Cutler's car, she hiked up her dress in order to run faster, exposing a large pair of women's underwear. They

The woman had shoplifted women's clothing from a store in the mall and then assaulted one of the managers.

were bulkier than normal, and Cutler could see a sleeve from a woman's blouse sticking out through the leg opening.

As the shoplifter sprinted away, the large baggy underwear stuffed with stolen merchandise slipped down over the suspect's thighs. At that point the officer noticed something extra that obviously didn't come from a store. The woman shoplifter, evidently, was not a woman.

By now the officer was having a difficult time calling in the report because she was laughing so hard. And the fleeing shoplifter was rapidly losing ground. With every step, the loaded underwear slipped farther down the suspect's legs. Finally, they fell to the ground and sent their wearer sprawling.

Still trying to make a graceful getaway, the fugitive scrambled back up, kicked off both the offending underwear and the high heels, and ran faster. But by this time Cutler had pulled the patrol car into the suspect's path, and the fleeing criminal slammed across the hood of the car. She/he was arrested and charged with shoplifting.

Cutler still speaks of that shoplifter-in-drag as the strangest criminal she ever—literally—ran into.

143. With One Hand Tied Behind My Back

(Germany)

In Hamburg, there is a small bank branch office that opens for business only three days a week. Locals don't have to fight the crowded roads to the city and the teller knows everyone by name. Almost everyone, that is.

One Friday afternoon a stranger walked in. The teller greeted him cheerfully, but the stranger didn't reply. Looking around to make sure no one else was in the bank, the stranger pulled a gun.

"This is a robbery. Give me all the money."

The robber grabbed the cash and tied the teller to a rolling chair. Oh, and he tied just one of her hands. After he left, she rolled over to a phone, reported the robbery, and untied herself with her free hand.

She literally thwarted his robbery with one hand tied behind her back.

144. Two-Dog Night

Twenty-three-year veteran Sergeant Dave Glover of the East Peoria, Illinois, Police Department told us of an incident that happened when he was just a rookie.

Officer Glover and his partner were called to a domestic disturbance one night and arrived at the scene to find a woman sitting on her front porch crying. The woman stated to the officers that her husband had been drinking heavily that night and had become physically abusive to her. He had run out the back door only moments before the officers had arrived. So while his partner took down her statement, Officer Glover decided to walk around back of the house to see if the man might still be around.

While searching the backyard with his flashlight, Officer Glover kept hearing a dog in the neighbor's backyard barking angrily. The dog was chained to his dog house and the officer assumed it was just doing its job, warning him off. The entire time the officer spent around back looking for the suspect, the dog kept barking. Eventually Officer Glover approached the dog and shined his light on him. The dog wasn't barking at him. He was standing outside his house, looking inside. "Why doesn't he just go back into his dog house?" the officer wondered.

As Glover neared the dog house he heard a second dog barking. This barking was coming from *inside* the house. Each time the chained dog would bark, the dog inside the house would begin barking in answer to him. Keeping a safe distance from the chained dog, the rookie shined his light into the dog house. No wonder the dog wouldn't go into his house. It was occupied: inhabited by a drunken, disheveled man who was barking louder than the real dog.

"Come out of there, you idiot!" Glover ordered.

"Okay, I'm comin' out . . . don't shoot me, man!"

"I'm not gonna shoot you," Glover responded. "Just come out of there!'

It took a few moments of wriggling and grunting before the drunken man was able to crawl out. "Are you taking me to jail?" he muttered.

"No . . . I'm taking you to the dog pound. *Of course* you're going to jail. But not in my car until you change your clothes."

A change of clothes indeed. The man was covered from head to toe with dog feces. He was allowed to clean up a bit before being transported downtown to face charges of assault and battery.

Sergeant Glover told me that, though it was many years ago, the arrest of that man was one of his more memorable *collars*. Ha!

145. They Always Return to the Scene of the Crime

It's amazing how many people don't know when they're well off—like the man whom former Baltimore, Maryland, policeman Frank Walmer stopped for erratic driving.

"There was no doubt the guy was drunk," Walmer says. "But he came out of the car just crying his eyes out. He told me he had just been notified that his elderly mother, who had been in Provident Hospital for some time, was about to expire, and he was trying to get there in time to see her one last time."

Walmer asked the man if he had been drinking, and he admitted he had. "I didn't intend to be driving," the man said. "But when the hospital called, I didn't have no other way to get there."

Feeling compassion for the man, Walmer told him to park his car and offered to drive him to the hospital. Blubbering his appreciation, the driver did as he was told. When the two men got to the hospital, the driver thanked Walmer effusively for his help, then dashed inside.

"I was glad to help him, but I have to admit I was a little suspicious," Walmer says. "There was just something about his behavior that didn't ring true."

Wondering if he was becoming too cynical, Walmer drove back to the man's automobile and parked a block away so he could keep an eye on it. Eight minutes later a cab containing the still-intoxicated driver arrived. Out he jumped, keys in hand, and headed for his car.

"I waited until he slid behind the wheel before I pulled in behind him and turned on my lights," Walmer says. "When I walked up to his car, he just shook his head and said, 'I knew this was going to be a bad day.' "

146. Honey, There's Someone at the Door

Dumb criminals are people like you and us. They put their pants on one leg at a time. They eat and sleep just like we do, and when the doorbell rings, they open the door, even when they're robbing someone's house.

A cleaning lady in Cambridge, Massachusetts, had arrived at her next appointment. She rang the doorbell before she used her key to get in. The man who answered was not the owner, and he was wearing white socks on his hands. Thinking fast, she gave the mystery man a sales pitch on her cleaning services.

"Not interested. Thanks."

With that, the burglar closed the door and finished his job. The cleaning lady alerted the police. Within moments the cops arrived at the house and caught Sad Sock as he was leaving with the loot.

Thinking fast, she gave the mystery man a sales pitch on her cleaning services.

147. Welcome to the Waltons

It all started when an elderly couple in Billings, Montana, hired two teenage boys for a couple of days of summer yard work. Seven months later, when the two boys were scheming for a way to make some cash, they remembered the couple. An old man and an old woman living alone—an easy mark. Or so they thought.

The two punks parked well away from the house and sneaked up in the dark. They kicked down the kitchen door with little concern about the noise, assuming they could handle the old coots physically, even if they were heard coming.

As they started up the stairs, however, they ran into the old couple's daughter, who had been awakened by the sounds in the kitchen. Her screams woke up her husband, as well as another of the old couple's sons-in-law and his two sons, including weight-lifter Bobby.

That made two grandparents, a daughter, two sons-in-law, and two grandsons—all pitted against a pair of scrawny teenagers. By the time the seven family members were pried off, the punks were bruised, bitten, and scared to death. The police had rescued them from a nice, old-fashioned Thanksgiving at Grandma and Grandpa's.

What a couple of turkeys!

148. Going out with a Bang

Kerry and David weren't very nice people. Their idea of a good time was to get drunk and drive some thirty miles outside their southwestern city and wreak havoc on whatever innocent desert creatures happened across their paths. Mainly coyotes.

From their new four-by-four Blazer, they would either run them down or shoot them, or both, leaving their mangled carcasses lying in the desert. Sometimes they even set traps for the unsuspecting creatures, ensuring themselves sufficient victims for a day of demented sport.

Yes, the whole thing was sickening and deplorable. But there finally came a day when one small coyote managed to get in a little payback.

Our two sickos had removed a coyote from their trap and taped two sticks of dynamite to its body. Then they lit the fuses and turned the coyote loose.

Scared, confused, and panicked, the hapless creature ran . . . for about ten feet. Then it turned and ran straight back toward its tormentors, the lit dynamite still hissing at its side. Kerry and David ran. The coyote followed. It would rush one way, zig and zag, then chase after the other guy. Finally, the coyote ran for the nearest cover, which was a five-by-eleven-foot shaded area—right under the new Blazer.

The situation had quickly turned from bad to worse. The terrible two were now the ones scared, confused, and panicked. And they, like their little victim, were helpless. They couldn't chase him off. They couldn't drag him out. They couldn't even get near him. In fact, they had to run even faster now . . .

Kaboom! Bye-bye, Blazer.

Dumbfounded, the two ghoulies were suffering the consequences of their evil. They were thirty miles from home and stranded in the middle of the desert. No guns, no beer, no water, no whatever else they had brought with them—not to mention the loss of a twenty-thousand-dollar vehicle.

When the two were finally rescued and the investigation completed, the two faced charges of animal cruelty and other violations against nature. And once the truth was out, the insurance company refused to cover the Blazer.

It wasn't enough. But that little coyote, although doomed, had at least managed to give them a small taste of what they deserved.

149. Robbery Returns

Investigator Lonnie Isom of Pensacola, Florida, had his case wrapped up in record time. Suspect, evidence, victim, and stolen goods were all coming together beautifully at the crime scene. It was almost like the ending of a Charlie Chan movie. And Officer Isom had made only two trips to the scene of the crime: first to take down the victim's report and a second time to nab the suspect with the goods.

On his first visit to the shopping center parking lot, a woman had reported to him that someone had broken into her car and stolen some merchandise that she had just purchased at an electronics store. This is an all-too-common call, and the clues were few to none, but Isom made as detailed a report as possible and began to check on other thefts in the area and links to the usual suspects.

He needn't have bothered. Less than twenty-four hours later, the woman called back and asked Isom to come quickly to the electronics store. He arrived to find her holding a suspect, assisted by an off-duty deputy and a clerk.

It seems that the woman had returned to the store to find out the exact value of the items for her insurance claim. While she was trying to describe what she had bought, a man came in to ask for a refund on several items.

"I had one like that! And that! Wait, those are mine!" she cried.

The thief was trying to return her stolen things right in front of her!

Isom, in his best Perry Mason-Charlie Chan investigative style, laid out the crime when he arrived. "*You* stole *these* items which *she* purchased at *this* store. *You* took them from *her* car in *that* parking lot and were trying to return them for money at the *same* store while *she* was trying to determine their value."

Everything sure seemed to jibe, and there was no way to deny the obvious, so the suspect didn't try. But later that night, when Isom was questioning him at the jail, the thief with the bad timing complained that someone had stolen his soap and towel from his cell.

150. Snob Appeal

(France)

The city of Paris boasts some of the world's finest hotels, catering to such notables as heads of state, oil magnates, and movie stars. Such guests usually expect individualized service, fawning attention, and total luxury. And the staff at these elegant establishments have learned to be patient with millionaire whiners and demanding divas.

Sheik Abdul Lama Ra appeared to be just such a spoiled brat when he first arrived at his Paris hotel. His entourage made a clamorous entrance,

153

The staff realized that there was something very odd about the sheik.

with the sheik wailing about lost luggage and demanding that the bellhop fetch a tailor immediately. But he also stuffed twenty francs into the bellhop's hand, an action that immediately disposed the bellhop in his favor.

Over the next few days, the staff realized that there was something very odd about the sheik. His demands were outrageous—a bowl of yellow M&Ms (just yellow!), a vintage wine flown in from Bordeaux, etc. But his tips were huge, and his open enjoyment of the services rather touching. He lacked the jaded quality the staff had come to expect from typical guests. And typical guests never guzzled their wine and enthused, "Hey, this stuff is great!"

Other evidence gradually began to mount that all was not as it seemed with the sheik. "Without his turban and sunglasses," the valet reported, "he looks like an English house painter." Several employees noticed that the sheik's accent would occasionally slip. And the desk clerk noted a number of phone calls to a working-class neighborhood of Brighton, England.

Then came the day when the seventy-year-old woman from Brighton appeared, asking for the sheik's room.

"Is he expecting you, madam?" the manager asked.

"Well, he would be, wouldn't he? He invited me here himself. I'm his mum."

The manager simply nodded and escorted her upstairs. Sheik Howie's jaw dropped to see his mum with the manager, but that consummate professional only let him squirm for a moment. "If your mother would like to order dinner now, sir," he said, "we could serve you here in your suite."

Howie swallowed, losing his accent entirely. "That would be lovely."

"Then, if you would be so kind, sir, I need to speak to you downstairs . . ."

Sheik Howie and his mum enjoyed an elegant dinner compliments of the hotel manager. He put his mum on her train back to Brighton, England. Then he surrendered to authorities and began the long process of paying off his hotel bill of seventy-six thousand francs.

151. Backseat Driver

When police pull over a driver, they're always ready to hear the "big story." Sergeant Doug Baldwin of the Pensacola (Florida) Police Department remembers a time when a van was swerving and weaving across the center line. When the officer approached the van, now stopped, he noticed that the driver had moved over to the passenger's seat.

The officer shined his flashlight across the front seat to the man who had suddenly become the passenger in a driverless van. The officer asked for the man's driver's license and registration.

"I wasn't driving," the man claimed and pointed to the backseat. "The guy in the back was."

The officer shined his flashlight in back and got a good look at the perpetrator—a huge teddy bear.

It didn't take the officer long to assess the situation. One of the van's occupants was stuffed. The other was obviously loaded.

152. Told You So

An undercover cop in a small Virginia town had a problem working undercover. The very nature of undercover demands a new identity, a new kid who becomes one of the gang. If you go to purchase drugs and the dealer turns out to be one of your old high school or neighborhood "gang," things begin to get sticky. This was the case for one officer we'll call WD-40.

WD-40 was working undercover attempting to buy cocaine from various individuals. WD-40 didn't know the dealer he was going to meet, just his street name, Graphite. Well, Graphite showed up on schedule to sell WD-40 some cocaine when his jaw dropped. Graphite immediately recognized WD-40 as a kid that grew up on his block. The kid that played hide-and-seek with you and your sister and rode the same bus. The kid you hadn't seen in six years until three months ago when you met at the grocery store. That's when he told you that he had gone through the police academy and become a police officer.

Hence, "WD! You're a cop!"

WD got his nickname by eluding sticky situations and, once again, he proved true to his name. He was quick to apply a layer of lubrication.

"Nah, I gave that up a month ago. Couldn't get high, way too much stress, and bad pay. What do you have?"

Graphite took it as smooth as you please. In a classic Keanu Reeves response, Graphite uttered a succinct "Whoa," and proceeded to sell WD-40 the cocaine. Imagine his surprise when WD slapped the cuffs on him.

Sure, he told you he was a cop, but hey, you never know.

153. Bad Excuse No. 53

Most folks probably have been stopped for speeding at one time or another and are usually ready with a perfectly good excuse for breaking the law. Sgt. Johnny Cooley of Birmingham, Alabama, has worked traffic on the local interstate highway for almost a quarter of a century, but the creative excuses he hears never cease to amaze him—as was the case with the following, which occurred just as rush-hour traffic on a Friday afternoon was starting to hit full stride.

Sergeant Cooley popped on his radar gun and sat back in his cruiser. It was a beautiful afternoon. Maybe this would be one afternoon rush hour that would just roll on smoothly like the swiftly setting sun. No such luck.

Within moments, Cooley's radar gun screamed. When he checked the speed, the gun read "102." That's one hundred two miles per hour in a fifty-five-mile-per-hour speed zone! The car blew by in the left lane, and Cooley peeled out behind with lights and siren on. Three miles down the road, he had the speeder pulled off to the shoulder.

"I always ask the motorists first why they were speeding, because you never know when someone's in the middle of a real emergency and might need help," Cooley says. "The last thing I want to do is impede someone who has a legitimate medical emergency. So I asked him if he had a problem."

The driver was very calm and almost sheepish when he answered Cooley, "Uh, no . . . no, sir."

"So I asked him why he was going one hundred two miles per hour in a fifty-five speed zone."

"Well, I just got my car washed and I . . . uh . . . well, I was trying to blow-dry it," the guy said.

Cooley asked him how much the car wash had cost him. The driver looked confused but told the officer "five bucks."

"So I handed him the ticket and told him the blow-dry was going to cost him one hundred twenty-five dollars."

154. Going My Way?

It seems that some people go out of their way to get into trouble. That's more or less what happened the night that Nashville Police Officer Floyd A. Hyde unexpectedly became involved in a high-speed chase.

"I was en route to a personal-injury accident in West Nashville, and to get there I had to enter Interstate 40 from I-440. As I merged, blue lights and sirens going, I fell in behind a gold Pontiac Firebird that suddenly seemed to sprout wings and take off down the interstate. The driver apparently panicked at the sight of me. He accelerated to more than a hundred miles per hour and began passing cars on the shoulder. It was obvious that he thought I was after him and was making a run for it."

But Hyde couldn't give chase, despite the driver's reckless behavior. Injured people always take priority over traffic offenders, so the officer had to stay en route to the accident. But he did try to keep the Firebird in sight as he drove, hoping another nearby unit would be able to step in and stop the speeding vehicle. As it turned out, keeping the Pontiac in sight was not that difficult. Every turn the Pontiac made was the very turn the officer needed to get to the accident scene.

Hyde followed the Pontiac all the way to his destination. At that point he found another unit had already arrived at the accident scene. His help wasn't needed. Now he was free to try to stop the nut in the Firebird, who by this time had developed something new to panic about.

"Just about the time my priorities changed," Hyde says, "I saw fire billowing out from underneath that car, with blue smoke and oil going everywhere. He'd blown his engine. Now he had to stop.

"After I arrested him, I asked him why he was running. He told me he had a suspended driver's license. When I told him that I hadn't been after him in the first place, that I would have simply gone around him if he hadn't taken off like that, *and* that I wouldn't have caught him if he hadn't made every turn I needed to make—well, he got pretty upset."

That incident cost the driver of the Firebird plenty—a thousand dollars for the new engine plus the expense of having his car towed—not to mention the charges for driving with a suspended license, attempting to elude, and reckless driving.

"I saw fire billowing out from underneath that car, with blue smoke and oil going everywhere. He'd blown his engine. Now he had to stop."

155. Pickpocket Panic

(Italy)

Tourists are always warned about the pickpockets in foreign countries. It doesn't matter if you're in Picadilly Circus or on the beach in Pago Pago, the stories of the pickpockets' exploits are by now mythical. In Rome, one such legendary pickpocket domain is the Spanish Steps. The beautiful steps climb upward forever, and in the morning sun or by moonlight, the steps and their surroundings have inspired many poets, film makers, and pickpockets.

It was on just such a day that Mark Burton and his new bride strolled around arm in arm, very much in love. Burton was blissfully suspended in time until the hand brushed his rear. He hoped it was Fran, his bride. When he felt the wallet go, he was hoping it wasn't Fran. They always say the first argument is about money.

It wasn't Franny. It was a fourteen-year-old boy who darted up the steps. Burton gave chase. The boy sped up. Burton cranked it up two notches and forced the boy into the corner of a landing, where he tripped him up. The teen gasped for wind as Burton stood over him, pleasantly warmed up and ready for more.

"Wanna race down? Last one to the bottom goes to jail."

Burton grabbed his wallet back and waited for the policeman who shuffled up the steps, huffing and puffing. The teen had picked the wrong guy—Mark Burton is a veteran marathoner.

156. Those Darn Trick-or-Treaters

The dispatcher in Many, Louisiana, received a call from a citizen complaining of the marijuana smoke billowing from their neighbor's apartment. The police responded to the address, and Officer Dean Lambert approached the front door while his partner went to cover the back.

Lambert knocked a little too soon—his partner was not yet in place at the back door. He could hear scurrying around inside after he announced himself, and his partner was almost hit in the face by a paper sack the

160

suspect tossed out a back window. Finally, the suspect opened the front door as innocently as any law-abiding citizen.

Lambert explained why he was there and asked if he could search the man's apartment.

"No problem. There are no drugs in my house. Never have been and never will be."

Peering around, Lambert spotted a paper bag on the kitchen table and walked over to inspect the contents. It was half-filled with marijuana.

"Well, then, what's this?" Lambert asked, looking down in the bag at the marijuana.

"Oh, that's just some candy I got for the little trick- or-treaters."

That's when Lambert's backup came in through the back door, holding the paper bag the man had tossed into the backyard.

"Hey, thanks for the candy." Then Lambert cuffed him.

157. Three Days of the Convict

Officer Kevin Studyvin of the Birmingham (Alabama) Task Force tells of the time he and his partner were working on a Saturday afternoon, wearing plain clothes and operating out of an unmarked car. As they pulled up to a red light, Studyvin noticed a familiar-looking man on the other side of the intersection. The man across the way made eye contact and began to wave as if he wanted them to pull over. So they did.

"I know you guys are cops, and Saturday must be your day off," he said, "so I figure y'all must be over here in the neighborhood wanting to have a little fun. I've got what you need right here. Y'all want somethin'?"

"Let's do it," Studyvin said, glancing at his partner.

So they did a deal right there.

"We handed him the money, he handed us the dope, and we arrested him," Studyvin says. "No wonder he looked so familiar. We had just busted him for selling us cocaine . . . on Wednesday!"

158. A L'il Chef Will Do Ya

(England)

There's a restaurant chain in England known as the L'il Chef, identified by signs that display a funny little chef character. He's three-dimensional, made of tin, and stands about four and half feet high. He's perched atop a sign which tops out about thirty feet above the ground on the roof of each restaurant.

L'il Chef is like the English cousin of the American "Big Boy." Like his American cousin, L'il Chef has been the target of many student pranks and much vandalism. Poor L'il Chef has suffered everything from a painted mustache to chef-napping.

One Saturday night a few college students who had downed several pints of ale decided that L'il Chef was probably bored and bloody well tired of seeing the same sights day-in and day-out. So they liberated him from the rooftop.

They carefully disconnected the bolts holding him to the sign and made off with him. Riding back to school in the vandals' old Triumph convertible, L'il Chef was having the time of his life. He was standing in the back seat of the convertible with the top down and the wind flowing through his painted hair.

The students made it back to their dorm. Their only mistake came the next afternoon when the students decided to take L'il Chef rowing. That's where they met the dean, who was escorting a prestigious alumnus around the campus. His heart sank as the still-hungover students rowed by with L'il Chef on the prow of their boat.

You see, the alumnus watching from the riverbank had amassed a fortune as the CEO of L'il Chef restaurants. He actually took it quite well though, since he had almost been expelled when he attended the college for a similar incident. When the big cheese of L'il Chef was a senior, he had helped kidnap and barbecue a rival college's pig mascot.

He saw the chef-napping as an improvement in the ethics of the students. At least the boys hadn't cannibalized L'il Chef.

L'il Chef was having the time of his life.

163

DUMB CRIMINALS' TOP-10 LIST

The World's Top Ten Alibis and Excuses

Almost every law enforcement officer we've met the world over has a personal list of outrageous alibis and excuses he or she has been fed by dumb criminals. Here is a list of our own favorites:

1. "They're not my pants!"

2. "I couldn't have robbed that house because at that time I was robbing the house a block and a half from there."

3. "I know I was speeding, but this is a Mercedes; it's the safest car in the world."

4. "I had to steal the car to get to court."

5. "Someone has been spreading my fingerprints all over town."

6. "I didn't steal it. It was already stolen." (This particular dumb criminal watched another crook steal the car, rip out the stereo, and run. So he went ahead and hot-wired the car for his own use. "It was like the laws of salvage," he told officers. "It was abandoned.")

7. "I wasn't really speeding. I just washed my car, and I was blowing it dry."

8. "No one could identify me in that stolen car because I had on a ballcap and the car's windows were tinted."

9. "I went to McDonald's with my friend from the guest house and then chipped a few golf balls in the dark. Then I left town right after the crime."

10. "I didn't do no Armstrong robbery, and I'll blow in a polygram to prove it!" (This brilliant comment came from a less-than-educated criminal being accused of a strong-arm robbery.)

159. If You Can't Beat 'Em . . .

Several years ago in Arkansas, a man robbed a pharmacy clerk at knife point. A few days later, the clerk picked the man out of a photo lineup and pressed charges against him. When the case went to trial, however, the man was nowhere to be found. He had fled the state, and officials had no clue where. They knew he came from New York City, but couldn't be sure that was where he had gone, and they didn't know where in New York to look. They really didn't have much hope of catching him.

Then they got the break they needed to find their criminal. Sure enough, the suspect had returned to New York and had applied for a job. Federal authorities were alerted when the man's prints were sent to Washington, D.C., as part of a standard check required for that particular job application. The man was soon arrested, charged, and convicted.

Oh, and he didn't get the job he applied for—that of police officer.

160. Hearts Breaker

Let's go east to Long Branch, New Jersey, where Patrol Division Sergeant Larry Mihlon told us about a case he was involved with that turned a winner into a loser.

A cat burglar had been plaguing the Monmouth County area for several months, leaving residents and the police very frustrated. On occasion, some fingerprints had been lifted from the scene, but police were unable to match them to any on file in the New Jersey State Police database.

He was good at being bad. Though he'd stolen a wide variety of stuff, computers were of special interest to him. Detective Mihlon told us that the thief had made off with a full desktop system including the monitor and joystick . . . on a bicycle! A lot of burglars who experience early success at some point get overconfident and careless. And that's what happened to this guy. He was seen leaving a house by a watchful neighbor who notified the police.

After his arrest and a lengthy interrogation, the man confessed to a myriad of home burglaries. Among the many items recovered from the thief's house was a laptop computer that had been stolen from a man's living room while he slept. When the rightful owner came down to the police station to identify his computer, he and Mihlon went through it to determine if any damage had been done. This is the funny part. When they looked at the games section, they discovered that the man was apparently a Hearts player, and a pretty good one at that. He was so proud of his skills that after each victory, he just couldn't resist typing his name in the winner's box. Ha!

The computer screen was photographed by Sgt. Mihlon and later given to a grand jury where the man was indicted.

Sometimes you just can't win for losin'.

161. A Funny Vent

It was 3:00 A.M. when Fort Worth, Texas, Deputy Sheriff Jim Reed answered a call to meet a complainant at his residence. The caller was standing outside waiting for the officer as he pulled up.

They exchanged greetings, and the man commenced telling the officer that, while walking his dog for a nature call, he thought he heard someone yelling for help. It was a quiet, still night, and both men cocked their heads to listen. Sure enough, the faint cry of "help" was heard floating on the soft night breeze.

"It sounds likes it's coming from that shopping center across the street," Officer Reed said. "I'll drive over and check it out."

The shopping center was L-shaped, and at the far right corner of the L was a drugstore. The officer turned the corner and stopped to listen. There it was again, and it was coming from the rooftop of the drugstore.

Climbing the old iron ladder bolted to the side of the building, Officer Reed swept his flashlight slowly across the roof.

"Help me," cried a somewhat pitiful voice. "Over here . . . help!"

Reed's flashlight threw its light onto one of the building's ventilator shafts. Half a nose, two eyes, and the top of a man's head were all that were visible above the top of the vent. Like a deer frozen in the headlights, the helpless man stared blindly from the darkness. Officer Reed burst out laughing so hard it took him several attempts before he could yell those famous words: "*Freeze. Police!*" Then he burst into laughter again.

The shafted man didn't find the situation quite so funny, and let the officer know. Reed then called in and requested a rescue team to the scene.

Sometimes laughter can be infectious. This was one of those times. A cop's job is a dangerous and high-stress occupation that welcomes a little levity. Backup units began arriving. And laughing. The fire department arrived, along with an ambulance. They tried their best not to, but they laughed, too. Eventually, even the suspect began to laugh.

After several attempts to lift the man out, a power saw was used to cut a hole in the roof and remove the man and the vent all at once. The man was then cut out of the pipe and placed under arrest.

A routine frisk of the subject was cause for another outburst of laughter. The reason the man entered through the small vent, yet couldn't escape the same way, was that all of his pockets and the front of his shirt were stuffed with prescription drugs. The grateful goofball went on to tell Officer Reed that he was so excited to find all those drugs, he just didn't want to leave any behind.

The judge prescribed two years and to call him in the morning.

162. Why I Hate Family Disturbances

Most law enforcement officers hate family disturbance calls. Not only are they frustrating to handle, but there is also the real possibility that one or both of the combatants will turn on the interfering officer. Many law enforcement officers have been injured or killed while trying to calm down family fights.

Don Parker was a deputy with the Escambia County Sheriff's Department in Pensacola, Florida, when he handled a memorable family disturbance call. The address was a second-floor apartment in a two-story building. As Parker climbed the stairs and started down the outside walkway, he heard yelling and screaming from the end apartment. The door was standing open about four inches, and the hoarse tones of an obviously drunken male were being drowned out by the shrill soprano of an enraged female. Parker pounded on the door and identified himself. There was instant silence but no response, so he pounded again.

"At that point the door flew open and the drunk came charging through like a fullback running for daylight," Parker said. "Unfortunately, I had been a little careless, and instead of standing to one side I was standing directly in front of the door. The drunk charged straight into me, carrying me backward with his rush.

"I had only a brief impression of a very large man wearing blue checkered pajama bottoms and nothing else. He had wild, bloodshot eyes, shaggy hair, and two days' growth of beard. He was at least six inches taller than me and fifty pounds heavier. At the moment of collision, he grabbed me by the arms, pinning them to my side, and we shot across the walkway and crashed into the railing. The force of the assault bent me backward over the rail, and my straw Stetson spun away in the darkness."

The man was so strong that Parker was unable to move. "Put me in jail!" the man shouted. "Just put me in jail!"

"I tried to think of something I could say to quiet him," Parker says. "So I asked him, 'Why do you want to go to jail?' I asked as calmly as I could.

" 'Because I'm drunk!' he shouted, giving me a shake with each word, 'and I belong in jail!'

"Although I was still completely helpless, I looked him in the eye and said sternly, 'Okay, that's it. You're under arrest.' "

Immediately, a big smile lit up the drunk man's face.

"'All riiiiight!' he said, releasing me abruptly. He turned and sprinted down the concrete walk, bare feet pounding, ran down the stairs, crossed the parking lot, opened the back door of my cruiser, jumped in, and slammed it behind him!"

By the time Parker got to his car there was nothing more for him to do. He holstered his gun and stood there breathing hard, trying to collect his shattered wits. After a moment the guy in the backseat yelled, "Hey, are we going to jail or what?"

Parker assured him he was indeed going to jail. The man settled back in the backseat and smiled, saying, "It's about damn time."

The drunk came charging through like a fullback running for daylight.

163. Flip-Flop Cop

(Australia)

A constable in Queensland broke a case wide open with an unusual investigative technique. It all started when the officer responded to a silent alarm from a small business. Someone had broken in, and several computers were missing.

While he was writing up his report, the officer noticed a pair of rubber flip-flops, or thongs, lying in one corner. The owner of the business said he had never seen them before, so the officer took them back to the station as evidence. Call it a hunch.

Later that evening at the station, the officer was doing his paperwork when three men were hauled in on a motor vehicle offense. Our deputy noticed that one of the men was not wearing shoes. Playing his hunch, the officer picked up the rubber thongs and nonchalantly dropped them to the floor as he passed the area where the suspects were being booked. As the officer continued on around the counter, the barefoot man walked over to the flip-flops, slipped them on, and walked back to his place.

"Those flip-flops belong to you?" the officer asked casually.

"Yeah, they're mine," the barefoot bungler replied. "I couldn't figure out where I'd left them. Thank you."

The officer couldn't hold back a smile. A minute before, he really hadn't had much chance of solving the computer-theft crime. Now he had a confession, the evidence to convict, and the three suspects in custody, all without leaving the station. "Oh, no," he told the casual criminal. "Thank *you*!"

164. Big Brother Is Watching You

Officer Pete Peterson, now an instructor at the Federal Law Enforcement Training Center in Brunswick, Georgia, was working patrol in a much burglarized Illinois neighborhood several years ago. There had been a robbery in the neighborhood and the perpetrator had been arrested, but the police were looking for a possible pickup car. Officer Peterson stopped a vehicle that fit the profile that had been circulated. He asked the driver for his license, and the man quickly complied.

Peterson glanced at the license, did a quiet double-take, then asked the driver to repeat the information on the license. The driver again cooperated. After several minutes of questioning, however, Peterson said, "I don't think you're Mark Peterson."

"What?" the driver protested. "No, that's me!"

"I don't think so," Peterson repeated.

"I don't know what you're getting at," the driver retorted indignantly. "But I can't stand here all day. I've got an appointment."

For several more minutes he kept insisting the driver's license was his and that Pete was wasting his time.

Finally, Officer Peterson showed him his name badge. "You see, my name's Peterson. I've got a little brother named Mark, and this is his driver's license. My folks live at the address listed here. So I'm pretty sure that you stole this license!"

The driver just sank. "This has been the worst day for me," he sighed.

The day got even worse when he heard the jail door slam shut. He had three outstanding felony warrants for his arrest.

165. Going Down

Sgt. Ernest Burt of the Birmingham (Alabama) Police Department has served hundreds of arrest warrants in his time. But few have involved cases as bizarre as this one, the moral of which suggests that a criminal's guilt can bear a heavy burden.

One morning, officers approached the door to one of the units in one of Birmingham's oldest apartment buildings and began knocking. They stood there for several minutes patiently rapping away, waiting for a response. Finally, an elderly woman opened the door a crack, revealing a dour expression and saying nothing.

"We have an arrest warrant for a Mrs. Sheryl Tary," Burt said. "Is she at home?"

"No, she's not here," the woman curtly answered.

Burt pressed on, politely telling the woman at the door that he and his partner would like to come in and look around. He was in the process of explaining himself to the uncooperative greeter when, suddenly, they heard a tremendous crashing sound from a room inside.

"I mean it was *loud,*" Burt said. "My partner and I quickly looked at each other, pushed open the front door, and rushed inside to see what had happened. When we got to the living room, we couldn't believe our eyes."

There, lying on the ground groaning, was a woman weighing about three hundred pounds, surrounded by and covered with pieces of plaster, some of which were still fluttering to the floor. She had fallen through the ceiling from the attic, where she had been hiding out.

Sheryl Tary, we presume.

"We told her to just lie still," said Burt, who by this time was biting his lip. "We dispatched an ambulance to the scene. Three paramedics carried her off on a gurney. At the time, her condition was quite serious, but after they told us she would be all right, we just had to laugh. I'll bet even *she* laughed about it later."

166. Con Descending

Known for its heavy winters, it's not uncommon in Fargo, North Dakota, to see someone up on a roof shoveling off the deep snow. And that's what this guy might have been doing, except for two things: He didn't have a shovel, and he was wearing only gloves and socks—in sub-zero weather.

Earl Buddly figured if he were going to break into the small five and dime, he would go in through the roof. Watching from the coffee shop across the street, he saw the employees file out at closing time. Twenty minutes later the owner locked up, got into his car, and drove away. Show time. Scaling a drain pipe in the rear corner of the building, our cautious criminal crawled to the skylight. He went to work with a crowbar, prying up a corner. With a little grunting and a big pop, the Plexiglas dome was removed.

Earl began to squirm and wiggle his way down. Hmmm . . . the opening was smaller than he had thought. Aha! Too many clothes. Boots off, he undid his pants and quickly pulled them down to his ankles. That done, he dropped his boots and pants down to the floor below. He'd be going out the back door when he left.

Naked from the waist down except for his socks, he tried his descent once more. His bottom half fit, but now his top half was too big. So he climbed back out, whipped off the sweater and shirt, and tossed them down, too.

Now with both arms scissored above his head, he tried to squeeze his shoulders through the open skylight. No go. Covered with cuts and scrapes and nearly freezing, he gave up. His shoes and pants were lying fifteen feet below him in a nice warm pile on the floor. He began running in place and flapping his arms to keep warm. He was still flapping when the police arrived.

The opening was smaller than he had thought.

167. Fashion Victim

(Australia)

It seems there was a young man in Melbourne who had a real obsession with the latest fashions. Whatever color was in, whatever fashion was hot at the moment, he *had* to have it. Unfortunately, this man's income couldn't keep pace with his fashion addiction, so he began to add to his wardrobe from outdoor clotheslines all over town. Usually it would be several days before the owner noticed a garment missing, if he ever noticed at all.

By all appearances, our fashion-plate perpetrator had found his ticket to Mr. Blackwell's Best-Dressed List on the cheap. But then he got careless. En route to the local cinema one day, he spotted a snazzy dark-blue shirt hanging on his neighbor's clothesline. It was a beautiful and very expensive shirt—irresistible to our dumb criminal. He slipped it right off the line and onto his back, then continued his walk to the movies wearing his new "off the rack" fashion statement.

Unfortunately for him, his neighbor was standing right in front of him in line at the cinema, buying a ticket with the girlfriend who had given him the shirt.

"Isn't that the shirt I gave you last week?" she quietly asked her boyfriend.

"If it's not, it's one just like it."

So the girlfriend turned and walked over to the man.

"I love your shirt," she told the unsuspecting loser, batting her eyes. "Where did you get it? I'd love to buy one just like it for my boyfriend."

The dumb criminal beamed. He was right: Clothes *do* make the man. "Oh, one of the shops downtown, I forget."

Another bat of the eyes. "May I see the label?"

Our rummage-sale Romeo couldn't resist a chance to show off, so he turned around and let her check inside his collar. Yep, there was her boyfriend's name, "Rodney," sewn in below the designer label.

"Wow, it's a designer label. This must have been very expensive, Rodney." She winked at her boyfriend as the dumb clotheshorse corrected her.

"*My* name's not Rodney, it's Frank."

Time for the real Rodney to step in.

"*My* name is Rodney. Remember me? I live next door to you, and that's my favorite shirt you're wearing."

"I paid good money for this shirt," the dummy protested, but the girlfriend protested louder and smarter.

"No, I paid good money for that shirt, and I sewed Rodney's name in the collar."

The jig was up. The police found several other "Rodneys" in Frank's closet, not to mention a couple of "Bobs," one or two "Toms," and a number of "Geoffs."

Now Frank just has the one suit, but it is monogrammed with his very own prison number.

168. Attack of the Fifty-Foot Idiot

One of the country's last drive-in theaters, this one in Washington, D.C., was the scene of one of history's worst-botched robberies.

The mishaps began when the two young thieves set out to steal a getaway car. They selected the easiest car to steal, not the best one to drive. Sure enough, it stopped dead in the road about a quarter mile from the theater.

Undeterred, the would-be criminals pushed the car off the road and walked the rest of the way to the theater. Only after several friends had waved at them on the way did they remember to pull the bandannas down over their faces. But that didn't stop the box-office clerk from calling them by name. She knew them from high school.

Determined to get on with their crime, the robbers denied who they were and stuck to their plan. One of the culprits pulled out an uninsulated pair of wire cutters to cut the phone lines, but he cut into a 220-volt electrical line instead. While he was lying senseless, his accomplice pulled a gun and demanded the box office money.

"This a joke, right?" she asked, then reached out and pulled his bandanna down. "See, I knew it was you."

Insisting that he was very serious, he set down his gun to adjust the bandanna.

Whereupon she picked up the gun and the phone and called the police—just like in the movies!

169. The Blind Being Signaled by the Blind

In Chino, California, Captain Harry Tooley has heard every excuse in the book and more than a few tall tales and bad alibis, but one sticks in his mind. A motorist sped through a new intersection without slowing down or even looking both ways. The officer quickly pursued the speeder and within moments had pulled him over.

The driver of the speeding car insisted that when he went through the intersection, the traffic signal was as green as green could be. The officer insisted that the motorist was mistaken. The usual argument ensued and, normally, the officer would have to end this discussion with something like, "Tell it to the judge." But this time the officer couldn't resist winning an argument at the scene, so he escorted the driver of the car back to the intersection.

The two of them stood and gazed up at the brand new stop light. It had not been connected, so it couldn't have been green when the motorist passed. To top it off, the lights were still taped over and completely covered with cardboard.

They stood silently until the motorist sighed and said, "Okeydokey."

170. Roll, Tumbleweed, Roll

It was a slow afternoon for Deputy McCracken near Ventura, California, when the call came that a car had been stolen and was headed in his direction. Within moments, Deputy McCracken set up a stakeout. Big as day, there he was, and as soon as he spotted McCracken, he was off to the races.

Before Lead Foot had gone a mile, he had blown his tires. Leaping a fence on the embankment, the crook took a tumble down a hill covered with cactus. At the bottom of the hill was a storm fence, which the bad guy couldn't have cleared on a good day.

So he hiked back up through the cactus to the waiting officers. McCracken was kind enough to take the hedgehog hoodlum to the hospital, where the medical folks removed the cactus spines, one by one.

Leaping a fence on the embankment, the crook took a tumble down a hill covered with cactus.

171. There's One Born Every Minute

Circus man P. T. Barnum is famous for saying that there's a sucker born every minute. Retired captain Don Parker of the Escambia County Sheriff's Department in Pensacola, Florida, reports an unusual incident that proves Mr. Barnum's point:

A resident of a quiet neighborhood was walking his dog in the woods one evening when the animal sniffed out a woman's purse. The man unzipped the purse to look for identification. Instead of a wallet, a comb, or a lipstick, he found several curious packages, about the size of small bricks, wrapped in plastic and sealed with duct tape. Suspicious, he called the cops.

A patrolling deputy soon arrived and took the purse and its contents back to the station. As suspected, the packages contained drugs—pure cocaine with an estimated street value of two hundred thousand dollars.

The narcotics division immediately set up surveillance at the site where the purse had been found, hoping that someone would try to retrieve the drugs. But there was no activity, even though the officers stayed until well after midnight. Finally, as they were about to give up, one of them had a brilliant idea.

"Give me a piece of paper," he whispered to his partner. Then he wrote, "I found your purse and the contents. Call me. Large reward expected." He listed one of the confidential phone numbers that bypassed the department's switchboard and rang directly in the narcotics office.

The narcotics officer quickly taped the note to a stick and placed it where the purse had been. Then he and his partner went home.

The narcotics officers' fellow workers were highly amused the next morning when they learned about the note. For the rest of the day, the two were teased unmercifully. But the jokes stopped abruptly when they got a call around three in the afternoon.

A female cop answered the phone and set the trap. She demanded ten thousand dollars in cash for the safe return of the purse and its contents. At first the person on the other end of the line balked, but she made it clear he would have to pay up if he wanted the dope back. Finally, he agreed.

The drop was set for a phone booth outside the local mall. Undercover deputies took up positions in the parking lot around the booth.

The male and female narcotics officers stood by the phone booth, the female cop holding the purse. Soon a car with three occupants pulled up.

One suspect got out of the car and handed the narcotics officers a shopping bag that was bulging with cash. The female undercover officer gave the suspect the purse, and the man turned to go back to his car. That's when the cops got the drop on the suspects.

When both cops drew their weapons, the suspect started to go for his own, but thought better of it. Seeing that his friend was in trouble, the driver of the car did what had to be done—he prepared to save his own tail. Before he could get the car in gear, however, he found himself staring down the gun barrels of about a dozen policemen.

The final score was six pounds of cocaine, ten thousand dollars in cash, three suspects arrested, one car confiscated, and a nice leather purse. And the bust might never have been made if that one narcotics officer hadn't posted the sign.

It just goes to show: There *is* a sucker born every minute. And it always pays to advertise.

172. One for the Road

Tampa, Florida, police officer David Shepler has won an award for arresting more drunk drivers in one year than anyone else in his department. His experience and skill stand him in good stead even when responding to routine traffic calls—like the one that took him to the scene of a traffic accident on Interstate 275 near the Tampa airport.

Arriving on the scene, Officer Shepler found a nearly demolished car up against the guardrail of the busy interstate. "The first thing I saw was about three hundred feet of red paint where the car had scraped and skidded all along the guardrail. The next thing I noticed was that the car was still moving—but barely."

Shepler ran to the car and found the driver still behind the wheel, doing his best to drive his wrecked vehicle away. "I told him to turn off the engine, but he said he was in a hurry and had to be someplace. It was then I realized he was heavily intoxicated, so I reached through the window and took the keys."

The driver staggered out of the car and stood by the door, swaying like a sapling in a strong wind. Shepler told him he suspected him of being drunk and was going to give him some roadside sobriety tests. "As soon as I told him this, the guy reached inside the car and hauled out a six-pack of beer. He pulled off two cans and offered me one. I refused it and told him again I was about to administer a roadside sobriety test."

The inebriated driver nodded and said, "Yeah, I heard all that. But I do much better on tests when I've had something to drink."

Needless to say, Officer Shepler had to inform the man that he had had quite enough to drink. The Breathalyzer reading confirmed this, reading his blood alcohol level at .31—which is more than three times the legal limit in Florida.

173. Free Mow, No Tow

(Australia)

Lyle Hannibal was just a regular bloke who lived in Sydney: He went to work, kept his nose clean, and paid his taxes. Like many Australians, though, Hannibal liked to quench his thirst with a cold brew. This was exactly what Hannibal planned to do on a hot summer Saturday, until his wife informed him that what he *really* needed to do was mow the lawn.

Hannibal rifled back the perfect excuse: "Can't, dearest. The mower's broken."

"Then get it fixed, luv," Martha fired back.

Hannibal awkwardly loaded the mower into the trunk of his car and set off for the shop. He hoped the diagnosis would be serious, involving parts being ordered or perhaps even waiting for a motor transplant. Unfortunately, the mechanic said he could have it running like a top in about two hours. While he waited, Hannibal went to the pub next door to drown his sorrows. Two hours and six beers later, he was headed home with his working mower and a pretty serious beer buzz.

Just a block and a half from his house, Hannibal spotted two police cars with lights on. Two officers were giving a field sobriety test to a motorist. Even in his impaired state, Hannibal realized that this DUI roadblock could become a big problem for him. He would be stopped, and he would fail the test. More importantly, his wife would kill him.

That's when Hannibal had his stroke of genius. He pulled the car over half a block from the roadblock, coolly unloaded his mower, and began mowing a total stranger's front yard.

After about forty-five minutes, the two officers loaded up their gear, took down the roadblock, and headed back to the station just as Hannibal, sweaty and tired, was finishing the front yard. That's when the owner of the house came out to confront Hannibal.

"Now that you're done with the front, you can start on the back." The man then got out his wallet and showed Hannibal his nice police badge. Hannibal had chosen the yard of an off-duty deputy for his hideout.

174. Collar around the Ring

One jewel thief learned the hard way that diamonds aren't *really* forever. Providence, Rhode Island, police chief William Devine explains:

"The suspect wasn't really a jewel thief. He was really just a shoplifter who bit off a little more than he could chew," Devine said.

It seems our two-bit thief had gone into a jewelry store and asked to see some diamond rings. The clerk obliged him and brought out a tray of the store's largest, most expensive pieces. Our would-be jewel thief tried on just about every ring in the place but just couldn't find the right one. He was about to give up and leave when the clerk noticed that one of the rings, the most expensive one, was missing. Naturally, the clerk mentioned this.

The thief was outraged at what obviously was an accusation directed at him. He denied any knowledge of the ring and accused the clerk of trying to pull a fast one. The clerk called the police anyway and, just before the cops arrived, she noticed her "customer" pop something into his mouth.

The police had a good idea that the man was in possession of the stolen ring, but they couldn't find it on him. Maybe it was *in* him. So they decided to search the suspect internally.

Sure enough, an x ray of the suspect's abdomen showed a ring cuddling up against the ham sandwich he had eaten for lunch an hour earlier.

But before the jewelry store owner could positively identify the ring, everyone had to wait for nature to take its course.

Like sands through the hourglass, the ring did materialize in due time. And, yes, it was the stolen one. The man was booked and convicted.

We just had to ask about the method of evidence retrieval used by the police in this case. But all Chief Devine would say about it was, "That job went to the officer who was low man on the totem pole."

Just before the cops arrived, she noticed her "customer" pop something into his mouth.

175. Drop in Any Time

A cat burglar entered a grocery store in Vermilion, Ohio, from the roof one night. Lacking the stealth and balance of a real feline, our creature of the night ended up falling through the ceiling and into the middle of a crew busy restocking the shelves for the next day's customers. Our falling star was quickly set upon by the startled crew and arrested by the local police.

Oh yeah, the store was an all-night market—it stayed open twenty-four hours. So did the front door!

176. A Hansel and (Burp) Gretel Story

(Germany)

The city of Munich loves its beer—and for good reason. Generations of the world's greatest brewmeisters, as well as the world's largest Oktoberfest celebration, call Munich home. With such a frothy history, though, it's no wonder that Munich has its share of alcohol-related crime. Some citizens, in fact, take their beer more seriously than the law—like the three thirsty citizens who thought they could have their beer free and drink it, too.

They broke into the brewery through a wall-mounted vent and headed straight for the large coolers in back, where each man grabbed a couple of cases. Then they all headed for the back door . . . blissfully unaware that they had tripped a silent alarm. An approaching officer shouted for them to halt as they came barreling outside. But they just dashed faster, not noticing that one of the beer cases had split and that cans of beer were spilling out behind them.

Like Hansel and Gretel in the forest, the officer and his backup then followed a trail of cans down the street and up the steps of a house, where an old lady let them in. A can of beer near the basement door told them where to go next. With guns and flashlights drawn, the officers followed the trail into the dark basement, where they found the three dummkopfs about half a can deep into their drinking binge.

Bottoms up, guys!

177. Store-to-Store Salesmen

In the Houston, Texas, suburb of Bellaire, a couple was arrested and charged with the theft of over $20,000 worth of jewelry stolen from Lucas' Jewelry Store. Jodee and Sandy Barnett pleaded guilty to the theft after they were arrested for trying to sell some of the stolen jewelry to another store.

How did they get caught, you may ask? The store they were trying to sell some of the hot ice was the downtown branch of Lucas' Jewelry Store, Lucas' #2.

I'm assuming they were happy to have had their rights read to them, because obviously neither of them could read.

178. Look Out! He's Got a Turtle and He Knows How to Use It!

It was a classic case of love gone wrong in Indiana. Boy meets girl. Boy falls in love. Girl doesn't.

In this case, she really did try to let him down easy, but he was distraught. He was fuming as he barreled out of her kitchen door and into the night.

The brokenhearted Romeo staggered through the fields in the throes of lover's angst. Then he saw his weapon, seized it, and started back to his girlfriend's house.

In a rage, Romeo returned and chased his ex-girlfriend around the kitchen with a large snapping turtle. He was much faster than Juliet and he easily caught her in the small kitchen, but he couldn't get the turtle to bite her. Finally, Juliet managed to call the police. The officers arrived, disarmed (deturtled?) the irate lover, and arrested him for assault with a reptile.

The incident marked the definite end of one relationship, but the beginning of another. Juliet thought the big turtle was cute, and she was ever so grateful that he hadn't bitten her. The girl and the turtle are still together and living happily in Pennsylvania, according to the policeman who retold the story.

He was much faster than Juliet and he easily caught her in the small
kitchen, but he couldn't get the turtle to bite her.

179. In Your Face

Police captain Mike Coppage of Birmingham, Alabama, remembers the time that one of his fellow officers was on his way home in a marked unit and had just stopped by Shoney's, a restaurant known for its strawberry pies. He picked up a whole pie to go and was just about to leave the parking lot when a call came through from the dispatcher. A break-in had just occurred in a small business right behind the restaurant.

Leaving his patrol unit behind in the restaurant parking lot, the officer walked around to the crime scene and began his investigation. While he was dusting for prints, the officer suddenly heard a desperate cry for help on his walkie-talkie.

"Help! Help!" cried the voice. "I'm in trouble. Help me!"

The call was coming from a police radio. It was an officer in trouble!

In response, the police dispatcher desperately tried to pinpoint the distressed officer's location: "Where are you? What is your location?"

"I don't know!" came the response. "Just send help."

"What is your patrol car number?" the dispatcher asked.

"I don't know."

Realizing now that it had to be a civilian on the police mike, and believing that the officer was too severely injured to respond, the dispatcher put out the call: "All units, officer down!"

"Sir," the dispatcher then said to the voice on the radio, "I need the number of the unit."

"Okay. I see it now. It's 412. Car 412."

By this time, our crime-scene officer was running back to his car at top speed when it dawned on him—car 412 was *his* unit. He raced back to his police cruiser, and there stood the man, still clutching the microphone. His face, neck, and the front of his shirt were covered with what had to be blood. He was breathing sporadically and obviously in a state of shock and confusion. The officer tried to calm the man down and was about to administer first aid when he noticed that the "blood" on his hands was thick and sticky. The man was covered with strawberry pie!

Wait a minute, thought the officer, *I just bought a . . . oh, man, don't tell me that. Noooo.* By now the cop was peering into his patrol car. It looked like an octopus had had a strawberry and whipped cream food fight in the backseat.

The "injured" man, a street person—and drunk out of his mind—had walked by and seen the pie in the cruiser's backseat. He had then crawled inside the squad car and helped himself to that strawberry pie without benefit of utensils. For some unknown reason, he had completely freaked out and called for help after eating the entire pie with his face.

"We laugh about it now," Captain Coppage says, "but at the time the officer was so mad he couldn't see straight."

180. Bloomin' Idiot

Police officers in Citrus Heights, California, responded swiftly to the 911 call. The man on the other end of the line told the dispatcher that he had just captured a thief on his property and was holding him at gunpoint. When police arrived on the scene, they found homeowner Payton Harrison still pointing a .38 caliber revolver at the young man he had just caught trying to steal his property.

"I caught him! I caught him red-handed," Harrison boasted proudly. "This little punk was trying to rip me off, but I was just a little too smart for him."

"Okay, sir," one of the officers said. "You can put the gun away. We'll take it from here."

"No problem, officer," he assured them.

"Is this your house?" an officer asked.

"Yes, it is. I've lived here about a year," he said.

"You want to tell us what's goin' on here?"

"Yeah, sure," the owner replied. "I was doin' some work in the basement, when I happened to look up and see this pair of legs go by the window. Well, my backyard is fenced in, and I'm the only one who lives here, so I know it's got to be somebody who ain't supposed to be here. I grab my .38, slip upstairs, and sneak out the back door. And sure enough, there he is comin' out of the greenhouse with an armload."

"An armload of what?" the cop asked.

"Of marijuana! Can you believe it? This little punk was rippin' off my best pot plants. The evidence is layin' right there by the porch. I want to press charges."

187

The stunned officer looked at the large pile of plants on the ground and asked the kid, "Is this really what you were stealing, son?"

"Yes, sir," the scared teen admitted.

As the young thief was being escorted to a patrol car by another cop, the officer turned to the man: "Sir, at this time I'm placing you under arrest. Turn around and put your hands behind your back."

"Me?" the dumbfounded felon asked. "What for? I didn't do anything wrong. I'm the one who was gettin' ripped off. I called you!"

"You're under arrest for felony possession of marijuana," the officer informed him.

"You've got to be kiddin' me," the man groaned in disbelief. "I call the cops on a burglar and I end up goin' to jail. This is one of the stupidest things I ever heard of."

The officer nodded at the man. "I couldn't agree with you more."

181. A Woman and Her Purse

(Australia)

In the parking lot of a large mall just outside Brisbane, a young woman was strolling to her car pushing a shopping cart. Her purse dangled from her shoulder. She didn't hear the car creeping up on her from behind.

Now, it's not unusual for a car to be moving slowly through a parking lot—maybe they were just looking for a space. On the other hand, maybe the car was actually a stolen vehicle with four out-of-control teenagers out on a joyriding crime spree. And maybe those teens had decided to sidle up to the woman as closely as possible so that one of the dudes in the back seat could lean out the window and grab the handle of her purse.

Such was the case. The girl driving the stolen car floored the accelerator and aimed at the lady's back. The boy in the back leaned half out of the window. *Whoosh!* The car brushed right by the woman's shoulder as a hand deftly lifted the purse. The teens laughed as they sped away, not knowing that this victim was not about to give up her handbag that easily.

The car screeched to a halt to avoid colliding with a car crossing in front of them. That's when the woman caught the boy in the back seat by his long hair. She began to pull him out the window of the car by his hair while he screamed in pain, *"Go, go, get out of here!"* No go. They had hot-wired the ignition of the car to steal it, but now the car had stalled. That's when the three boys jumped ship and ran, with the one still clinging to the woman's purse.

The girl was struggling in the front seat. She had the driver's side door open, but the strap of her own purse had gotten wrapped around the little knob used to adjust the seat, and she was trying to pull it free. But when the victim came around and began pummeling her with her fists, the driver simply abandoned her purse and made a run for it.

Imagine the officer's surprise when he arrived at the scene of the crime and the victim presented him with one recaptured stolen car and a photo I.D. of one of the culprits.

The moral of the story? Never come between an Australian woman and her purse.

182. But, Mom, You Said I Needed to Show Initiative!

(England)

Magistrate Pam Mills of Devonshire raised three boys of her own, so she knows mischief when she sees it. She was also very direct and strict with her boys, so it comes naturally to her to "Just say no"—even to a bungling bank robber.

It happened the morning Magistrate Mills went to the bank to deposit the proceeds from a weekend charity event. The teller counted out the pounds and pence while Mrs. Mills looked on, thrilled that the event had been so successful. She and the teller were so intent on the transaction that they barely heard a gruff voice saying, "Give me the money."

On reflex Mrs. Mills shot back, "Don't be so silly." She pushed the would-be robber's gun aside. "That's a toy gun. Just go away."

Mom Mills had been in this situation dozens of times before, when her own young ruffians confronted her with broom handles and sticks, demanding that she raise her hands and surrender. "I was in my own little world," she remembers about her bank showdown. "I spoke to the robber as if he were one of my boys."

She was right. The "gunman" was holding two metal pipes taped together to look like a shotgun. He kept trying to convince Mrs. Mills his weapon was real while the teller hit the silent alarm and the police arrived.

He couldn't even convince her that he was "old enough to know better."

He kept trying to convince Mrs. Mills his weapon was real.

183. The Clothes Make the Man . . . Dumb!

Dwayne Carver was a maintenance man at the Cedar Wood Apartments in Virginia Beach, Virginia. He had a good job, his own tools, and a blue uniform that read "Cedar Wood" on the back and "Dwayne" on the front.

Now, if you were going to rob a 7-Eleven store, as Dwayne did, you would probably wear a ski mask, as Dwayne did. But you probably wouldn't wear your work uniform . . . yes, as Dwayne did.

When he approached the clerk, his face was completely covered. He even made his voice sound deeper as he ordered, "Give me all the money." The clerk stared at Dwayne and his name tag and handed over several hundred dollars. Dwayne fled to a carefully concealed rental car that he had rented just for the day so that he couldn't be traced.

The police arrived shortly, and the clerk was asked to give a description of the robber. "All I can tell you is that he was wearing a ski mask and a blue maintenance uniform with "Cedar Wood" on the back, and "Dwayne" on the front."

The two officers looked at each other. Surely not . . . no, this was too easy. Maybe the thief stole the uniform or purchased it used at Goodwill. . . .

But it was Dwayne, all right. When the officers appeared at his apartment, he hadn't even changed clothes. The ski mask? It was in his back pocket. The gun? It was in his other back pocket. The money? It was in his front pocket.

You know, this guy's story would have made a great B horror movie back in the fifties. Can't you just picture the title now, slowly dripping down the screen?

Now Showing: The Dwayne with No Brain!

184. Thumbthing's Wrong

Back in Peoria, Illinois, some band members, buddies of mine, were setting up in a small club. The PA system was being tested while the drummer twisted the last wing-nut onto his cymbal stand. About then, the guitar player hurried in wheeling a large amplifier in front of him.

"Need some help?" the bass player called out from the stage.

"Nah, I got it. I just gotta get my 'ax' out of the back seat."

Moments later, the casual calm was shattered by a blood-curdling scream coming from the parking lot. "What the heck was that?" everyone asked in unison. Another scream cut through the air. The group scrambled from the stage and rushed outside. A man standing next to the guitar player's car was frantically pulling on the door handle with one hand and screaming bloody murder, dancing in place.

"*Hey!*" someone shouted, "*what the hell are you doin'?*"

More screams. The guitar case was lying on the ground at his feet. "Help me, please!" he begged. "Open the door for God's sake!"

My friend walked over and picked up his guitar. He looked at the man writhing in agony. "Damn, I'll bet that hurts," he said slowly.

"I think I'm gonna' faint!" cried the thief, "but I can't!" No he couldn't—not unless he wanted to lose an appendage.

While my friend was taking his amplifier inside the club, he was being watched. He had no more than gotten inside the building when the thief made his move. He opened the back door and, with his left hand on the roof, leaned inside and grabbed the guitar out of the backseat with his right hand. The thief swung the door shut. On his left thumb. And the door locked. It wasn't unlocked until the police arrived and arrested the guy.

Thumb fools never learn.

185. One in a Million

Lila Desatoff is one smart cookie, normally. Normally, Lila would never carry more than $20. Normally, Lila would never leave her purse in the kitchen. That's normally, but this was a holiday weekend. Lila had lent her brother $3,000 to buy a motor home about six months before. The good news was that he had just dropped off the huge wad of cash. The bad news was that because of the holiday, the banks had closed early and wouldn't open for three days.

Lila was working at her computer late that night, and at about 1:00 A.M. she thought she heard her husband in the kitchen, where she normally never leaves her purse with $3,000 in it. She peeked into their bedroom as she went to the kitchen to join her husband for a late night snack and saw—her sleeping husband. She heard another noise in the kitchen and woke him. He charged down the hall clutching a huge flashlight just in time to see the culprit sprinting out the back door with Lila's purse, smartly accessorizing his hip hop outfit.

Lila's husband pursued him over two fences. The thief escaped, but he dropped Lila's purse.

Normally, stolen purses are found completely empty. This thief had grabbed Lila's wallet, but not the envelope containing $3,000 in cash. Lila immediately canceled her credit cards and reported the theft. The cops tried to prepare her for the worst, explaining that, normally, wallets are never recovered. The cards are stripped out and sold, and the I.D. and wallets get ditched. Normally.

Normally, the police don't call to say that your wallet was recovered intact, except for the seven dollars that was missing. Normally, thieves don't keep every wallet they ever stole, either. This guy was definitely not normal. He was caught when a bystander saw him snatch a purse, followed him to his apartment, and then called the police. The police found over 60 wallets in his apartment. Some dated back twenty-three years, judging from the driver's licenses that were still in them.

186. A Real Drunk Driver

A California police officer told us about the time he was especially worried about the car weaving in front of him. It was nighttime, and the road was not well lit. The driver obviously was having a difficult time staying in his lane. He would drift over the double yellow line to his left, then edge over almost to the ditch on his right. The officer had been behind him for nearly a mile with lights flashing and siren wailing when the man finally made a crude stop on the side of the road. He slumped forward onto the steering wheel as the officer approached his car.

"Sir," the officer said, tapping on the driver's window with his flashlight, "turn the car off for me, and step out of the vehicle, please."

The man was dangerously drunk. As he got out of the car, he staggered back against the fender and slid nearly to the ground. The officer kept him from falling.

"How much have you had to drink tonight, sir?" the officer asked.

"I haven't dren binking, occifer," the man slurred.

"Lying to me isn't going to help you, sir. Now, how much have you had to drink?"

"A couple uh beers," he muttered. "Zat's all."

"A couple of beers? Do you take any medication, sir?"

"No. Not that I know of."

"Not that you know of? I need to see your driver's license, sir."

The man fumbled through his wallet and produced a license. As he handed it to the officer, there suddenly was a terrible crash nearby. Two cars had crashed into one another and been knocked to the side of the road.

"Wait right here!" the officer ordered the drunken man. "Don't you move!"

With that the policeman ran forward to the crash site. He was talking with the people involved in the accident when he suddenly saw the drunk man driving past him at a high rate of speed. "Hey!" the officer yelled at him as the man sped by.

Thirty minutes later the police were at the man's house and had it surrounded. Six or seven squad cars sat out in front, and several officers with guns drawn were positioning themselves around the front yard. They were pounding on the door and shouting, "Police! Open up!"

A still-drunk and very groggy man finally answered the door and was immediately seized by the officers, handcuffed, and arrested.

"Hey, what the hell is goin' on here?" he asked belligerently.

"Where's the car?" the officers demanded to know.

"The what?" he asked. "I've been home all night sleeping."

"Where is the car?"

"It's in the garage, I guess. That's where I usually park it." The man seemed totally befuddled.

"Here it is!" an officer shouted from the now-opened garage.

Sure enough, there it sat. The garage was filled with exhaust fumes. The engine was still running. So were the blue lights on the top of the squad car. The guy was so drunk he hadn't even realized that he'd driven off in the police cruiser instead of his own car.

"I haven't dren binking, occifer," the man slurred.

187. Be Careful What You Invent

(England)

George Musgrave was ticketed not long ago by a traffic bobby in London for parking on a yellow line. It was a minor offense and a minor fine, but there was something unusual about the crime.

You see, George Musgrave was responsible for the very existence of the yellow line. In 1947, George had suggested that the Motor Vehicle Department use yellow lines for no-parking zones and the like. It was all part of a road-safety competition.

George's suggestion netted him a three-pound prize.

George's parking ticket cost him a thirty-pound fine.

DUMB CRIMINAL QUIZ NO. 367

How well do you know the dumb criminal mind?

While robbing a gas station, the attendant asked the robber for a favor, and the robber complied. Did the attendant ask him . . .

a) to hem his pants?

b) to let him make one phone call?

c) to play the guitar accompaniment for "Dueling Banjos"?

d) not to rob the store?

If you answered (b), then you know the criminal mind. The attendant at the Reno, Nevada, gas station was nothing if not bold. "Remember," he told the man who was holding him up, "every victim is allowed one phone call." The robber agreed, and the attendant called the police. Before you could say "reach out and touch someone," the Reno police were asking that dim-witted robber to do *them* a favor: "Would you put your hands in these cuffs, please?"

---

188. Five Will Get You Ten or Twenty-Five

With a long sigh, Janice Patterson finished writing her check on her account and received the five-dollar bill from the bank teller. She actually needed more, but her balance was far too low at the moment. She wouldn't get her next paycheck for two more days. Until then, she would just have to get by on those five dollars.

Janice got into her car, swung the door shut, and put the key in the ignition. Just as she was starting the engine, a man jumped in the front seat beside her and pointed a gun right at her face. "Give me all your money—right now!" he demanded in a harsh voice.

Reluctantly, but obediently, Janice turned over her five-dollar bill.

"It's all I have," she explained.

"You're kidding!" The bad guy put the gun down. Incredulous, he searched her purse and the glove compartment before he finally realized she was telling the truth.

"Damn—wouldn't you know it! All those people comin' out of the bank, and I have to pick the one that don't got no money!"

All Janice could do was shrug. But now her would-be robber decided to take a different approach. "Write me a check!" he ordered.

But Janice had to shrug again. She had just written the last of the checks in her checkbook.

Obviously, this was not going well at all for our criminal.

"I gotta think!" he mused, then ordered her to drive around the block. Janice obeyed.

They had just turned the corner when another problem apparently occurred to the worried criminal. His victim had seen what he looked like and presumably could relay his description to the police.

"Don't look at me," he warned. "You keep looking at the floor, hear me?"

"That would be difficult," she told the crook. "I'm driving, remember?"

"Well, you just look straight ahead. Don't look at me."

She didn't.

Momentarily frustrated, the bandit then remembered that banks keep counter checks available for customer use. He directed his victim to drive back to the bank.

They went inside to one of the desks, where he directed her to write a check for eighty-five dollars. She didn't bother to tell him she didn't have that much in the account. But she did try to communicate with the teller. As the bandit fidgeted and glanced around, Janice gestured, mimed, made faces, and even pointed at the man, but her dramatics had no effect on the teller.

Resigning herself to the victim's role, the woman handed the check to the bandit, but in her nervousness she neglected to sign it.

The teller, finally tipped off by the omission of the signature, slipped back to the manager's office, where a call was made to police. The robber was arrested, convicted, and sentenced to ten years in jail.

Janice Patterson barely escaped punishment herself.

"It's a good thing you didn't sign it," the teller pointed out to her. "The check would have bounced, and we would have had to charge you a twenty-five-dollar processing fee."

189. A Self-Inflicted Drive-By

Drive-by shootings are the scourge of lower-income neighborhoods. Gangs use this cowardly and costly practice to retaliate against enemies and rival gangs—with deadly effect on innocent children and adults who just happen to be in the wrong place at the wrong time. Drive-bys also escalate the cycle of violence as one act of revenge replaces another. But we did hear of a drive-by shooting in Oklahoma that ended with some poetic justice for a change.

A carload of gang members had set out to avenge their honor by taking a few potshots at their rivals on a city street. Their car was a "low rider" loaded down with six young gang members. They cruised the dark night streets, patrolling their "turf" and searching for some stragglers from another gang.

Finally, they spotted their prey—three kids walking and apparently not aware of the car behind them. The setup was perfect. Nobody else was on the street. All was quiet, no stores were open, and no cops were anywhere to be seen. The cruising shooters cut off their headlights, killed the radio, and silently idled up the street, barely moving.

Just as the shooter in the backseat was ready to pull the trigger, the car's front right wheel rolled into a huge pothole. The car bounced, the gun fired, the front left tire blew, and the young men on the sidewalk scattered. The driver gunned the engine and rode the rim for about half a block; then the wheel came off the axle and the car screeched to a grating stop. The gunman inside the car had foolishly shot out his own tire.

When the police arrived to apprehend the gang members, they found them arguing and fighting amongst themselves over the flat tire.

190. Buried Treasure

Retired Escambia County (Florida) Sheriff's Department captain Don Parker knows that modern-day pirates still sometimes bury their loot in the sand. He has some firsthand experience in the matter.

It happened on a quiet summer's night on Pensacola Beach, as Parker and reserve deputy David Stanley were patrolling in Parker's unmarked car. Traffic was light, and there were plenty of tourists and locals walking around enjoying the balmy evening breezes.

As they approached a stop sign, Parker noticed a car behind them in the other lane and coming up fast. To his surprise, the vehicle, a rusted and battered four-door sedan, shot through the intersection, ignoring the stop sign. Unfortunately, a Volkswagen bug was in the wrong place at the wrong time, and the larger car broadsided the VW, spinning it around like a top.

"Luckily, there were no injuries," Parker says, "but it all happened so fast we didn't have time to react."

After the sounds of breaking glass and screeching tires subsided, the two officers jumped out to render aid. Then a strange thing happened.

"The guy sitting on the passenger side of the big sedan came out of the car like a jack-in-a-box, ran to the side of the road, and began digging a small hole," Parker recalls. "David and I watched in amazement as he pulled two sandwich bags full of marijuana from his pocket, dropped them in the hole, and quickly covered the dope with sand.

"Now, it's true we were driving a plain car, but both of us were in full uniform and no more than ten feet from where the man was digging in the sand. Apparently, though, he didn't see us."

Satisfied that the damning evidence had been successfully hidden, the guy casually strolled back to the accident scene. Parker told Stanley to go and stand on the spot where the dope had been buried. Then he went to direct traffic until a trooper could arrive to work the wreck.

A highway patrolman was soon on the scene, and the driver of the sedan freely admitted that he had run the stop sign. Both he and his passenger were friendly and cooperative, and the investigation was quickly completed. The trooper wrote a citation to the at-fault driver, then closed his notebook. "Well," he said to Parker, "I guess that does it."

Parker smiled. "Not quite." He nodded at Stanley, who quickly dug up the two little bags and held them up for everyone to see. "We found some buried treasure, and I think we know who buried it."

The two dumb (and dumbfounded) criminals were quickly handcuffed and placed in the back of Parker's car for the short trip to the beach jail.

**He pulled two sandwich bags full of marijuana
from his pocket, dropped them in the hole,
and quickly covered the dope with sand.**

191. About Face

Here's a guy who really isn't a dumb criminal but could be considered criminally dumb.

Jeffrey Miles of North Wilkesboro, North Carolina, turned the key to his front door and entered the foyer. The house was dark except for the small kitchen light shining down the hallway. As he turned after closing the door, Miles saw a strange man—apparently an intruder—facing him in the dim light. With a loud yell, the homeowner bolted from his house, ran to neighbors, and phoned 911.

The officer who arrived was met at the curb by Miles and the neighbor. "He's still in there, I think. I haven't seen anyone leave since I called you. Be careful, officer," Miles advised.

"Did you get a good look at him?" the officer asked.

"I wasn't in there long enough for a good look, but I can tell you this, he was one ugly SOB!"

The cop crept up the front steps and entered the house cautiously with weapon drawn. Miles and the neighbor waited outside at a safe distance. Thirty seconds later, the officer emerged from the house laughing uncontrollably.

"What is it?" Miles asked anxiously. "What'd you see in there?"

"C'mon up here, I want to show you something," the officer said, wiping tears of laughter from his eyes.

As the three men entered the house, the officer shined his light down the hallway. "There's your burglar, sir," the officer said.

"Well, I'll be damned," Miles said. The officer was still laughing. Miles and the neighbor joined in.

"I feel like a complete idiot," the homeowner said. "My wife told me she was going to do something with that full-length mirror she bought at the yard sale, but I didn't know she was going to put it at the end of the hallway! I guess I was wrong about an intruder in the house. . . . I'm sorry, officer."

"Well, you were right about one thing, though," the neighbor chimed in. "He was one ugly SOB!"

192. I Scream, You Scream

(United Kingdom [Isle of Man])

Between Wales and Ireland in the Irish Sea lies a tiny island known as the Isle of Man. It has the longest continuous parliamentary form of government in the world. The Isle of Man is also the home of the Manx cat. It is a beautiful little island, with white cliffs rising up out of the green sea, lovely rolling farmland and sand beaches covered in stones worn smooth by the tides.

Every summer the island hosts professional motorcycle racing. Literally, the one road that circles the whole island is the race course. Farmers pile up haybales on hairpin turns to pad the crashes of the cyclists, and thousands of fans invade the island for a week of squealing tires and shrieking engines.

This particular year there was a particular Italian racer entered, whom we'll call Giuseppe. Giuseppe was easily angered and had a reputation on the circuit as a hothead. He had a tendency to push the bike too hard in the corners. So it was no surprise to the other racers when Giuseppe totaled his bike on the first day of time trials.

Giuseppe's greatest nemesis and arch rival on the tour was a German, Klaus. Klaus couldn't help but smile broadly when he saw the "Scratched" on the leader board beside Giuseppe's name. Words were exchanged and, had it not been for their crews, they would have come to blows.

It was also no surprise when Giuseppe blamed Klaus for his crash, claiming his bike had been tampered with. His accusations were groundless and the officials dismissed them immediately, but Giuseppe would have his revenge.

That night Giuseppe partied with the fans who were camping all over the island. At campfire after campfire, Giuseppe drank the wine at each one, playing, in almost operatic style, the fallen hero, the sad clown. He was just drunk enough and mad enough now to do something really stupid.

It was two in the morning when Giuseppe finally stumbled into the alley of garages in the business district of Castletown. Klaus and the German contingent were staying on the next street over, but their bikes were in one of these garages. Giuseppe found the German insignia.

Without hesitation, Giuseppe put his fist through the glass pane of the door and opened the door from the inside. He was still wearing his leather motorcycle gloves so the shards of glass didn't leave a scratch. He fumbled in the dark, groping for a light switch, but found none. Feeling his way forward, he bumped into something about knee high that felt like a tire. He thought it was the front tire of a motorcycle, so he pushed it hard to knock the whole bike over. But when he did, it *kicked* him real hard. Giuseppe went down howling as "the thing" caught him square in the chest. Then the lights came on.

There sat Klaus and three crew members eating ice cream. Knowing Giuseppe, Klaus had a feeling the idiot would try something. They didn't turn Giuseppe in to the officials, even though by the time they got done with him, Giuseppe wished that they had.

193. It's Only Pretend

Out in Arizona, there's still an incredibly large group of people making their living as hired gunslingers. These crack marksmen are cool customers. They have nerves of steel and steady hands. The gun is their best and only friend. They're cold-blooded, ruthless murderers.

Well, not really. They play cold-blooded, ruthless killers in movies, television shows, and Wild West shoot-outs. One group, doing business as "Guns for Hire," will actually stage a shoot-out at your next backyard barbecue for a fee.

These guys shoot straight and they always get their man. Mainly because their victims always fall down on cue when they hear the blank pistols pop, but it looks just like the real thing. Maybe it's too real for some folks.

One lady called, interested in hiring them. She seemed a little confused about their act though.

"I just need one of you." She explained. The "Gun for Hire" taking the call tried to explain to the lady that for a gunfight, you really need at least two people.

"I don't want a gunfight. I just want one guy to shoot my husband." The "Gun for Hire" thought she was describing a gag she wanted to play. You know, like a singing telegram. "Happy Birthday to you. Blam! Blam!

203

You're dead." But the more he tried to explain their group rate to the caller, the more adamant she became about killing her husband for real. She thought that the listing in the phone book she had called, "Guns for Hire," was just that—hit men for hire, Murder, Inc., by a new name.

The faux gunslingers notified the police and set up a meeting with the lady. Sure enough, this lady was serious. She had the cash and she made it clear in no uncertain terms that she meant business. No pretend shootouts with chicken blood for her, no sirree, she wanted the real deal.

The cowboys believed her. The police believed her. The judge believed her, and the jury gave her four years. Obviously, her brain was napping while her fingers did the walking.

194. An Alarming Realization

People with guilty consciences do things to give themselves away. Let's head East, where a shoplifter captured herself.

As is the case at most retail stores, merchandise at Norton's Department Store in Lakehurst, New Jersey, is tagged with those pesky security clips that trip the alarm if the clerk hasn't deactivated them at the checkout counter. A woman had just purchased some clothing and was passing through the exit door at about the same time as another woman, who wasn't carrying anything. The alarm was triggered, and strident beeping filled the air.

The smiling store manager and the security guard at the door had seen the first woman pay for the articles and knew the clerk had merely forgotten to deactivate the tags. But before either had a chance to speak, the woman standing next to her began pulling out several skirts and blouses from beneath her bulky clothing. She was detained by the officer and manager until the authorities arrived to take her to jail.

The real kicker came when she was taken to the manager's office, and it was discovered that none of the clothing she was stealing had any security tags on 'em!

So clothes, and yet so far away.

The alarm was triggered, and strident beeping filled the air.

195. Read Between the Lines

(Germany)

A genius in Hamburg had concocted a nifty scam. He would park alongside a motorway and take potshots at passing cars. Then he would send a note to the local government, threatening to continue the random shootings until his demands for money were met.

Instead of giving in to the extortionist's demands, however, local detectives used a simple child's trick to locate and arrest him.

The extortion letter had been written by hand on notepad paper. By gently rubbing the surface with the side of a lead pencil, they were able to detect the last thing the extortionist had written on the pad *before* the note—including, as if by magic, his name, address, and phone number.

All they had to do then was drive by and pick him up at the address he had provided them with.

196. He Can Hide, but He Can't Run

Terry Jarnigan was a troublemaker. He was always having brushes with the law, and he was especially well known for starting fights and somehow managing to get away just before the police arrived.

One Friday night Terry tried to pick up another man's wife in a local tavern in a Midwest town, and a fight ensued. Soon the whole place was involved in an old-fashioned barroom brawl, with chairs and glasses being thrown and broken amidst a frenzied free-for-all.

Then someone yelled "Cops!" The crowd broke for the door, and Jarnigan was one of the first ones out. But the squad car pulled in, lights flashing, just as he was making his way across the parking lot. With no time to think and few places to run, Jarnigan opened the door of a brown Pontiac Bonneville and stretched out along the back floorboard.

In a matter of minutes, more officers and squad cars had pulled into the parking lot. Jarnigan would have to sit tight for a while. He just lay there in the back of the Pontiac, watching the shadows of the flashing lights and listening to the voices outside. He couldn't hear everything that was said as the police began arresting the people involved in the donny-brook. But he did hear his own name over and over as bar patrons explained the origins of the fight.

Then Terry Jarnigan heard voices coming closer to his hiding place.

"It's not fair to arrest me!" a man was protesting in a shrill voice. "I didn't start the fight. Some jerk was hitting on my wife, and she didn't like it. Well, I didn't like it either, so I just . . . "

"Yes, sir," another voice answered calmly. "We'll get all of that sorted out down at the police station. But we don't have any more room in the cruisers, so you'll have to follow me downtown in your own vehicle."

"He's the one you ought to be arresting . . . " The man was still mutter-ing as he swung open the door of his brown Pontiac Bonneville. Terry Jarnigan blinked as the dome light came on, and the car's owner jumped back and yelled.

"Hey! Here he is—here's the punk that started the whole thing! You just wait till I get my . . . "

The officer stopped the furious husband just before he took hold of the cowering troublemaker. Jarnigan was duly booked for inciting a riot and for committing illegal trespass in entering the man's car. And then he was thrown into the same holding tank with the people he had provoked into fighting in the bar only an hour earlier, including the enraged husband of the woman he had flirted with.

They were all very glad to see him.

197. "Don't Call the Police"

Officer Timothy Walker of the Birmingham (Alabama) Task Force let Amer-ica's Dumbest Criminals in on one of his personal favorites:

"I was working the eleven-to-seven shift at the time. After running a few errands that morning, I got home around one in the afternoon and went in to get some sleep. I'm lying there on the bed about half-asleep when I hear the sound of glass breaking in the living room.

"I sleep with my gun right next to the bed, so it was already in my hand as I cautiously slipped down the hallway. I heard more glass break as I spun around the corner. I'm just five feet from the window when I see the top of this head and shoulders comin' in. By the time he gets his hands on the floor and looks up, he's staring right down the barrel of my loaded .38.

"He went cross-eyed for a moment. Then I reached out and grabbed him by the shirt with my free hand, and in one swift pull I dragged him into the house."

"Don't shoot me! Please don't shoot me!" the burglar cried, perhaps remembering that old adage that says if you shoot somebody on your property, you'd better drag 'em into the house.

"I'm not going to shoot you," Walker told the frightened man, "but you're damned lucky that I didn't!"

"Don't call the police," the man pleaded. "Please don't call the police."

Walker just stared at him. The brilliant break-in artist obviously hadn't noticed the framed photos of Walker in uniform placed on a nearby table . . . or Walker's police cap in a chair . . . or the police badge on his belt . . . or the police-issue firearm nestled in Walker's hand.

"Man, look around," Walker said. "I *am* the police!"

198. They're Sitting on Top of the Loot

Cracking ATMs is a crime ripe for dummies. It's what we call the "Impossible Dream."

A couple of fellas in Portland, Oregon, decided to take the ATM challenge one night. They had a powerful 4 x 4 and had a stout chain for towing cars, so they were ready for anything.

About two in the morning, they backed up to a free-standing ATM kiosk. One of the slick dudes wrapped the chain around the ATM and signaled the driver. That sports utility vehicle groaned in the lowest gear and then screeched off. The front wheels popped off the pavement when the slack snapped out of the chain. With a grinding rip, the ATM came free from its foundation.

Phase 1 was complete and they gave each other high-fives. Phase 2 now began. The plan was to tow the ATM until it cracked open. They towed the metal ATM five or six blocks, and every time it bounced into the air and came crashing back down on the pavement, it made a horrible racket. The farther they went, the more impenetrable the ATM seemed to be.

A brilliant solution came to them. They would release the ATM and smash into it with their 4 x 4. Surely, that would free up the cash inside. They took a running start half a block from it. They must have been doing fifty or sixty miles per hour when they hit. *Wham, bam,* and suddenly silence.

They were sitting three feet in the air with their wheels barely touching the road. Their 4 x 4 was suspended in the air, stuck on top of their loot, the ATM. They were still spinning their tires when the police arrived.

This is the only known case of an ATM solving its own burglary and physically holding the culprits at the scene until the police arrived.

The plan was to tow the ATM until it cracked open.

199. The Bare Facts

Working radar on a blistering summer's day is not the job assignment of choice for most law enforcement officers. It was just such a day that Officer Bill Cromie was running radar in a small town in upstate New York.

"I was sitting right by the side of the road with my air conditioning running, letting the sight of my marked car slow the speeding drivers and actually blinking my headlights at some of the faster ones," Cromie says.

So far he had been able to avoid having to actually write a single ticket. But he could see off in the distance a car approaching at a high rate of speed. Cromie blinked his headlights, but the vehicle didn't slow.

Cromie set off in pursuit. By the time he caught up to the speeder, she was still doing over fifty miles per hour. When she saw his blue lights, she pulled over. Cromie got out of his car, ticket book in hand, and then did a double take.

"Looking through the rear window I could see she was alone in the car, but she seemed to be shrinking. With each step that I took, she slid that much lower in the front seat. I was about to ask for her driver's license, but I only got as far as, 'May I see your—' because I suddenly realized I could see her—*all* of her. The woman was stark naked."

At that point it was hard to say who was more embarrassed and, blushing furiously, Cromie turned his back on the cringing woman. "I suppose I was taking a risk, but I was fairly sure she wasn't carrying any concealed weapons. Of course, I asked her how it was that she came to be driving her car, naked, at a high rate of speed."

The woman told him that she had been driving beside a river, and it had looked so cool and inviting that she just had to take a quick swim. Picking what she thought was a deserted section, she had peeled off her sweaty clothing and dived in. The water had been wonderful, but as she floated with the current she had seen two fishermen emerge from bushes and sit on the bank only a few feet from where she had left her clothes. Intent on catching fish, they hadn't seen her or her clothes, but they obviously had posed a major problem for the swimmer.

From the looks of things, they had settled in for the day.

Luckily, the woman's keys were still in the car, so she had swum around a bend in the river and waded ashore, creeping past the unsuspecting fishermen. She had been able to get to her car undetected and was headed for home when Cromie stopped her.

Convinced she had to be telling the truth, he said he would let her go without writing her a ticket. The woman expressed her gratitude, but wanted to know if Cromie had a coat she could borrow. He didn't. Unhappy with his answer, she insisted that he help her.

"I told her the only thing I could give her was my uniform, but that would have been pretty hard to explain if she got stopped again. She finally drove off, still hunkered down in the seat. But at least she was doing the speed limit."

200. Jean-Claude "Damn Van"

(France)

It had been raining for a week straight and Jean-Claude Bouchet was glad of it. Bouchet was a thief and he loved this time of the year in Paris. People stayed indoors to keep dry, windows were more difficult to see out of, and any inadvertent fingerprints left behind were washed away by the steady rainfall.

Ah, April in Paris.

Breaking into cars and trucks was Bouchet's specialty. He could case a vehicle, quietly pop out a window, and be gone with the contents in less than thirty seconds. The last week had been a treasure trove of cameras, purses, wallets, and even a bass fiddle.

From the darkness of the alley, he studied the white van parked directly across the street as he strolled toward it. Without breaking stride, he casually placed his hand on the hood of the van as he stepped up on the curb. The engine was cold, meaning it had been parked for a good while, and the windows were darkly tinted. This usually meant there was something in there to hide.

This wasn't the safest of neighborhoods, and whoever parked here either didn't know it or had mechanical trouble. *They'll be in for a surprise when they get back,* he chuckled to himself as he slipped the pry bar from his pant leg via his waist.

Walking to the rear of the van, he gave a quick look around and tried the handle. Locked. Next he slid the bar into the door seams beside the lock and pulled sharply. The metal bent and the pry bar popped out. He dug in a little deeper with the edge and gave a strong grunt and, suddenly, *pow*! The door burst open with such force that it knocked him to the pavement. He was instantly set upon by no fewer than four Paris police officers, handcuffed, and placed under arrest.

Bouchet had just broken into a police surveillance van. The French speak a different language, but if you mention *idiot,* people understand what you mean. *Au revoir.*

201. If You Can't Trust a Three-Time Felon, Who Can You Trust?

Back in 1982, Officer Steve Stafford, only three weeks out of the academy, responded to a robbery call at an all-night convenience store in Saraland, Alabama. When the clerk described the getaway car—a blue Toyota minivan—Officer Stafford recalled passing it. While his backup took the rest of the report, the first officer sped down the street. There at a gas station was the blue minivan, and two men arguing as they gassed up.

Stafford quickly announced himself as he drew down on the two spatting armed robbers. One of the men started to go for the back of his belt when the officer told him to freeze. Stafford patted the man down and found a .25 caliber pistol in the man's belt. It wasn't loaded—much to the surprise of the crook.

"You sent me in there to rob that place with an empty gun!" this bad guy said to his cohort.

The driver was slightly embarrassed. "Well, I didn't want anybody getting hurt."

"And you forgot to get gas before we rob the place! I don't believe you!"

The driver was very embarrassed. "I know. It was on my list."

202. "Not by the Hair of My Chinny-Chin-Chin!"

Charlie Hackett, chief of police in Kokomo, Indiana, tells this story about dumb criminals determined to live high on the hog:

"Someone called in a complaint about some rustling going on out in the country. My partner and I were working organized crime at the time, but we were the only ones on duty, so we had to go. We found that this farmer had been losing big time—twenty-five or thirty hogs in all—but not all at once. Those hogs had been disappearing one at a time, one a night. And each time the rustlers had managed to take the whole pig. The farmer had found blood, but no carcasses."

Hackett and his partner staked out the area the next night. Before long, they saw a big station wagon rolling down a little lane near the hog pens. Three or four men got out. The officers used night lenses to watch the suspects walk down the lane toward the hog pens. Then the commotion started.

"They were running," Hackett remembers, "and the hogs were running. Then one of the guys pulled out a .22-caliber rifle and popped one of the hogs. He shot again, and the hog went down.

"Well, we backed off at that point, knowing they would have to come back down the lane with the hog they had shot. So we're sitting there waiting for them to get onto the highway so we can stop them. Sure enough, they came zipping down. We pulled them over."

The two officers approached the vehicle and peered inside, expecting to catch the rustlers red-handed. But all they saw were two men in the front seat, three men in the back—and no sign of a recently deceased hog.

One of the officers peered into the rear of the station wagon. "Nothing back there but an old seat," he said. Then they looked more closely and realized it was the backseat of the station wagon. The officers asked the men in the backseat to get out.

"Now, it didn't look too bad," Hackett says. "There was a seat cover over what appeared to be the backseat. One of our guys reached in and pulled off the cover."

It wasn't a seat at all. It was a very large, very dead hog. "We don't know how they did it, how they got that hog into the backseat—it must have weighed around five hundred pounds."

213

But that's not the end of our little pig tale.

"Later on, we got a search warrant to go back to the house where one of these guys lived, and we found a small, live pig this guy had previously taken. We kept her for evidence, and one of our officers took her home to keep for the trial. By the time the trial came around, however, the officer had grown quite fond of the pig. He even had her paper-trained! The 'evidence' remained at the officer's home as a pet until she weighed about four hundred pounds, then she moved to a local farm."

Presumably, she never had to serve double duty as the backseat of a station wagon.

Those hogs had been disappearing one at a time, one a night.

203. Little White Hot Lies

Captain Vincent Detrolio of the Union County (New Jersey) Sheriff's Department sent an officer out to serve a routine warrant at the suspect's residence. When the officer arrived at the address, the suspect's mother answered the door and the officer explained the reason for his visit. After the officer had mentioned the suspect's name, a voice from the living room was heard to say, loud and clear, "Tell him I'm not here!"

204. The Car Dealer, the Card Dealer, and Mom

One crazy story told by Officer Bruce Harper and still making the rounds among Las Vegas, Nevada, police officers concerns two brothers and their seventy-year-old mother who stopped by a car dealership in Las Vegas. They asked the salesman if they could test-drive a particular new car. He threw a set of tags on it, climbed in the backseat, and they were off.

After they'd gone a few miles, one of the men asked his brother to pull over so he could drive the car. When they stopped, they ordered the salesman out of the backseat and forced him into the trunk. Then they shut the lid and headed out of town.

Another motorist had witnessed the entire event. He followed them to a casino outside of Vegas and phoned the police. The officers arrived and freed the shaken salesman, who was able to give them a good description of his unlikely kidnappers.

The officers couldn't be sure just how many people might actually be involved, so they acted with caution. A S.W.A.T. team was dispatched to the scene. The team entered the casino and went directly to the security room filled with closed-circuit television monitors. Moments later they spotted one of the brothers seated at a blackjack table.

To apprehend him and the rest of his family, several members of the S.W.A.T. team dressed up like waiters and carried towels and drink trays concealing their weapons. Three of the disguised officers came up behind the brother who had been spotted. Surrounding the guy, they pulled him straight back off his chair and onto the floor. No one else at the table looked up. They were too interested in their card game to care about anything else, but that's Vegas.

Meanwhile, other members of the team had located and arrested the remaining brother. With both brothers now in custody, the focus was on Mom. They'd gotten her name from her sons, so catching her was simply a matter of paging her on the casino intercom system.

The three were charged with grand theft auto and kidnapping. Why an entire family would kidnap a total stranger, put him into the trunk, and then stop to gamble is beyond logic. But then, these weren't exactly the Waltons.

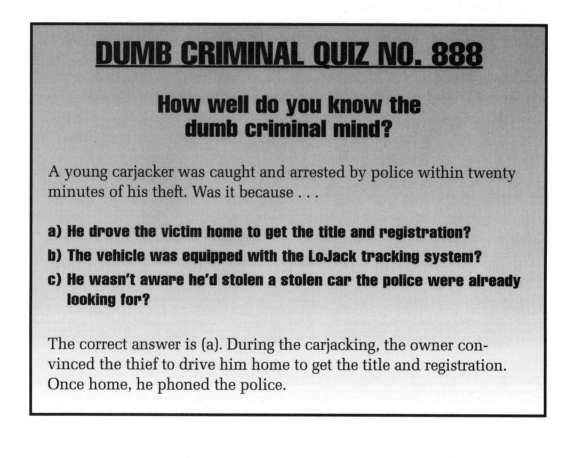

DUMB CRIMINAL QUIZ NO. 888

How well do you know the dumb criminal mind?

A young carjacker was caught and arrested by police within twenty minutes of his theft. Was it because . . .

a) He drove the victim home to get the title and registration?

b) The vehicle was equipped with the LoJack tracking system?

c) He wasn't aware he'd stolen a stolen car the police were already looking for?

The correct answer is (a). During the carjacking, the owner convinced the thief to drive him home to get the title and registration. Once home, he phoned the police.

205. The Safe That Held Up Two Robbers

In Lake Oswego, Oregon, a couple of bad guys found out the hard way that "two out of three" ain't bad . . . but it ain't good enough.

The plan to steal the safe was sound; the two men in the parking lot agreed to that. They would back up the big truck to the front of the store, run in, and wrap the thick chain around the floor safe and pull it right out of the store. Unless something unforeseen happened, they figured their chances of a clean getaway were pretty good.

They'd done their homework. They were familiar with the store, knew on what day the safe was full, and had tracked how often the police made their rounds. Both men were keenly aware that their success depended on three things—expedient execution, split-second timing, and a little luck.

Their execution was flawless. By screaming "Everybody down!" as they entered the store, they got what they were counting on—confusion, fear, and compliance.

Their timing was impeccable. In less than thirty seconds the heavy chain had been wrapped twice around the safe and held fast by the large hook placed over the taut links.

Their luck, however, was terrible. With his adrenaline pumping, the driver mashed the pedal to the metal and he didn't let up. The force of the initial thrust jerked the safe off the floor and sent it sliding out the front door at about twenty miles an hour. When the safe had cleared the entrance way, the driver slammed on the brakes. The truck stopped. The safe didn't.

To the amazement of our two Robin Hoodlums, that big ol' safe just kept a' comin'. Out the door, across a short sidewalk, into the parking lot, and straight for the rear end of their pickup.

"Go, man, go!" the guy ridin' shotgun screamed.

"I'm goin', I'm goin'!" snapped his partner. The driver hit the gas at the exact same moment the safe hit them. With the grating screech of metal on metal, coupled with a bone-jarring crash, the rear end of the truck was lifted off the ground as the safe wedged itself beneath the frame.

The smell of burning rubber filled the air as blue smoke rolled from the squealing back tires. The speedometer said ninety; the thieves said nothing. As for the plan, five points for loyalty, five years for stupidity.

206. Nip Nap Sap

(Australia)

A deputy in Melbourne answered a call from a man who could only whisper his address into the phone. Responding immediately, the deputy was surprised to find the householders outside, hiding in the bushes. "The bad guy is in our den, asleep," the husband explained. "We hid out here in case he woke up before you arrived."

The deputy called for backup, and two officers soon arrived on the scene to initiate the search. Sure enough, there was the cat burglar curled up in the den—purring in alcoholic slumber next to the wet bar.

The suspect confirmed the officers' suspicions the next day after he had slept off a wicked drunk and was moaning from an equally wicked hangover. He had only begun ransacking the house when he discovered that the owners' bar was stocked with exotic liquors and beers from around the world. Well, this was too good to pass up, so our dumb criminal decided to have just one little taste of the light, fruity, and yet incredibly potent English elderberry wine. While enjoying his first taste of elderberry he noticed some Greek ouzo, another drink he had never tasted. The ouzo left him feeling warm and adventurous, so why not try the unique flavor of dandelion liqueur . . . and then some ice cold chili pepper-flavored beer from Texas . . . and well, you get the picture. He was head down at the bar by the time the householders arrived home.

Maybe we have a new crime deterrent here. Because many studies have found that a vast majority of crimes are committed under the influence of alcohol, why not apply that knowledge and create the dumb-criminal equivalent of a roach motel? The dumb criminal is attracted to the wet bar like a moth to a flame. He sits down and has a nip. Then he simply naps until the police come around to collect him—all nice and cozy, ready for his stretch in jail.

The owners' bar was stocked with exotic liquors
and beers from around the world.

207. Life Is Like a Pair of Brown Shoes

An immigration officer was sick and tired of dealing with illegal aliens who would pretend not to understand any English for several hours and then suddenly speak it fluently. So on this particular evening when the agent stopped a truck filled with thirty illegals, he decided to try something different.

"Do any of you speak English? *¿Habla Inglés?*"

Every head shook no, and every face looked very quizzically at the frustrated officer.

"Okay, well, look, I'm really tired of this. I'm gonna shoot you all, and I'm going to start with the people wearing brown shoes."

As the officer drew his pistol, three men looked down quickly at their feet. They quickly and gladly accepted the role of translator for the group.

208. The Jewel Fool

It was late in the afternoon when a seventy-five-year-old woman entered the Las Vegas, Nevada, police station accompanied by her thirty-five-year-old boyfriend. She was dressed nicely and spoke in a quiet tone as she spoke to an officer about a robbery that had just occurred. Her diamond jewelry was missing.

"If you'll step over to this counter, I'll be glad to take your report," said Carolyn Green, the clerk at the front desk. "Your friend will have to sit over there, though, because only one person at a time is allowed in this area."

The woman's young male companion complied and took a seat in one of the chairs against the waiting-area wall.

"You were robbed, ma'am?" Green asked.

"Yes, I was," she replied. "At my house . . . about ten thousand dollars' worth of diamonds was taken from my house."

After taking down the rest of the necessary information to start the paperwork, Green asked the woman, "Do you have any idea who it was that robbed you?"

"Yes, I do," came the response.

"Do you know the person's name?"

"Yes, I know his name."

"Would you know him if you saw him again?"

Again, the answer was in the affirmative.

"Do you know where the person is and where we might be able to find him right now?"

The elderly woman looked over her shoulder. "He's sitting right over there against the wall," she said, pointing to her male companion. Green stood up and looked over at the man who had just brought the woman to the station.

"*He's* the man who robbed you?" Green asked in shocked disbelief.

"Yep. My jewels were missing, and I told him I was going to go down to the police station to report it. I asked him to come along, and he said yes, he'd even give me a ride down here. So he did, and here we are."

Green shook her head and called over to the young man. "Sir, will you step over here, please?" The man stood and walked over to the counter.

"Yes?" he said nonchalantly.

"Did you steal this woman's jewelry?"

"I did," he said.

"One moment please, sir," the clerk said. She turned to summon an officer. "This man just admitted that he robbed this woman of ten thousand dollars' worth of jewelry, and now she's signing a complaint against him."

The summoned officer shook *his* head. "Didn't you just come in here with her?"

"Yes," the young man answered blankly.

"She says you're responsible for her missing jewelry."

"She's right," he admitted. "I did it."

"Well, then, you're under arrest for robbery," the still-stunned officer told him.

"Okay," the man sighed, placing his hands over his head and surrendering without incident. He was later sent to prison.

The police probably could have recovered plenty of rocks had they been able to open the man's head.

209. "Ask a Simple Question..."

Several years ago, as a rookie deputy sheriff in New Mexico, Captain Billy Hillgartner was practicing lifting fingerprints with rubber fingerprint lifters. Having successfully lifted one of his own prints from his desk, he tossed this print into his briefcase and forgot it.

About a month later Hillgartner was interviewing a burglary suspect at his desk and getting nowhere. The guy was not admitting to anything, and Billy really had nothing on him. This guy was a pro and Hillgartner was just a rookie.

At wit's end, Billy just happened to glance over at his briefcase and he spotted the old fingerprint lifter. He pulled the lifter out and showed it to his suspect.

"Do you know what this is?" he asked, and tossed it across the desk to the suspect.

The suspect picked it up and, after looking at it, replied, "Yes."

Hillgartner then asked the suspect a simple question: "Do you know where I got that?"

The suspect lowered his head and again replied, "Yes, 4712 Donaldson Lane."

Hillgartner couldn't believe his ears. The guy then gave a full confession.

In fact, Hillgartner's ploy has worked with six guys. His own fingerprint helped him solve at least six different burglaries.

210. The Honeymoon's Over

Police officer Mary Wiley was used to working undercover. She had been involved in more than a hundred prostitution stings in and around Birmingham, Alabama. So she pretty much assumed she had seen it all—until she met the man in the tuxedo.

When working a sting, Officer Wiley would pose as a streetwalker while other officers monitored, from down the street, her conversations with potential clients. Once a deal was struck with a "john," or client, she would direct him to meet her around the corner, where he would promptly be arrested for solicitation. If he was married, the first question out of his mouth was likely to be, "Will my wife find out about this?"

That's more or less what happened with the tuxedo-clad gentleman. He pulled his car up to the curb, rolled down the window, stuck his elegantly groomed head out the window, and propositioned her. Wiley did her job, and it wasn't until after the tuxedoed man had been arrested that she found out why he was dressed so nicely. It was his wedding day!

Believe it or not, the man had taken his wedding vows only four hours earlier. He'd left the reception, still dressed to the nines, to buy more beer, and he then apparently decided to stop for one more purchase.

"Is my wife going to find out?" he asked.

"I wouldn't worry too much about that," Wiley responded. "If she does find out, you probably won't have a wife anymore."

At the very least, we'd bet she threw a lot more than rice at him when he returned to the reception.

Believe it or not, the man had taken his wedding vows only four hours earlier.

211. A Bad Day at the Mall

It's probably safe to say that everyone in America goes to the mall at least a couple of times a week. But I'll bet of all those millions of people, only a handful of them go to the mall totally drunk. Of that drunken handful, I'll bet there's only one couple that gets shnockered before strolling the concourses. Of course, we found that lucky couple. Or rather, they found us.

A clerk in a music store first got suspicious of this toasted Bonnie and Clyde when Clyde claimed to be a deejay and bought some cassette tapes for his radio show. The clerk thought all deejays used CDs these days. He had a sneaking suspicion that the drunken duo were writing bad checks all over the mall. So he called security.

Security took the man to their office for questioning and released the woman with all of her purchases. Unfortunately, this lady was too inebriated to remember where they had parked. In tears and at wit's end, she came back to mall security to ask for help. She described their brand new sport utility vehicle, and in moments security had located it. They thought it was odd that the brand new vehicle was badly damaged, but then they opened the door for the lady and a case of beer shattered on the parking lot.

This was enough red flags for any law enforcement officer, so security ran the tags on the car and sure enough, it was stolen. And yes, all the checks they'd written that day were bad, too. Oh, and the damage to their car was traced to a hit-and-run with a parked car.

212. Easy Come, Easy Go

(Germany)

A trio of troublesome fellows in Hamburg were playing cards one night. Hand after hand, they all folded. None of them had a bit of luck. Frustrated by the dullness of their game, they finally decided to up the stakes and rob a large grocery store around the corner. After a few beers, it all seemed so simple. *We wear masks and pull our guns, they hand us money, and it's over.*

It did turn out to be very simple. They pulled off the robbery exactly as planned and got away with twenty-three hundred deutsche marks. (It helped that the host had an automatic weapon in the closet.) Now the intrepid trio decided to celebrate. They parked their car on a seedy side of town near the red-light district and started out on foot to find some female companionship.

While these stooges were partying and spending all their stolen money, however, a passing policeman happened to notice the automatic weapon lying in plain view in their car's back seat. He also noticed that they were illegally parked. He called to have the car towed away.

When the tired threesome finally came straggling back to where they had parked, they found themselves staring at an empty curb. They finally figured out that their getaway car had been towed, so they did what any good citizen would do—they cussed a little and then called to find out where they could pick up their vehicle.

Sure enough, the police had their car. They had the gun, which a witness had already identified from the robbery. The police also had the masks used in the robbery, which had been left in the car as well.

The police had everything connected with the robbery, in fact, except the stolen money and the criminals themselves. That's what Moe, Larry, and Curly provided when they showed up for their car—with twenty-one hundred deutsche marks still wadded up in their pockets.

213. Big Mac Attackers

Retired Officer David Hunter of the Knox County (Tennessee) Sheriff's Department tells this story of two very hungry holdup men:

After an evening of partying and smoking dope, the two very high potheads decided they would kill two birds with one stone. They were broke, and they had the "munchies," so they agreed that the best thing to do would be to rob a hamburger joint. Armed with loaded shotguns, they burst through the door of the first place they came upon.

"Give us all the money," the dim-bulb duo demanded, "and a dozen hamburgers with everything—to go!"

"I'll get you the money, man," one frightened employee replied, "but the grill's already been shut down. It'll take about ten minutes to reheat."

"Do it," came the gunman's reply. "We'll wait!"

Meanwhile, a passing motorist noticed that the two men sitting in the burger shack were holding shotguns. Suspicious indeed. The motorist phoned police.

"Here's your food," the shaking worker said.

The burger bandits grabbed the greasy sack and hit the door just as the sound of police sirens and squealing tires filled the night air. In their haste, they left the stolen money sitting on the table.

Panicked, the two robbers ran across a highway, slid down an embankment, and tried to hide under a bridge, which is where the K-9 unit found them. The hamburger heist was over.

"What really pisses me off," one man said to the other as they were being led away in handcuffs, "is that those damn dogs ate all our burgers. I didn't even get one bite!"

The officer responded, "You ought to be glad those are the only buns the dog bit."

214. Nice Pry

Now here's a guy who gets ten points for best comeback—and four years for burglary.

It all began when retired security guard Chris Hughes of Columbia, Tennessee, responded to a silent alarm at one of the warehouses he was hired to patrol. When Officer Hughes arrived at the building, he saw a man with a crowbar, prying on the large overhead door.

"Hey, partner, what are you doin'?" Officer Hughes asked.

The man nearly jumped out of his shoes. "Me? I . . . uh . . . well," he stammered, "well, I'm trying to straighten out this bend in my crowbar!"

The man was arrested, convicted, and given three years for burglary and a fourth for possession of burglary tools. Plenty of time to get things straightened out.

"Me? I . . . uh . . . well," he stammered, "well, I'm trying to straighten out this bend in my crowbar!"

215. Calling All Cops

Beepers can be a disadvantage for dumb crooks in more ways than one. Such was the experience of an undercover narcotics officer in Florida nurturing a relationship with a known drug dealer who was a first-class slimeball and a major source of crack cocaine.

Making a narcotics buy without entrapment and with as much admissible evidence as possible is the goal of every undercover narcotics investigation. This particular officer had socialized; that is, he had seen and been seen in all the right places by his target. Gradually, over a two-month period, he had developed a relationship with the dealer. Finally, the officer had made his first buy, and he and the dealer had exchanged pager numbers so they could arrange future transactions.

The stage was set for a second buy. If this operation was done properly, the cops would then have cash, drugs, audio recordings, still photographs, and video on this guy—hopefully enough to convict him of drug trafficking and put him away.

But then the suspect made an interesting mistake. He called the undercover officer's pager to alert his "customer" that the stuff was in and the deal was going down, but he got the last number of the officer's beeper number wrong. The number he accidentally dialed just happened to be the pager number for the police department's S.W.A.T. team. Eighteen heavily armed, highly trained, sharpshooting officers answer that number.

Luckily, our undercover officer was also a member of the S.W.A.T. team, so he got the beep. And like all of the other seventeen S.W.A.T. team members, he answered the page by calling the number that appeared on his pager. Only when he recognized the answering voice as his dealer did the officer figure out what was going on. He quickly switched into his undercover persona.

"Hey, man, is it going down?"

By now the dealer was totally confused and totally paranoid, because by now he had already talked to about five officers who were answering the S.W.A.T. team page by calling the dealer's home number from the page and identifying themselves. Every cop in town seemed to be calling his number, and he had no idea why.

"Who is this?" he demanded of the undercover officer.

"It's me, Jimmy T.," the narcotics officer said, giving his drug-buying pseudonym.

"Man, I beeped you about ten minutes ago, and then the cops started calling. I ain't kidding, man. Five cops have called here in the last five minutes!"

Now the officer was scrambling to fix any possible damage. Luckily, he had himself a bona fide dumb criminal. "Wait, what number did you call?" he asked.

The dealer told him, and he laughed. "You got the last number wrong. My pager number ends in seven, not eight. You must've called the cops!"

"I must have."

"Did you say anything?" the officer said, fearing his cover had been blown and fishing for information.

"No! I just told them that it must've been a wrong number."

"Whoa, dude. Close call. So, do you have the stuff?"

The dealer and the undercover officer met within the hour, and as they did their business they both laughed about the erroneous beep. Their laughter was captured on audio and videotape along with the deal that convicted the dealer.

216. The Telltale Hat

Will Rogers once said, "God picked up the United States and shook it, and everything that was loose fell into California." He wasn't kidding, as in the case of the Oakland, California, robber who victimized an elderly woman.

The thief came out of nowhere. "Give me all your money!" he demanded.

Fearing for her safety, the victim complied, giving up her pocketbook and some rings. Running hard, but still in full view of the victim, the thief felt his hat blow off his head, and it (the hat, not his head) landed in the middle of the sidewalk. The police were called, and the hat was picked up and marked as evidence.

A few days later the elderly victim was asked if she would come down to the station that afternoon to view a police lineup of potential suspects. She agreed, but it all happened so fast and scared her so, she really didn't get that good a look at the man. But she would try.

At the police station, she was taken to a small room and seated behind a two-way mirror. Seven men stood lined up on the other side of the glass. One by one, the men were ordered to place the mugger's hat on their heads, step forward and say, "Give me all your money!" After the last man had spoken, the detective turned to the lady and said, "Well, do you recognize one of them as the robber?"

She shook her head slowly back and forth while biting her lower lip. "I . . . I can't be certain. . . . I'm sorry, young man, I'm just not sure."

"I understand," he said gently. He then picked up the microphone. "All right, fellas, that'll be all, thank you."

The victim rose up from her chair, still shaking her head. Suddenly, the man in the middle of the lineup yelled to the officer just offstage, "Hey, can I have my hat back?"

Now, we're curious: Just what size hat fits a pinhead?

217. Halle's Bomb-It

(Germany)

A nefarious duo in the town of Halle hatched a heinous plot that entailed sending a letter to a store owner, and threatening to bomb his grocery store. They would then go into the supermarket, pick up a quart of milk and some ham, and inconspicuously leave a small bomb on a shelf. Once outside, they would make a call and demand payment from one of the store managers, threatening to blow up the store.

They got the bomb planted all right. But things started to go awry when they called to voice their demands. The first two managers they talked to thought the bomb was a hoax and refused to pay. Their first two bombs were duds and never even fizzed. The third manager did pay off, but then the bomb went off by accident. No one was injured, but it did damage several rows of canned yams.

This was the perfect time, of course, for our brilliant bombers to leave town. They had their money, and police were already swarming the crime scene, searching for clues, dusting for prints, and lab-testing every shred of evidence. Someone was sure to find something soon.

Did they leave? Such a sensible strategy was apparently more than their dumb criminal minds could even begin to fathom.

In the middle of the investigation, a traffic cop passing by the supermarket happened to come upon a parked car with two men asleep in it. Looking closer, he realized they were passed-out drunk. The backseat of their unlocked car was crammed with clothes, papers, and miscellaneous junk, which the suspicious officer rummaged through while they slept.

Within moments he had unearthed originals of all the extortion letters, the cell phone used to make the calls, and a bag of loot.

"It was like an extortion office on wheels," he said.

Oh yes, he finally did awaken the suspects and inform them that their goose was, in fact, cooked.

Looking closer, he realized they were passed-out drunk.

218. Stop Me When I'm Warm

A couple of punks, who had already had a few, threw an empty beer bottle from a train. The bottle hit a car windshield, and the owner reported the incident. When the cops met the train at the station, the conductor knew exactly who the officers wanted to see, because these jerks had made the whole train ride miserable for all the other passengers and the staff.

Detective Greg Allen of the Henryetta County Sheriff's Department in Oklahoma was the officer who questioned the train slobs. It was an unusual interrogation, to say the least.

"We know what you guys did, so you may as well just go ahead and tell us your side of the story." The detective felt the boys were ready to confess. That's when one of the suspects broke down.

"Okay, Okay, we broke into that car!" The other suspect just nodded.

Detective Allen didn't miss a beat. "No, no, the other thing you did." Now it was the silent partner's turn to confess.

"Okay, Okay, we're the ones who set that fire and burned down the house." His partner nodded in agreement.

Detective Allen was now surfing a wave of confessions. "No, not that, the *other* thing." The two suspects looked at each other and then at the detective, and then it dawned on them.

"Oh yeah, we threw some beer bottles off the train." They agreed on every crime.

"Exactly. Now, let's go back to the car and the house." Detective Allen got three confessions for the price of one.

219. More Than a Swap on the Wrist

A small town in Mississippi was honored to be home to the county's high school. This meant that the tiny burg of fifteen hundred citizens actually grew twice its normal size during school hours. And like any growing metropolis, the town began to have crime problems.

One night the high school was broken into by thieves who entered through a kitchen fan. The sheriff and his deputies arrived just after the thieves departed the building through the front door, tripping the alarm.

There were very few clues and no suspects. It was about six the next morning when the local radio station went on the air with news of the daring high school heist, which was followed by the station's most popular show, *The Swap Meet*. The on-air personality would take calls from people who wanted to trade items for what was offered over the air.

The sheriff and his deputies were doing paperwork on the crime when the disc jockey started the swapping. "All right, our first item, or should I say items, are ten space heaters that Bobby Monet has to trade for a late-model Corvette or Trans Am. Bobby also has four trombones that he would like to trade for a VCR."

One deputy was writing the words "space heaters" on the list of missing items when he heard Bobby Monet put the missing items up for trade on *The Swap Meet*. One of the deputies owned a 1969 Trans Am, and within two hours the deputy, dressed in plain clothes, met Bobby to show him his vintage Trans Am. Within moments four deputies had apprehended Bobby Monet and swapped him five years in jail for the space heaters and trombones.

220. The Kickstand Caper

Dennis Larsen was a motorcycle cop in Las Vegas in the seventies when he ran into a unique law enforcement situation.

Larsen was making a routine traffic stop in Vegas at about ten o'clock one night. He pulled over a speeding pickup and parked his motorcycle on the side of the road with the kickstand down on the semi-soft shoulder. Officer Larsen was at the driver's-side window of the pickup asking for the man's driver's license and registration when he heard the horrible, unmistakable sound of a heavy, well-equipped police motorcycle crashing to the pavement. His kickstand had broken.

Now, police motorcycles are not your little, lightweight dirt bikes. They are big, heavy machines. Larsen asked the speeding motorist to help him get his bike up off the shoulder of the road. Then Larsen hopped on and began to make a beeline for the police garage.

On the way to the garage, unfortunately, he spotted a little street bike zipping in and out of lanes, cutting people off, and generally being extremely reckless. There was no way Larsen could stop anyone without an operational kickstand on his bike, but the guy driving the street bike was being a real jerk.

Finally, Larsen flipped on his lights and siren and gave chase. The biker pulled over in the next block. Larsen pulled over behind him. Larsen, still sitting on his bike, raised one hand and motioned for the man to come over to his bike. "I want you to straddle the front tire of my bike and grab my handlebars with both hands," Larsen said.

The man looked puzzled but did as he was told. Then Larsen finally was able to let go of his bike and step off. He asked for the man's license, and the gentleman explained it was in his wallet in his back pocket. Larsen retrieved the wallet and the license, while the man kept a firm grip on the handlebars. Larsen then began writing the ticket.

After the paperwork was done, he placed his ticket book on his bike's front bumper and again took the handlebars.

"Now, please sign the ticket, sir," Larsen said.

The man let go of the handlebars and signed his ticket.

"Now, please put your hands back on the handlebars, sir."

The man did exactly as he was told and grabbed the bike again. Larsen tore off the man's copy of the ticket and stuffed it in the guy's shirt pocket. He then took the handlebars back from the biker and hopped onto his bike.

"You know," the man said, "I've been stopped before, but nobody has ever made me stand like that and grab the handlebars. Is that some new thing the cops do now?"

"No, sir. My kickstand broke about ten minutes ago, and I was on my way to the police garage to get it fixed."

The man scratched his head again. "So, what would you have done if I hadn't stopped?"

"All I would have been able to do was radio it in and follow you until I ran out of gas."

"What would you have done if I had dropped your bike and made a run for it?"

"Well, my bike weighs too much for me to pick it up and chase you, so I couldn't have followed you."

221. The Titanic Coupe De Ville

Officer Will O'Diear answered a traffic accident call late one night. It seems two drunks in the southern city had gone through a stop sign and had swerved to miss a car in the intersection. They took out a fire hydrant that began spewing water under their car. Being in the condition they were in, the two drunks weren't about to exit the car anytime soon, either.

The front wheels of the car had climbed up a guy wire that supported a telephone pole. So the two drunks were facing the sky, with the car standing on its rear bumper. And they were sinking.

The broken hydrant was pouring out hundreds of gallons of water and eating away at the mud beneath the car. The car was slowly oozing down into the sinkhole. Officer O'Diear got there just in time to help the two muddy drunks to safety, as they watched their Titanic Coupe De Ville go down for good.

Imagine explaining that to the insurance company. "No. I didn't total it. I sank it at an intersection."

222. Once a Soldier . . .

Occasionally, we receive a story here at *America's Dumbest Criminals* headquarters that doesn't involve a dumb criminal, but does involve the police and their ability to defuse potentially volatile situations. There's no criminal in this case, just an unfortunate fellow whose straw, so to speak, didn't go all the way to the bottom of his glass—and an experienced cop who handled a delicate situation with creative efficiency.

"Sometimes an officer has to fly by the seat of his pants," says C. R. Meathrell, chief of the Salem City Police Department in Salem, West Virginia. "And being able to ad lib at the drop of a hat can be a real plus."

Several years ago, when Meathrell was a sergeant working the night shift, he was called to a rest home to take care of a disturbance. An elderly patient had refused to take his medication and had mentally reverted to his days as a private in the army. The old soldier had raised enough pure hell that everyone on his floor was awake. For well over an hour he had paced the hallway, ranting and raving about the expected German attack.

The home had called the police to help them with a transfer to a nearby hospital.

"I had a rookie with me who was still trying to find his way around our little town," Meathrell remembers, "and all the way there he was plotting how we would take this guy. I had to remind him that it was just an old man with a bolt or two loose, not a Charles Manson."

When the officers arrived, staff members were waiting to escort them to the old fellow's room. When the rookie and the uniformed sergeant entered the room, the old man stared at the sergeant's rank stripes and then snapped to attention.

"Sergeant," he blared, "I've been a good soldier. Let me show you my medals." With that, he popped open a cigar box with several figurines in it.

Here's my chance, Meathrell thought.

"Private," he barked, "we are here to get you out of enemy territory. But we must hurry; the enemy isn't far behind."

The elderly "private" snapped to attention again, gathered his duffel bag, and marched out the door.

All the way down the hallway, the sergeant called cadence, and the little group marched out the front door as if they were going to war. Five or six elderly ladies cheered. One elderly gentleman simply muttered, "Nut."

Things went well until the officers and their charge emerged from the door of the rest home. There the good "private" stopped dead in his tracks. He had spotted the fire department ambulance that stood waiting to transfer him. An attendant opened the side door and offered him a hand, but he wasn't having any part of it.

"It's okay, private," the sergeant assured him. "That's a tank I ordered to get you safely across enemy lines. I'll stay behind and guard our flank."

Like a shot, the good old soldier was up and in the ambulance. Meathrell closed the door and waved good-bye.

As the ambulance drove away, the rookie turned to the sergeant with a slack jaw. "A tank?" he asked in disbelief.

"Don't gripe," the sergeant said. "He's on his way, isn't he?"

The elderly "private" snapped to attention again, gathered his duffel bag, and marched out the door.

223. Bigger *Is* Dumber

Three off-duty soldiers with girlfriends in the tiny hamlet of Ellensberg, Washington, had already imbibed before picking up their dates. Whether it was the brewskies, the night air, or young love, the soldiers lost all control when they saw a vision above the We-Sak-It-Git-'n-Go shop. There she was, larger than life, and yet so real, so near. She was ten feet off the ground. They gazed up at her with mouths hanging open. She was a fifty-foot-tall, inflatable beer bottle on top of an Ellensberg convenience store.

Like a top-secret mission behind enemy lines, the three silently went to it. Within seconds, they had formed a human ladder and vaulted onto the roof, where they were now positioned to secure the area and take their prisoner. *Poof!* They deflated the bottle and leaped back to the sidewalk, the proud owners of the ultimate party decoration: Paul Bunyan's Bud, the mother of all cold ones.

Just like Privates Moe, Larry, and Curly, they had to blow it up for the guys back at the barrack. The M.P.'s just followed the huge Long Neck in the sky to find them.

It's hard keeping military intelligence bottled up.

224. Usin' Your 'Ead

(Australia)

Now we venture to Queensland in the Land Down Under for a comically bizarre tale.

Police officer Colin Walker received a call from dispatch about two suspicious men walking around, looking into parked cars. When he arrived, Officer Walker turned off his lights and parked in an alley between two houses, from where he could clearly see the two men. Something was awry. One man was walking backward, dragging the other toward the passenger side of a running 1958 Oldsmobile. As any movie-goer might be wont to say, *What's wrong with this picture?*

"Police! Don't move!" shouted Walker, his weapon drawn. As the officer approached the suspect, the man on the ground was moaning. He had

a very large purple and red knot on the top of his head. Officer Walker quickly frisked the first man for weapons, then handcuffed him to the passenger-side door handle of the still-running car. Next he attended to the man on the ground who was now sitting up.

"Just take it easy man, an ambulance is on the way," he told him. "What's going on here?"

Seeing the cop and hearing more sirens on the way, the man's nerve broke and he began to babble.

"We were going to rob the owner of this bar, who always carries a lot of cash on him, but I don't have a car so we—"

"Shut up, you idiot!" screamed his partner.

"Go ahead, mate, you were going to rob this bar owner but you needed a car and—"

"And since I don't drive, I told Aldo if he'd drive I'd cut him in for half. Well, he said he'd drive but we'd better steal a car in case someone saw us pullin' off and uhh—"

"Well, what happened to you? Did you two get into a fight or something?" Walker quizzed.

"Oh no, nothin' like that. See, we was walkin' about lookin' for a fast getaway car when we spotted this big ol' V8 Olds. So Aldo popped the hood and hot-wired it. After it started, he was lookin' at the engine with his hands up on the on the hood, sayin', 'Man, they just don't make 'em like that anymore.' Well, I stuck me 'ead in to grab a peek just as he was slammin' it shut. That's the last thing I remember."

Officer Walker shook his head in disbelief. "You blokes might want to consider getting into some other line of work when you get out of jail."

So ends the blunder from Down Under.

225. A Limited Athletic Supporter

When questioned about the luxury of his prisoners' athletic program at the State Correctional Institution at Pittsburgh, the Activities Director stated, "There are some limitations to the program. No pole vaulting, no cross-country running, and no away games!"

226. Fail Safe

It was after midnight in Illinois when two thieves finally made it to the second floor of an old office building. It had taken them more than an hour to cut a hole in the roof big enough for the two very large men to squeeze through.

It was a hot summer night, and they were already sweating profusely by the time they found the three-hundred-pound safe in the manager's office. Within minutes, one was cutting around the door frame with an acetylene torch while the other was attempting to knock the tumbler off the safe with a sledgehammer. After forty-five minutes they were exhausted. They couldn't get it open.

"I've got an idea," one of them said. "Let's take it over to the window and drop it into the alley. With all the damage we've done to it, it should bust wide open when it hits!"

After pouring some water from the office cooler on the safe to cool it down, they dragged, pushed, and lifted the steaming safe up to an open window and shoved it out.

The safe landed below with a tremendous crash and clanging sound as it hit the garbage cans. The men quickly ducked down as if they were two little kids who had just beaned somebody with a water balloon. After a moment or two they peeked out. Apparently, nobody had heard.

The two persistent thieves huffed downstairs and broke out through a back door. They hurried down the alley, jumped into their pickup, and pulled up next to the safe. With their adrenaline still pumping hard, they managed to hoist the hot safe into the back of the truck. Then they drove it out of town about twenty miles until they came to a railroad crossing.

"It's 2:20 now," one of them said to the other. "In about ten minutes the CSX [train] out of Decatur is gonna come roaring by here at about sixty miles an hour. So we put the safe on the tracks, the train hits it, and, *pow*, it busts wide open. The engineer will never know he hit anything."

"You're a genius, man," his friend acknowledged.

So with some more huffing and puffing the two brainiacs managed to wrestle the safe out of the truck and onto the railroad tracks. And not a moment too soon.

"Here she comes!" the first man announced. Both of them hurried off the tracks and ran to duck behind the truck.

It happened just like the crook had predicted. The train's engineer never knew he'd hit anything. He didn't slow down a notch. The speeding train struck the safe at sixty miles per hour just as planned. But instead of bursting open and being tossed aside, the safe caught on the front of the train and was carried off down the tracks into the night. The two men stared in silent disbelief at the fading caboose light. They looked at each other. Neither one spoke. They got into the truck and went home.

But the story was not yet over. Unbeknownst to the two men, a woman had heard the two thieves as they were loading the safe into the back of the truck in the alley. She had taken down their license number and phoned the police, who showed up the following day to arrest them. The safe was found at a switching yard in the next town.

"With all the damage we've done to it, it should bust wide open when it hits!"

227. A Con a Sewer

Gary Michaels of Chicago liked the finer things in life: fast cars, fine art, and expensive jewelry—stuff he couldn't begin to afford. But while peering through the window of the jewelry store, he reckoned his luck was about to change. This was the heist that would get him out of the hole.

Simple: Smash the window, grab the jewelry, and run. Quickly, Michaels spotted a street manhole cover. He pried out the one-hundred-pound disk, hauled it to the window, and heaved it through. Michaels grabbed all the rings, watches, and diamonds he could carry, then took off running. Turning the corner, he almost bowled over a couple doing some late-night window shopping. Panicked, he bolted back into the street, heading for an alley, and then disappeared from sight . . . down the open manhole.

DUMB CRIMINAL QUIZ NO. 178

How well do you know the dumb criminal mind?

While we were taping another episode of *America's Dumbest Criminals,* the person we hired to play a drug dealer didn't show up on the set that day because . . .

a) he was waiting for a call back from Baywatch.

b) someone had stolen his car.

c) he was doing missionary work.

d) he had been jailed for possession of drugs.

The correct answer is (d). True story: The guy had been popped with twenty pounds of Wacky Tobacky the day before the shoot! How's that for typecasting?

---

228. Cousin Ninny

Every region of our country has its own set of stereotypes when it comes to how they regard residents on the other coast or even in the neighboring county. One of the reasons these stereotypes live on is, every now and then somebody comes through town who really does embody the worst characteristics of a strange and alien culture.

Everyone in the world can describe an obnoxiously direct and arrogant person who (allegedly) typifies the Big Apple. One officer in Virginia met an incredibly blunt New Yorker who talked himself right into jail.

The man had been clocked at eighty in a sixty-five zone. He had to appear before a judge and pay a fine if found guilty, and then he would be back on the road. The judge immediately noticed the young man's accent and asked him where he was from.

"New York, of course."

The judge nodded. "And you're here for a traffic violation, correct?"

"Yes . . . yes, your honor," the impatience in his voice creeping through.

"Well, what brings you to Virginia?" the judge asked, making cordial conversation while stamping the guy's file.

"I'm running some coke for a friend and I really need to get moving."

Everyone in the courtroom stopped for a moment in disbelief, and then burst into laughter. A subsequent search of Broadway Bozo's car proved his story beyond the shadow of a doubt. He was in jail in a New York minute.

229. Jag Drag

On the beautiful islands of Hawaii, it's not hard to believe that you are in paradise. The combination of perfect weather, the world's most beautiful beaches, and friendly people bearing fruit and frozen daiquiris can make for a most satisfying experience. But there are some who must drive an expensive convertible through paradise to be truly satisfied. Our next dumb criminal is just such a man.

He was driving a Jaguar XK8 two-door convertible with the top down in the brilliant Hawaiian sunshine. If car commercials are a vision of the afterlife, then this man was already in heaven. He interrupted his heavenly cruise, however, for a stop in a public park. There he met a gentleman who couldn't help but admire the beautiful automobile, which at the time was worth well over seventy thousand dollars.

"I'll sell it to you for five thousand dollars," said the driver, grinning at his dumbfounded new friend.

"You're kidding, but . . ." The prospective buyer was stunned, to say the least.

"But you've got to get the cash in the next hour," the driver added. "Can you do it? This is the car of a lifetime."

"Yeah . . . uh, can you meet me at the bank in Kapiolani?"

"In one hour. Be there with the cash, and the car is yours."

Exactly one hour later, the Jaguar jerk was arrested for grand theft auto at the Kapiolani bank. It turns out the Jaguar had been stolen the day before on a test drive from a Honolulu car dealership. It also turns out that the stranger in the park happened to be an employee of the very same dealership. He called the police as soon as he left the park, and Honolulu's finest did the rest.

230. Funky Footwork

Pensacola, Florida, police officer Marsha Edwards was dispatched along with another marked unit to respond to a disturbance call one afternoon in a usually quiet neighborhood. The officers arrived at the location and were walking up to the door when a man came out brandishing a pistol. The officers scattered across the yard looking for the nearest cover. They drew their weapons and ordered the guy to drop his gun and lie down on the ground—which he did.

"There's three guys still fighting upstairs," he told the officers. So Officer Edwards and two other cops cautiously entered the home while a fourth officer handled the man in the yard.

As soon as they got through the door, they heard scuffling and shouts coming from upstairs. They quickly ran up the steps and found three men punching and kicking each other in a writhing heap on the floor.

Officer Edwards grabbed the first man she could get her hands on. "I wrestled him to the ground and placed my foot on him between his shoulder and neck and told him to stay put." Meanwhile, the other cops were trying to break up the fight between the other two men.

"Lady, please," the man on the ground pleaded.

"Be quiet and stay still," Edwards told him sternly.

"But lady—"

"Just shut up and lie there," she countered, her foot still pressing down on him.

"Oh, lady, lady, please—"

"What?" she finally shouted at the man. "What do you want?"

"You've got dog poop all over the bottom of your shoe!"

The officer lifted her foot. "Ooooh, you're right. Sorry about that. I must've picked it up out in the front yard. Man, that's nasty."

"That's what I've been trying to tell you," he moaned.

All four men were then arrested for disturbing the peace. For the poor guy on the floor, it turned out to be a pretty crappy day all the way around.

231. Go Figure . . .

An officer in Florida told us about a dumb criminal who showed up too late to be caught in a "sting"—but still managed to work his way into jail:

"The sheriff's department had set up a fake pawnshop that bought stolen goods. We videotaped all our transactions for several months, then shut the whole operation down and arrested thirty or forty people who had sold things to us. That sting attracted national attention, and the press was having a feeding frenzy—almost nonstop coverage—because the audio and video were so good. We recovered everything from sets of silverware to an eighteen-wheeler."

About a week after the pawnshop sting had been closed, sheriff's department personnel went in to unload their equipment and dismantle the operation.

"We arrived in an unmarked cruiser car that, of course, clearly looked like a police car, with antennas and all. We used a huge truck from the jail with the jail's name printed on the side, two guards, a couple of prison trustees to do the hard labor, and a couple of plainclothes deputies."

Then the bearded man reached into his pocket and pulled out
three stolen Social Security checks.
"I'll sell these to you for ten cents on the dollar."

They pulled up to the "pawnshop" to find a bearded man sitting on the front steps. He looked at the entourage, recognized one of the undercover agents who had worked the operation, and signaled him to come over.

The agent strolled over to the guy and asked, "What's up?"

"Where've you been?" the bearded man asked.

"We've been around. Why?"

Then the bearded man reached into his pocket and pulled out three stolen Social Security checks. "I'll sell these to you for ten cents on the dollar."

Needless to say, they soon had that man in handcuffs. But as they were putting him in the squad car, the officer couldn't resist asking him a question.

"Didn't you recognize the police units and the security guards and the truck with 'County Jail' on the side?"

"Well, yeah," the dumb criminal answered. "But I just figured you'd stolen the truck and were bringing it down here to sell."

232. Wishful Thinking

(Italy)

It was the late 1950s, and Emilio Puccini was a rookie on patrol in Rome during the wee hours of the morning. The city was very still and beautiful at this hour, the dark, quiet time just after the late-night revelers had turned in and just before the fish market came to life. It was usually so quiet during Puccini's watch that he could hear a drunk mumble a couple of blocks away. One night, however, he was startled to hear somebody suddenly screaming in English.

"I wish . . . I wish . . . I had some money!" The voice was clearly that of a young man, coming from the direction of the famous Trevi Fountain. Puccini heard a big splash as he trotted toward the voice. He arrived just in time to see the young man surface with his two hands filled with coins.

"Thank you. But . . . but . . . I wish I had more money!"

Apparently oblivious to his surroundings, the inebriated young man shoved the coins into his pockets and submerged again to gather up more from the bottom of the fountain. Puccini watched him dive for money several times before he hauled the dripping, sloshing lad to the sidewalk. When Puccini rattled off several terse comments in Italian, the young man gave Puccini a very puzzled look, then grabbed a handful of coins from his pocket and threw them back into the fountain while he screamed, *"I wish I spoke Italian!"*

It seems he had simply enjoyed too much wine and had run out of money. When the officer described the charities the coins were intended for, the young man quickly returned his pounds of loot. The loony part, he gets to keep.

233. It's Safe in the Water

This is another good story given to us by our police buddy, Sergeant Larry Mihlon, a detective with the Long Branch, New Jersey, Police Department.

One morning he was called to the scene of a robbery at a Burger King restaurant. The owner stated that sometime during the night, thieves had made off with the store's safe. According to the detective, there was no sign of forced entry and to add to his suspicion, he was told that the safe had been bolted to the floor from within. So whoever stole the safe had access to the building and knew the safe's combination "You didn't have to be Sherlock Holmes to realize this was definitely an *inside* job." Detective Mihlon told us.

The manager was brought in for questioning and shortly thereafter confessed to the crime. He admitted that he and a friend had entered the building after hours and that he had opened up the safe and unbolted it from the floor. He and his partner took the entire safe out near a lake and ransacked it. When they'd finished looting it, they stopped on a dark bridge and threw it into the lake where no one would ever find it. No safe, no fingerprints, no case.

Afterward, the soon-to-be-ex-manager led detectives to the bridge. "That safe is at the bottom of the lake," the man sighed.

"I wish you could have seen the look on that guy's face when we stopped on that bridge and looked over the side," Mihlon said. There in broad daylight stood the safe in about three inches of water. It had been an especially dry summer and the lake had dwindled down to little more than a few inches."

In an update on this story, Detective Mihlon told us that the last he heard of the guy, he was working somewhere as a security guard! Go figure.

234. High-Tech Bomb Threat

It's entirely possible for even high-tech bad guys to be dumb criminals—as in the case of the Florida teenager who decided to use a fax machine to make a bomb threat to his high school.

Although it might have been a stupid idea—even *he* knew that the phone number of the originating fax machine is automatically printed on the fax—this young genius wasn't about to use his own machine. His unbeatable idea would be to use another fax machine and a toll-free number that he had been told could not be traced.

He called a large computer company and asked the person answering for technical assistance. One of the services the company provided was a computer faxing service. The customer could type in a fax number, and the information would be automatically transmitted to that number. Of course, the customer was also expected to put his name on the message. But the kid was too smart for that. In the message box intended for the sender's name, he typed a long message about a bomb being in the high school, along with a few other threats. He then typed in the fax number of his high school, transmitted the message, and quickly disconnected. Immensely pleased with himself, he sat back to see what sort of chaos would transpire.

Unbeknownst to the young man, most of his message was lost in transmission. Because the name box accepts a total of only twenty characters (including spaces), all that went through were the words, "There is a bomb in—"

The school authorities called the cops and, when they arrived, turned over the fax. Lo and behold, it contained the toll-free number of the computer company's technical support line. From there, it was a simple matter for the company to check its records and find where the call had originated.

Within a half-hour the young prankster was in custody. In the presence of his parents, he was soon confessing all and was eventually charged with making the bomb threat. Sadder but wiser after being expelled, the young computer whiz learned that a little knowledge can indeed be a dangerous thing.

235. Flight to Freedom

(Albania)

Before the Iron Curtain came crashing down, Albania's dictatorial government had been particularly brutal and paranoid. Travel for the average citizen was unthinkable. But Ivan Ruzica had hope—hope inspired by a bootleg videotape.

Ruzica had seen a black-market copy of the American film *Iron Eagle,* in which a sixteen-year-old boy flies an F-16 fighter behind enemy lines to rescue his imprisoned father. Ruzica thought, *If this child can fly such a plane, so can Ivan.* Ruzica was probably inspired a bit by the fifth of vodka he had just knocked back.

A muddled plan formed. He stumbled out of his barracks and down to the hangar. True, Ruzica was in the Albanian air force. And yes, for the last seven and a half months, he had worked around the big MIG fighters. But Ruzica was the base landscaper. He was not a pilot, nor had he any training to fly.

When he sneaked up to the fighter, the sentry was at the other end of the hangar. The canopy was open and Ruzica slid down into the pilot's seat. He slipped on the helmet. He pulled the crank on the side of the cockpit and the canopy began to lower. He gave thumbs-up to his imaginary crew just like the kid in the movie. Then he reached down and hit the big red button on the right.

Ruzica was instantly hurtled into space. His face pulled back from the G forces as he shot right up toward the stars—without his plane. Ruzica had ejected from the parked plane. Unfortunately, he did not get high enough for his chute to deploy fully. After his seat hit the tarmac, the chute quietly fluttered down to cover Ruzica, sitting upright, unconscious in the pilot's seat. They found him about fifty feet from the parked plane.

Which goes to show, some people just can't handle ejection.

The canopy was open and Ruzica slid down into the pilot's seat.

236. Lassie to the Rescue

Frank Wise of Cordele, Georgia, tells us the story of a patrolman who one night came across two young men acting strangely in a cemetery. After backup arrived, the officer began a search of their car for drugs, when, suddenly, one of the suspects bolted, dodging headstones. He leaped over a ditch and darted into a nearby residential neighborhood. It looked like his speed and luck would lose the police.

Within moments, however, the chase abruptly halted. When they caught up, the officers approached the man, flat on his back screaming for help. Over him was a vicious-looking dog, growling and snarling with one paw firmly planted on the fugitive's neck. The grounded suspect complained that the dog bit his leg and tripped him. Every time the suspect tried to get up, the dog would snap at his face and push him down with a paw to the throat. He begged the police to call off their K-9 officer, but they couldn't. It wasn't their dog.

Their K-9 officer was on sick leave. The dog that so deftly apprehended the fleeing felon was a stray. The owner of the house came out to see what all the fuss was about. When he heard how the dog had protected his property, the home owner adopted him, built him a doghouse, and fenced in his backyard. He figured any dog that protected him so well deserved a home for life. The criminal found a home as well, but only for five to seven years.

237. Step by Step

If we were stupid enough to risk jail or prison by breaking into a business and stealing something, we'd go for something big, and we'd take every precaution to cover our tracks. But we're not that stupid. That's why we're writing a book and a certain man in Wisconsin is writing his wife.

It had snowed off and on for most of the day. There wasn't a lot of moisture in the air, but there was enough to keep the snow from being blown away by the gusty winter wind.

Toward evening, the police received a call on a 2-11, a burglary. When they arrived at Bernie's Barbershop, they saw that the window had been broken out in the front of the small free-standing building. There really wasn't that much in there to steal. It was a modest two-chair shop.

Bernie the barber was called down to the shop to meet with the officers and take a look at the damage.

"Can you tell us what's missing from your shop, sir?" a young uniformed officer asked the man.

"What's the matter with people today?" the barber mused disgustedly. "I'm a working stiff. What's some jerk doing stealing from a working man?

"Sure, I can tell you what's missing, Officer," Bernie steamed. "My brand new portable color television set that I haven't had long enough to even have to dust yet—that's what's missing! I'd just like to know where the bum that took it is right now!"

It didn't take the officers long to find the answer.

While Bernie talked with the officers, one of the detectives on the scene had discovered something. Footprints. Not the footprints of the officers and Bernie; they were all mixed together in front of the store. No, these footprints led away from the others. Around the corner, past the row of dilapidated houses that lined the block, and down the snowy sidewalk.

Pedestrian traffic had been light that evening, so this particular set of prints was easy to follow. They continued across the street and down the opposite sidewalk. The detective followed them. The uniformed cop followed the detective. Bernie followed the officer.

The prints led to an apartment complex, then to a door, and disappeared behind it. The detective rapped sharply on the door. After a short wait, a nervous woman appeared.

"Yes?" her voice quavered. The detective was looking down. A set of wet footprints still covered the carpet and led right to a large sofa where an even larger man sat watching a hockey game on Bernie's TV.

The reception on Bernie's stolen television was perfect. The only snow was on the man's shoes, the only fuzziness was between his ears. And before the game was over, the larcenous hockey fan was looking at a different station . . . the police station's penalty box.

238. Sprechen Sie Deutsch?

Officer Arnold Hagman of the Boise (Idaho) Police Department was born in Germany and speaks fluent German. Working a traffic detail one day, he stopped a woman for speeding. When he walked up to the car to obtain her driver's license, she gave him a helpless, melting smile and said, in German, that she didn't speak any English.

Officer Hagman was more than just sympathetic. Nodding politely, he said, *"Heute ist ein glücklicher Tag für Sie,"* which means, of course, This is your lucky day.

Evidently, she disagreed, because the smile disappeared much faster than it had appeared.

239. Like a Duck on a Pond

(Canada)

Let's go north of the border to Dalhousie, Ontario, for a crime with a happy ending, starring a young man who stole a mountain bike—in broad daylight, downtown.

The daring young Dalhousian grabbed the bike from a store display and pedaled off down an alley—that dead-ended into a community police station parking lot. Now, you see where this is going, even if the bicyclist didn't. An officer just pulling in didn't see the frantic felon. The kid, thinking he was about to be cornered, ditched the bike and dove into a pond. He swam for his life to the other side to avoid capture. (Remember, no one is chasing him yet.)

Exhausted and dripping wet, the dumb creature from the black lagoon emerged at the very moment another officer was pulling into an adjoining fast food restaurant for lunch. Likewise, he didn't notice the walking pond scum. Still, our harried anti-hero was convinced a S.W.A.T. team of cops was closing in on him. He dove back into the pond. Gasping for air, he dragged himself out again and ran for freedom. He burst onto the street and ran right into, yep, another squad car.

The officer could barely understand the soggy suspect's weeping con-

The kid, thinking he was about to be cornered,
ditched the bike and dove into a pond.

fession as he gave himself up to a third cop who wasn't looking for him and had no idea what he was talking about. Wet behind the ears.

240. Safer than Cash
(Democratic Republic of the Congo)

A good job is hard to find in Kenshasa. Millions of people compete for a handful of jobs, so most workers are very conscientious. That was certainly true of a worker named Abdulai. For three years, he had come to work on time and with a smile. Manning a cash register on the deadly night shift, Abdulai had pulled down double- and triple-time wages. He had also received every raise possible for his perfect work record.

One night, however, Abdulai came down with something—chills, fever, weakness. He dragged himself to work anyway, determined not to break his record. Halfway through his shift, however, Abdulai had to call a cousin for help. The kind relative was more than willing to man the register while Abdulai rested in the back room. After his nap, Abdulai felt strong enough to relieve his cousin and finish the shift on his own.

Abdulai felt much better when he reported for work the next evening—until he saw his enraged boss and the two police officers. It seems that someone had pocketed two money orders on Abdulai's shift and used them to pay a traffic fine! Abdulai wasted no time in taking them directly to his cousin, who at that moment was returning from court . . . and was immediately returned there.

241. Hair Today, Scalped Tomorrow

Dumb criminals make all sorts of mistakes, not the least of which is their choice of targets. We've heard stories of nonvampires breaking into blood banks in search of cash. We reported the story of the man who chose to rob a Manhattan bank that was located in the same building as the FBI. He also happened to choose the day the FBI agents got paid. But why would anyone rob a hair salon? Sure salons don't have the greatest security, but then they don't have that much cash to protect either. Maybe we could understand one hair salon robbery, but a string of them?

This is the case of a wiggy robber in Brunswick, Ohio. The police were confronted with seven break-ins at hair salons in a five-week period. Wigs, cash, and various hair care products were stolen in each case. The method of entry was the same in each one, but the cops had almost nothing to go on. There were no prints and no clues. The investigation was going nowhere fast, until another salon got hit late on a Friday night.

Police responded immediately when the alarm went off. There were wigs missing, the cash was gone and shampoos and rinses had disappeared. Then the officer who responded to the scene found a clue that could nail the suspect. It was a chunk of his scalp on the broken window he had used to enter the salon. The officer radioed dispatch to put out an all points bulletin for a man carrying wigs, shampoo, and cream rinse who was bleeding from a wound to his scalp.

Forty minutes later, a man was stopped for speeding about ten miles from the crime scene. The officer noted several wigs in the back seat and several cases of shampoo. He put the driver in custody and ran his plates. Turns out the car was stolen as well. In Cinderella fashion, the chunk of scalp left on the window fit the divot in the thief's head perfectly.

Oh, and it turns out the thief was a hairdresser who intended to open his own place with his stolen small business loans from the other salons.

242. Perception Versus Reality

For some teenagers, committing dumb crimes is an occupational hazard that goes with the hormones. But two teenagers in Mesa, Arizona, deserve some sort of special recognition for their moronic accomplishment.

These two bozos shared a teenage paranoia—they were constantly checking their rear-view mirror for the lights of a police cruiser. This fear of cops gave them a brilliant idea for what they thought was a great gag. They stopped by an auto parts store and purchased some emergency lights for the roof of their car that were almost exactly like the ones on a police patrol car. Dumb and Dumber told the clerk they were volunteer firemen and needed the lights to answer calls.

With their blinding new emergency lights, the two teens began to freak out their friends with bogus "pullovers." In a rear-view mirror in the dark of night, they looked like the real deal to their friends—until they got right up to the driver's window and had a good laugh on their terrorized buds.

One night they were following a truck that looked just like one of their friend's pickups. The two pretend cops hit their lights and within moments the pickup had dutifully pulled over to the shoulder of the highway. But as Starsky and Crutch approached their "perp," they were stunned to see that the driver was not their friend, but a uniformed police officer who had just gotten off duty.

Dumber and Dumbest ran back to their "emergency" vehicle to beat a quick retreat, but the officer was too fast for them. They were quickly apprehended and arrested. Impersonating an officer is a serious offense, especially when the sucker you're trying to fool is no fool, but a uniformed cop.

243. They Didn't Get Clean Away

(Thailand)

Police in the Thai province of Ayutthaya had for some time been stumped by a rash of break-ins in affluent neighborhoods. Forty houses had been hit. In each case, the only clue had been a broken cement sewage tank under each house—and no hint of a suspect.

In need of a break or at least another clue, investigators were granted their wish when they were told about a free-spending group of suddenly wealthy eleven- and twelve-year-old boys. Working carefully but aggressively, police followed the gang of skinny youths to their meeting place under a bridge. From there the group split up and started out into a neighborhood that had already been victimized many times in recent months.

The cops watched as one youth slithered through an opening under the house that was no more than twenty inches high. About fifteen minutes later, he appeared at the front door, freshly showered and with his arms full of loot. His accomplices raced off in one direction with the loot while he strolled away in the other.

At the next house, the police moved in as soon as the point man slid under the house. Inside the house, they found the culprit half out of the toilet hole—the porcelain opening that Thais squat over instead of using a standard toilet bowl.

It seems our potty robber would break into the sewage tank, slide through the waste, and come out head first through the toilet and into the house. After a quick shower, the tiny thief would scoop up all the valuables and, in a matter of minutes, meet his friends at the front door.

But not anymore. Once caught, these kids were literally and figuratively in deep doo-doo.

They found the culprit half out of the toilet hole.

244. Never Talk to Strangers

Retired police captain Don Parker told *America's Dumbest Criminals* about a man named Simon Bolivar McElroy. He was having a bad day. After being freed from a Florida jail, where he had served time for a drug conviction, McElroy was on his way to catch a little sun at the beach. More to the point, he was going there to sell four plastic sandwich bags of marijuana. But en route to the beach, McElroy heard a metallic *clunk* when he hit the gas after stopping for a traffic light. The engine in his rusty old van had died.

McElroy grabbed his cigarettes and his lighter, shoved the bags of marijuana down inside his underwear, and walked away from the van, leaving the keys dangling from the ignition. McElroy stuck out his thumb and quickly caught a ride. Although he would miss the van, he didn't want to be anywhere near it when the cops showed up.

His ride took him all the way to the beach. He was beginning to feel better as he sat on the sand enjoying the warm breezes and the passing bikinis. The bags were making him itch, though, so he transferred them to his front pockets and started walking down the beach, looking for potential customers.

McElroy had just topped a sand dune next to a big hotel when he stopped dead in his tracks. Spread out in front of him were at least a hundred guys who looked just like him, with scraggly beards, long, stringy hair, and pasty-white bodies. They were lying on blankets, throwing Frisbees, or splashing in the surf. It looked like a druggie's family reunion.

He walked over to a couple of likely prospects and casually asked if they'd be interested in purchasing some weed. They not only were interested, but they also wanted to buy his entire supply! They dickered over the price and finally settled on an amount at least three times the going street price.

The guy he had been talking to called several others over, and in no time there was quite a little pile of greenbacks on the blanket beside the marijuana. McElroy started to reach for the money, but the guy stopped him. He told McElroy that they were now permanent friends and that he was going to sign his initials on every single bill as a token of his admiration for McElroy's kindness. Someone produced a pen, and the guy did exactly that. Although McElroy thought this behavior bizarre, he wouldn't have cared if the idiot had danced an Irish jig.

When the last bill had been signed, McElroy was given the money. He was about to take his leave when the guy told him he had some bad news. Before McElroy could react, each of the long-haired spectators suddenly produced a badge. They were of all shapes and colors and represented a variety of local, state, and federal law enforcement agencies.

As he was being escorted to the hotel to await the arrival of a uniformed patrol officer, McElroy was told he had managed to find an entire convention of narcotics investigators, in town to attend a training seminar.

The guy who had marked the bills was one of the instructors. He slapped McElroy on the back and told him to cheer up. "Look on the bright side," he said. "At least we'll have a really great story to start off tomorrow's session."

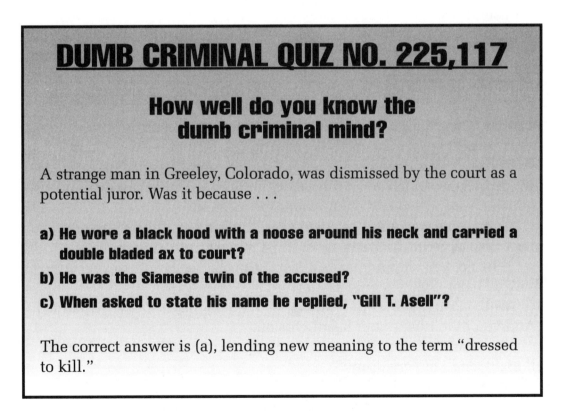

DUMB CRIMINAL QUIZ NO. 225,117

How well do you know the dumb criminal mind?

A strange man in Greeley, Colorado, was dismissed by the court as a potential juror. Was it because . . .

a) He wore a black hood with a noose around his neck and carried a double bladed ax to court?

b) He was the Siamese twin of the accused?

c) When asked to state his name he replied, "Gill T. Asell"?

The correct answer is (a), lending new meaning to the term "dressed to kill."

245. Wingnut

One day during Officer Dennis Gillum's stint as a police officer at Plattsburgh Air Force Base in upstate New York, the base exchange (BX) was robbed of more than fifty thousand dollars. The description of the thief was ambiguous, and according to Officer Gillum, he "left no fingerprints, and no one saw which way he fled."

Well, you gotta know something went wrong or Mister Mastermind wouldn't be in this book. But what could it be? He'd already gotten away with it. Three weeks after the robbery, Gillum received a phone call from a local car-dealership owner. Someone from the base had strutted into the showroom, picked out a new car, and paid cash for it. The bills were stacks of tens and twenties, still neatly wrapped in paper bands bearing the BX logo.

Busted!

246. Good Thinking

To police officers accustomed to hearing outrageous lies and absurd alibis, a truly honest answer can feel like a breath of fresh air—even if that breath has a distinct smell of alcohol. Captain Don Parker of Pensacola, Florida, received such an answer late one night when he stopped a woman he suspected of driving under the influence.

"By the time I got out of my patrol car," Parker says, "she was already out of her car, staggering back and forth, and obviously very upset with me."

"Why are you stopping me, Officer?" the obviously intoxicated woman drawled before Parker could say a word.

"Well, ma'am, you were weaving all over the road," Parker explained. "And you didn't have your headlights on."

"Oh, I can explain," she replied smartly. "You see, I've been drinking all night, and I'm very drunk."

Parker merely nodded.

"Considering my condition," she finished with unerring and incriminating logic, "I think I'm doing very well."

He had to agree, even as he took her in.

"Oh, I can explain. You see, I've been drinking all night,
and I'm very drunk. . . . Considering my condition,
I think I'm doing very well."

247. The Early Bird Gets Nothing but the Worm

(Canada)

It was a winter holiday, and the whole town of Burnaby was sleeping in, including the shop owners. Even the convenience-store owner was about forty minutes late to open, knowing that no one would be in for another couple of hours.

No sooner had he opened the doors, however, then a young man wearing a ski mask strode in. The owner wasn't alarmed. It was cold outside, and many Canadians are accustomed to donning ski masks, even when they're not committing a crime.

When the man in the mask produced a gun and demanded money, however, the owner finally understood he wasn't looking for the ski lift. The store owner explained that he didn't have much cash on hand because he hadn't had any customers yet. The would-be robber just kept waving the gun around, so the owner gave him the fifty dollars from the change drawer. Then, as the dummy turned to leave, the owner coolly popped him in the head with a baseball bat before calling the police and an ambulance.

"I would've let him go," the owner told police, "but he insisted on robbing me. I don't know why he tried to do it at opening on a holiday. Maybe he never had a job, so he just doesn't know about these things."

The convict would have been wise to hang on to his ski mask so that he could stay warm while chilling out in the cooler.

248. The Perfect Witness

After picking up a few items at a convenience store in Birmingham, Alabama, a middle-aged man was halfway out the door, when a young man in his twenties barged past him, looking a little nervous and certainly in a big hurry.

From his vantage point directly in front of the store window, the man watched as the kid suddenly pulled a knife on the cashier. The clerk reached into the cash drawer and handed the robber a fistful of bills. Stuffing the money into his pants, the kid raced from the store and into a pickup truck parked right beside the stunned man. Tires squealing, the truck sped away. The man was shaken. He had just witnessed an armed robbery.

Within moments of the clerk's shaky 911 call, the police arrived in force. The witness related to the officers exactly what he had seen and was able to describe the robber and the getaway truck in vivid detail. Police thanked him and he went straight home.

About ten miles from the robbery, the pickup was found abandoned on the side of the road, where it had apparently broken down. At about the same time the police were going over the truck, the eyewitness received a phone call from his son. It seems his truck had broken down on the side of the road and he needed someone to pick him up.

Well, needless to say, someone did. And it wasn't Dad. After a heated conversation, the son was persuaded to surrender to the authorities. Which he did.

The young son couldn't offer his father one good reason for robbing the store. But had the young man taken just a moment to look around, a good reason for not robbing the store would have been, shall we say, "apparent."

249. Type Ohhhhhhh!

When Charlie Beavers broke into a plasma center one Saturday night in Pensacola, Florida, he didn't get much—primarily because he didn't get too far.

Now, to a normal, rational mind, breaking into a plasma center might not make much sense. But to Charlie, it seemed like a good idea at the time. So after checking out the building, Charlie removed the top from an air vent on the roof and entered feet first. *Great*, he thought. *I'll just slide down this air vent, steal everything in sight, and make a clean getaway.*

His master plan was going flawlessly until the shaft did a nine-foot vertical drop, causing him to lose his grip. Charlie shot down the duct at a high rate of speed. The experience must have seemed like a ride at the fair—but the ride came to a sudden and painful stop.

Charlie's air shaft ended approximately three feet above a cross beam that separated two offices. And Charlie reached terminal velocity at about the same time he reached the cross beam. With a force hard enough to break through two ceilings (one leg on each side of the beam), he came to a crushing halt.

Charlie's legs were now in separate rooms. His arms were wedged tightly inside the shaft, straight up over his head. He was snugly straddling a cross beam.

Charlie spent a long weekend waiting for help. It arrived two days later, in the form of the police responding to a "breaking and entering" call. But then the police had to wait for the fire department to come and extricate Charlie from his predicament. As the luckless burglar was led hobbling away, Officer Pete Bell noticed that "part of his anatomy had swollen up to grapefruit size. And being from Florida, we know our grapefruits."

Beavers was arrested and charged with breaking and entering. Most officers on the scene agreed that Charlie had served his sentence long before the police ever arrived.

Oh, did we mention that it rained all weekend, right down the shaft and onto Charlie's face?

250. Do You Know Where Your Children Are?

Deputy Bill Cromie was patrolling the deserted streets of Phoenix, New York, around two in the morning when he noticed a fifteen-year-old boy pushing his bike along the street. Although it was unusual to see someone of that age out on the street at that time of morning, it was something else that drew Cromie's attention. Balanced on the kid's bike was a huge, glass-fronted china cabinet.

Cromie knew the boy. He pulled up beside him and asked the boy what he was doing with the china cabinet. Clearly nervous, the lad stumbled over his words but finally said he was taking the china cabinet home to his mother. Realizing how lame this story sounded, the kid eventually admitted he had stolen it from a house down the street.

"Those people have been away for a long time," he said, "and I didn't think they would miss it. Besides, my mom has always wanted one of these things."

Because they were only a block from the boy's house, Cromie followed him home so Cromie could talk to his mother.

The mother answered the door, and Cromie explained he had apprehended her son with a stolen china cabinet. She in turn asked the boy why in the world he would break into that particular house. The kid gave his mother a surprised look. "Don't you remember, Mom? You told me to go get it."

Clearly flustered by his reply, she mumbled and stuttered for a minute, then finally used the same words her son had: "Well, they've been gone a long time, and I always wanted one of those china cabinets. I didn't think they'd miss it."

The kid eventually admitted he had stolen it from a house down the street.

267

251. Reading Is Fun-Dumb-Mental

Sometimes, investigative police work can be a little like fishin' . . . you throw out a little bait, and you never know what you're gonna catch.

Our old friend, narcotics investigator Lynn Flanders of the Escambia County Sheriff's Department, told us this classic story of a sting operation they once set up along I-10 South, just inside the Florida state line.

In an effort to curb the illegal drug and money trafficking passing through Florida, the Sheriff's Department had a large official-looking sign painted that read, "NARCOTICS CHECK POINT 2.0 MILES AHEAD—ALL VEHICLES MUST STOP!" The sign was then posted on the side of the road by the Highway Department. There wasn't *really* a checkpoint ahead, but the criminals didn't know that, and it wasn't long before the fish began to bite.

Investigator Flanders, along with a chase unit, positioned her unmarked car on an overpass less than an eighth of a mile away. From their vantage point, they could see the passing traffic and the sign. With a hand-held video camera, they waited for the show to begin. They didn't have to wait long.

The first car was running about seventy when the driver saw the sign. He locked up his brakes so hard that he nearly lost control of the car as he fought to keep it on the road. Blue smoke bellowed from the tires as he screeched to a nearly dead stop on the highway. The driver then hooked a hard left and cut across the sloping grass median. That's illegal. He was of course pulled over and . . . surprise! An assortment of drugs and drug paraphernalia were found in the vehicle leading to the arrest of the driver and his two passengers. This idea was working well already.

The next car to see the sign had a different reaction. The lone driver applied his brakes and slowed down gently. He then pulled over to the shoulder. There he began pitching small plastic bags out the passenger window alongside the road. When he finished, he calmly pulled back onto the highway and continued heading south. But not for long. All his actions were being taped by the police, who leaped to collect the evidence. The bags contained several ounces of marijuana. Another arrest was made. This continued throughout the afternoon. Personal stashes, drugs for resale, guns, stolen merchandise, and a host of other illegals were tossed.

The big bust came later that day when two men who'd read the sign pulled over to the side of the road and just sat there. While they were debating the right course of action, the officers pulled up behind them. After some initial questioning, it was obvious that the men's stories didn't gel as to where they were from and where they were going. After a thorough search of the vehicle, Investigator Flanders and her team discovered $380,000 in cash stacked in some old diaper boxes hidden in the trunk. It was confiscated as drug money and as a result, $200,000 was eventually signed over to the Escambia County Sheriff's Department.

"All in all, it was a good day for law enforcement," Investigator Flanders told us, "and a bad day for lawbreakers."

252. A Clean Getaway

(Austria)

Something just wasn't right on the night train from Vienna to Brindisi, Italy. The conductor had been feeling that way ever since the train made its midnight stop. He had moved through the cars as usual to punch tickets. The sleeping passengers had left their tickets out so he wouldn't have to wake them. He was sure he had punched a ticket for every passenger . . . or had he?

Shaking his head, the conductor made his way back through the cars, even stopping to check the bathrooms. When he pounded on one bathroom door, an older woman's voice cried out for him to be patient. No surprise there. He moved on.

After the train made its next stop, our conscientious conductor repeated his rounds. This time, he found, a different bathroom was occupied—and the one that the woman had been in seemed unusually clean for this stage of the journey.

The train stopped again at around four in the morning, and the conductor still had the feeling that something was wrong. Making his rounds a third time, he found yet another bathroom occupied, the previously occupied bathroom beautifully clean . . . and now the little light bulb went on over his head.

Returning to the now-occupied bathroom, he rapped on the door and heard a gruff male voice telling him to "Try the next car." He waited a few moments and knocked again lightly. This time a *woman's* voice called out, *"une momento."* After a third knock, he heard an *old man's* voice protesting. Aha! The conductor's master key quickly revealed a teenager who had a talent for accents.

It turned out that the young man had been moving from bathroom to bathroom to avoid buying a ticket. Feeling guilty and bored, however, he had cleaned while he rode. In fact, he had done such a good job on the toilets and sinks that the conductor decided not to call the *carbineri.* Instead, he instructed the hygienic stowaway to finish latrine duty throughout the train.

253. Otis Takes a Shortcut

Officer Brad Burris of the Pensacola (Florida) Police Department once answered a drunk-driver call at a local go-go club late one night, only to find the driver still in the parking lot—sort of. The way the club parking lot was designed, you could see the interstate below, but you had to drive out of the lot and down to the road to get there. Otherwise, there was an eight- to ten-foot drop-off.

When Burris pulled up in his cruiser, he saw that the two front wheels of the drunk's car were hanging in midair over the edge of the parking lot. He had gotten stuck trying to take a shortcut. The rear end of the car was still on the pavement, the back tires still running at about sixty miles per hour producing clouds of blue smoke.

"I walked up to the driver's-side window, and there behind the wheel was a man who looked just like Otis Campbell from *The Andy Griffith Show,*" Burris says. "He was steering with both hands on the wheel and was, for all he knew, driving down the highway. His arms were rockin' a little, and he was staring intensely out the windshield. I mean, this guy was drivin'!"

Burris knocked on the window. The man gave a quick look to his left and went back to his driving, then jerked his head back left and jumped up out of his seat.

"Hey! What the . . . ?" he shouted, wide-eyed and bewildered, as if he couldn't understand how someone without a car could be running along-side him while he cruised down the highway.

"Pull over," Burris told him. The drunken man blinked widely and complied. He shut off the engine.

"Was I speeding, officer?" the man slobbered.

"Probably. Step out of the car, please."

It was all Burris could do to keep from laughing. "This guy was so drunk that he still didn't get it. As it turned out, he was a really nice guy; he'd just had too much to drink that night. Way too much." He was arrested for D.U.I.

254. No Fair

Detective John Crain of Birmingham, Alabama, and his partner were working undercover, doing drug buys and arresting prostitutes. One night they happened to be down by the state fairgrounds, when a citizen flagged them down.

"I been seein' y'all out here cruisin' around," the man said. "Guess you must be workin' at the fair. I just wanted to let y'all know that I can get you anything you want. Anything! I can get you drugs, prostitutes, hous-ing—you name it. I'm the man to see."

Not wanting to pass up a good opportunity, Crain asked the man, "Can you get us some crack?"

"No problem, man; just run me down the street here."

So Crain and his partner gave him a lift to a certain house, where he went in to get the drugs. Then he said, "Hey, I've got two women in my motel room. Let's go over there and do some partyin'."

"So we take this guy over to this sleazy motel and go into the room," Crain says. "But instead of two women waiting there, we met three more men."

This changed everything. Suddenly, the odds were four to two, and the officers had no backup. Crain and his partner didn't know if this was a setup or how many of these guys had weapons or what. So they just con-tinued to play along.

"Hey, let's smoke some of that rock you just got," one of the men finally said to Crain.

"Hold your positions; we are in control!"
Crain barked into his, uh, microphone.

"I want to wait for the girls," Crain coolly answered. "We'll smoke it when they get here, and then we'll go get some more."

"We don't have to go get more," one of the others said. "We've got plenty right here."

At that point, everybody started pulling out rocks of cocaine. They were arguing with each other about who had the best stuff. It was definitely time to end the party.

"Police officers!" Crain yelled. "Everybody freeze!"

"This was a tense situation," Crain remembers. "At any moment, one of them could have pulled a gun and started shooting. I'm thinkin', *We need some backup,* but I didn't know how we could call for backup without the means to do so. It was a standoff for a minute. Then I took hold of my collar and began talking into one of the buttons on my lapel."

"Hold your positions; we are in control!" Crain barked into his, uh, microphone. "All units, hold your positions!"

While this charade was going on, Crain's partner managed to slip out of the room and call for real backup. All of the men were arrested.

Says Crain, "The one who thought we worked at the fair asked me later, 'What was that button you were talkin' into? Man, you guys are comin' up with some neat stuff nowadays.'

"*Yeah,* I thought, *we sure are.*"

255. A Shining Example

To some people, image is everything. There are those who would not dream of leaving the house (even someone else's house) without making sure their appearance was in order. And different people have different priorities when it comes to appearance. Some people can't relax unless their hair is neatly combed. Others want to be sure their clothes are in style. For Cecil Warren, shiny shoes were everything.

Cecil was well known on the streets of Roanoke, Virginia, as a small-time thief and occasional burglar. He was just as well known for constantly shining his shoes. It wasn't uncommon for him to put on the spit and polish several times a day. In the end, his particular form of vanity proved to be his downfall.

Cecil had decided to burglarize a house, and he had no trouble getting in. He simply climbed up and over the back porch. Unfortunately, this feat also required him to scramble onto the roof. And roof climbing, as one prosecutor later put it, creates "a great probability of shoe damage." Our vain criminal couldn't get on with the job until he made some repairs.

Cecil escaped from the home with some five thousand dollars' worth of jewelry, but he left behind his can of shoe polish and, more importantly, his *monogrammed* shoeshine rag.

"The can of polish and that rag with the initials C. W. on it were as good as a set of fingerprints," one detective noted.

The vain Mr. Warren was found guilty of breaking and entering and grand larceny. He is now cooling his heels—and probably shining his shoes—in jail.

256. Safe . . . at First

"Go west, young man, go west!" Horace Greeley wrote those spirited words of wisdom a hundred years ago, and people have been headin' west ever since—drawn to the land of milk and honey with the cry of "There's gold in them there hills!" still ringing in their ears. Most are honest. Some are not.

In Corvallis, Oregon, the two men entering the large, two-story brick building from the roof that night were not honest. On the contrary. Their cry was, "There's gold in that thar safe!" This wasn't some spur-of-the-moment caper. While in prison, one of the men became friends with an inmate who used to work in this particular building. Both now knew the floor plan, when security made its rounds, and, most importantly, that there was a large safe inside. A payroll safe—and tomorrow was payday!

After climbing down a rope ladder to the second floor, they proceeded to the first floor and found the safe. It was huge. Break-in proof. But they had an equalizer. Why spend four hours hammering and drilling trying to knock off the tumbler when a few sticks of dynamite would do the job in seconds?

Why, indeed. Thirty seconds after lighting the fuses, they had their answer. In a tremendous explosion that practically leveled the building, the two were buried in a salvo of brick, wood, dirt, and debris. And that's where the police found them. After a stint in the hospital, both men were tried, convicted, and sentenced to prison.

What our two "dumbolition" experts didn't know was that the company that used to occupy the building had relocated. The old safe was too costly to move, so they sold it to the incoming construction company, which found it perfect for storage of their dynamite!

257. You Want Some Fries with That?

(Canada)

Carjacking is a terrifying crime, but it's also an incredibly dumb one. Why risk being dragged, run down, or even shot when you could just as easily hot-wire an unattended vehicle? Almost any crime, in fact, seems smarter than carjacking—except perhaps the taxijacking perpetrated by two guys in Vancouver.

It's one thing to hail a cab when you're in a legitimate hurry to get somewhere; quite another when you can't seem to get to jail quite fast enough.

They began by calling the cab to their house, thus leaving their address on record. Then they pulled a knife on the driver, who was still in radio contact with his dispatcher. They directed him through the drive-through window of a hamburger joint, where they refused to pay. Then they just rode around aimlessly until the police, alerted by both dispatcher and restaurant manager, were able to rescue the driver and arrest them.

We don't know what their lawyer advised them, but they could have pleaded not guilty of having brains!

258. The Bigger They Are, the Harder the Door

Officers use every trick in the book when it comes to taking control of someone who doesn't like the idea of being controlled. Here's another from that bag of tricks.

An off-duty officer in Las Vegas was working store security one night when a large college student shoplifted a pint of gin. Detectives met the shoplifter at the front of the store. A peaceful solution was not to be. The huge student ducked his head like an interior lineman on the football squad and barreled toward the only exit not covered by a store detective—the exit was locked.

The bull rhino hit the door going full steam. *Crash*! Door 1, Dummy 0.

The bull rhino hit the door going full steam.
***Crash!* Door 1, Dummy 0.**

259. What's Wrong with This Picture?

In Roxbury, Massachusetts, a man tried to rob a gun store with a knife. "Tried" is obviously the key word here. When police arrived, the suspect had five automatic and semi-automatic weapons aimed at him with five laser sights, little red lights dancing on his face like happy measles. The cops had to ask the obvious question, and the suspect shot back the obvious answer:

"If I already had a gun, why would I rob a gun store?"

260. Quick Comeback

Officer Dan Leger, a southern undercover narcotics officer, was always quick with an ad lib. One story Leger told us really showed the importance of the quick comeback in police work. A creative impromptu answer can be an officer's best tool for handling the situation by controlling the conversation.

"I was working undercover, and I was making a buy. You've got to record everything you can for evidence when the buy goes down, and this means you almost always have to be wearing some sort of 'wire' for recording your conversations. Unfortunately, every dealer knows that, too. Hollywood has always shown the undercover cop putting a wire right on the chest area, so for starters you want to be creative in where you put the wire. But you've also got to be prepared to talk your way out if the bad guys happen to find it. You'd be surprised at what they'll believe."

One criminal, for instance, went straight to Leger's wire and confronted him, blowing the officer's cover sky high. In less than a minute, however, Leger had managed to convince the criminal not only that he wasn't a cop, but also that he was one of the baddest and smartest criminals that particular dumb criminal had ever run into.

When the criminal shouted, "This is a wire! You're a cop!" Leger looked at him like he didn't have a lick of sense and then explained the facts of life.

"Of course it's a wire," he said patiently. "My lawyer told me to wear this so I'd have evidence to prove entrapment if I ever made a buy from an undercover officer. You ought to be wearing one, man. If a cop busts us and we go to court, it's our word against the cop's . . . and who do you think a judge is going to believe? But if you've got them on tape you can blow their case right out of the water."

The dumb criminal was stunned by the logic.

"Wow, that's really true, man. Great idea! Where did you get yours?"

"I told him where he could get a wire, and I also gave him some tips on how to wear it. He thanked me warmly for the information, then he went ahead and sold me the dope. I eventually proved my point in court."

The judge and jury did take Leger's word over the dumb criminal's because Leger had the recording from his wire and that was the evidence that convicted him.

261. Two-Way Radio . . . One-Way Ticket

Responding to a silent alarm at an industrial park in Aurora, Colorado, police officer Dave Leonard arrived at the location along with two other units. It wasn't long before he noticed a large garage door with a panel broken out of it.

Officer Leonard went around to the side of the garage and looked in a window. Not two feet away from him he saw a man with a black stocking cap atop his head, stacking up boxes by the side door.

"Hey, you supposed to be in there?" Officer Leonard asked calmly.

"No," the man replied matter-of-factly.

"I want you to come out here and talk to me."

The man did as he was instructed, exiting the garage by the side door.

"What are you doing in there?" he was asked.

"Nothin'," he stated. After a brief interview, the subject was placed under arrest for burglary.

As the fool was being read his rights, a whispered voice came over a radio. "Unit One to Unit Two. Unit One to Unit Two. Come in, Unit Two." But the source wasn't a police radio. It was coming from a walkie-talkie set the suspect was wearing on his belt.

"Who's that?" the officer asked.

"That's my partner," the guy admitted. "He's driving around while I steal stuff. I'm supposed to let him know when I'm ready for him to come back and pick me up."

Without looking at the suspect, Officer Leonard played a hunch. "Tell him that you're ready for him to pick you up."

"Okay," the man complied. "Unit Two to Unit One. Come in, Unit One."

"One here," came the reply.

"Come and get me. Over."

"On my way."

He was on his way all right—to jail. Unit Two was arrested as he pulled up. The car was impounded and both U–nitwits were taken into custody.

262. Ahhh . . . Baloney

Here's a tale about a sport diver whose good luck went out with the tide.

It had been a good day for Jerry Crain in sunny California. He'd only been diving for a few hours and had already filled two burlap bags with abalone. One bagful was within the strict limits set by the local fish and game department, while the over-the-limit other was stuffed with under-sized abalone, a double legal no-no.

California fish and game warden John Dymek had been watching the diver from the cliffs above with a pair of high-powered field binoculars. He knew that at least half of the diver's "catch of the day" was in violation of California law because of the one-bag limit.

Dymek watched as the loaded-down diver began his ascent up the steep hills above the beach. It wasn't an easy climb. The ground was soft and sandy and the footing loose.

He was still catching his breath when he heard someone approaching—Dymek, in uniform. Without a word, the diver picked up one of the sacks of abalone and, like an Olympian hammer thrower, began spinning in circles, swinging the sack in circular gyrations above his head. With one loud grunt, he sent it flying over the cliffs to the ocean below. Almost. By now the evening tide had rolled out, and the bag landed solidly on the dry tide bed a good ten yards from the water.

If that weren't dumb enough, when the officer checked out the contents of the unthrown bag, he discovered that "INeptune" had dropped the bag containing the under-sized abalone; the diver had hurled the bag with the *legal catch over the cliff.*

According to Warden Dymek, "The discarded bag was recovered, and the poacher was also charged with, and convicted of, attempting to destroy evidence."

Surfs him right!

The loaded-down diver began his ascent up the steep hills above the beach. It wasn't an easy climb.

263. Mission Improbable

(Canada)

Justice Spyros D. Loukidelis of Sudbury recounts a tale of two buffoons from British Columbia who pulled into a strip mall to rob a small branch bank. They were as well rehearsed and well choreographed as a movie cast, but the end effect was more Marx Brothers than *Mission Impossible.*

It began smoothly enough. The black sedan slid silently along the curb and eased to a stop. Two darkly clad figures slithered out, crouched behind the car, and snapped out two black ski masks. Simultaneously, they slid the masks over their heads and stood.

That's when they realized they had both put their masks on backward.

Blindly, they knelt and spun their masks around, then each drew a pistol with a silencer. Darting single file behind the car, they leaped up onto the sidewalk, flattening themselves against the wall as they scanned the area with their guns. The leader whipped open the door, and they were inside.

They squeezed off a round into the ceiling to maximize the element of surprise, but no one even turned to look at them. They looked puzzled for a split second, then both mouthed the word *silencers.* So the leader screamed, *"Freeze! This is a bank robbery!"*

An elderly woman behind the counter felt obliged to respond, "No, it's not."

The two men spun to face her. "What?"

"This would be a Singer Sewing Center robbery," she explained. "If you were two doors down, now that would be a bank robbery."

Cursing, the two men darted out the door and made their way commando-style down the sidewalk and into the bank. Breathing hard, they demanded, "We want all the money! *Now!*"

The single teller on duty immediately started to empty the money from her drawer.

"Put it in the bag!" the leader demanded.

The teller looked perplexed. "What bag?"

"Do you have the bag?" the lead gunman asked his partner.

The guy had to set his gun down to check all his pockets. "It must've fallen out when I pulled out my mask."

His partner sighed. "Do you have a bag, ma'am?"

The teller looked through several cabinets to find a bag. Then she made a great show of stuffing in fistfuls of money, mainly smaller bills. Quite tense by now, the less-than-dynamic duo grabbed the borrowed bag, bolted from the bank, and sprinted to their car. Now, it was the lead gunman's turn to look through his pockets.

"Wait," he said, "I'll be right back." His partner just stared as he jumped out and raced back into the bank. He never noticed that the teller was on the phone to the police. He was too intent on grabbing the car keys off the counter and hurrying back to the car where his partner waited. Finally, they got the car started and pulled away—just in time to be cut off on all sides by squad cars.

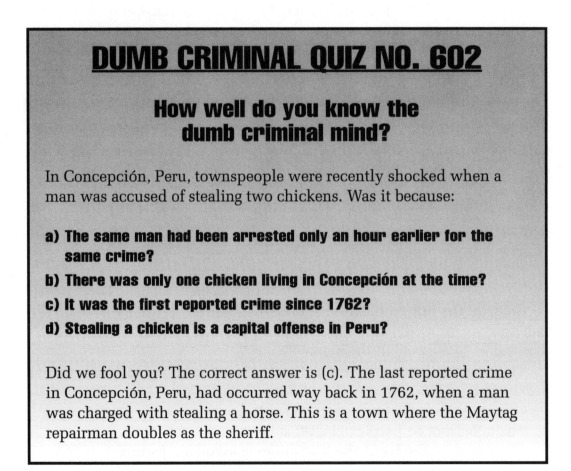

DUMB CRIMINAL QUIZ NO. 602

How well do you know the dumb criminal mind?

In Concepción, Peru, townspeople were recently shocked when a man was accused of stealing two chickens. Was it because:

a) The same man had been arrested only an hour earlier for the same crime?

b) There was only one chicken living in Concepción at the time?

c) It was the first reported crime since 1762?

d) Stealing a chicken is a capital offense in Peru?

Did we fool you? The correct answer is (c). The last reported crime in Concepción, Peru, had occurred way back in 1762, when a man was charged with stealing a horse. This is a town where the Maytag repairman doubles as the sheriff.

264. Always Wear Your Seat Belt

Like any safety-conscious motorist, West Texan Dwight Ketchum put on his seat belt before driving off. Nothing wrong with that, except for the fact that the car he was driving away wasn't his. When the police spotted him, Dwight took flight. The police gave chase.

After a few minutes of weaving through traffic at high speeds and still not being able to shake the police, Ketchum decided to bail out from the stolen vehicle. Pulling over, he flung open the car door and attempted to get out and run. But try as he might, he couldn't free himself from the seat belt.

The police were closing in on him fast. Too fast. Our car thief was apprehended while he was still struggling to get out of the stubborn seat belt.

265. An Open and Clothed Case

Duty du jour for Deputy Greg Deivert in Oregon was to transport inmates from the county jail to the courthouse for appearances. One inmate scheduled for trial was up on a stolen car charge. As the deputy waited for him to get dressed, the man held up two shirts and studied them. "There's really not a lot to think about, I guess; I've only got two shirts anyway," he said out loud. Choosing the old U.S. Navy shirt, he pulled it on.

The victim told the jury that, on the morning in question, he arrived at work on the construction site where he was a foreman. As he was closing his car's trunk, he looked over at the car parked beside him and saw a young man. The victim said that the man waved at him as he walked by. Approximately fifteen minutes later, he returned to his car for some blueprints, and it was gone. That was four months ago.

The district attorney then said, "Please look at the young man seated at the defendant's table and tell the court if this is the man who waved to you that morning."

The victim hesitated, then asked the defendant to stand. He studied him for a moment and said, "Yes sir, that's him."

The defense attorney went volcanic. "*Wait a minute!*" he shouted. "Do you honestly expect this court to believe that you can positively identify a man that, by your own testimony, you saw for no longer than ten seconds, four months ago?"

The victim answered, "If you look real close at the shirt he's wearing, you'll see my name under the navy insignia. That shirt was in the trunk of my car!"

The courtroom exploded with laughter, the defense attorney collapsed into his chair, and the prosecution rested. The judge pronounced the defendant guilty.

"The clothes make the man." In this case, they also make him guilty.

266. Choo-Choo Boo-Boo

(The Netherlands)

The setting was a very expensive department store in Amsterdam, filled with exotic delights for the Christmas shopping season. The time was after midnight, and nothing was moving in the dark store except for a lone dark figure in the jewelry department—an old pro at breaking and entering. Scooping up diamonds and watches with nonchalant skill, our man filled his bag and started to leave just like any tired shopper. Our man would be the first to testify that the holiday season sure was a wonderful time to shop, especially after hours, when the price is right.

Then he saw it, in the toy department—the model railroad of his youthful dreams. He couldn't resist. Using his flashlight to find the transformer, the thief lay flat out on the floor and opened up the throttle on the big locomotive. It pulled twenty cars—passenger cars, dining cars, even a few freight cars filled with presents and a bright red caboose!

Ol' Casey Jones was having the time of his life when two strong hands lifted him right up off the floor. Although the thief had set off a silent alarm, he had been too engrossed in his play even to hear the police arrive!

Then he saw it, in the toy department—
the model railroad of his youthful dreams.

267. The Write Name

Good friend Adrian Breedlove, a patrolman with the Brentwood Police Department in Tennessee, got his dumb criminal story to us just under the wire.

One evening during a routine market check at a local Kroger store, Officer Breedlove was making one last sweep of the somewhat empty parking lot when a suspicious man in a dark trenchcoat seemed to appear out of nowhere. Breedlove knew that no one had just pulled into the lot, and he hadn't seen anyone walk up, so his curiosity was piqued. He watched as the man entered the store. Something didn't feel right. The officer decided to check out the rear of the store. As he pulled his car around to the back, he spotted a black Camaro sitting behind the building without tags. The motor was still running, but there was no key in the ignition. Officer Breedlove radioed in the VIN (vehicle identification number) and the car came back reported stolen. The man in the trenchcoat was arrested and charged with the theft when he walked around back to get the car.

Not that driving a stolen car with no license plates isn't dumb enough, that's really where this story starts. The man had no identification on him, but told the officer his name was Richard Norton Hudson. He also gave the detectives that same name when he was questioned downtown. When they ran the name he'd given them, nothing showed up in the computer. Patrolman Breedlove told us that Hudson spent several days in jail unable to post bond. Eventually he was able to reach someone to bail him out. They arrived with the bail and showed Booking a check-cashing card and a picture I.D. with Hudson's name on it. Everything looked in order, so they sent an officer to get him.

Now when you make bond, you have to sign yourself out. And that's just what Richard Norton Hudson did. He was a free man. Almost. Just as he was about to exit the police station, a sharp-eyed clerk spotted Hudson's fatal blunder. He had signed a different name at the bottom of his release form. His real name. Kevin Scott Shane.

When they ran *that* name through the computer, it was a different story. Shane had a lengthy police record and was wanted for parole violations. He was rearrested on the spot, and later sent to a maximum security prison to serve out the remaining twelve years of a prior sentence.

268. Dudley Do-Wrong

(Canada)

Ken Simpson is a correctional officer in the Canadian province of British Columbia, and he sent us a detailed report of a not-so-Great Escape by one less-than-lucky inmate.

This particular prisoner was actually fairly well-behaved. In fact, he was what Ken would call a model inmate. He was allowed to go outside the prison on daily work details, which are breaths of fresh air to a prisoner who has been cooped up in a workhouse.

One day on work detail, one of our gent's fellow inmates fell ill. While the guards were busy attending to the puny prisoner, Mr. Model Behavior seized the moment and was able to slip off and make a run for it. Within five minutes the escapee had broken into a car and hot-wired the ignition. He headed down the freeway toward what seemed to be a flawless escape.

There were only two problems:

Number One: The stolen car had virtually no gas in it.

Number Two: The freeway entrance he had chosen was on a steep hill, with the Royal Canadian Mounted Police Station right there.

As soon as our Steve McQueen started up the steep hill onto the freeway, his getaway car stuttered, lurched, and coughed its way to a stop, out of gas—directly in front of the police station. As he frantically tried to restart the stolen car, two officers came out of the station and noticed the nervous guy with car trouble. Always ready to help a citizen in distress, the two officers approached the man to render what assistance they could. Of course, the motorist insisted he was fine.

Unfortunately for Stevo, one of the officers had already noticed the car had been hot-wired. It was at that moment the report of the escape came across the other officer's radio. The three of them all listened to a perfect description of the motorist in distress.

The prisoner just put out his hands to be cuffed.

269. Peekaboo, We Saw You!

(Japan)

Unfortunately, it would seem that the dumbest criminals in Japan are Americans. A retired United States Air Force security policeman stationed in Okinawa believes he has evidence to support that claim.

It was Christmas Eve back in 1979, and the security officer on watch was making his rounds around the base. Walking past the base bank, he decided for some reason to take a peek in the window. He cupped his hand against the glass and was shocked to see another face right up against the same window on the inside. Both faces jerked back quickly.

The patrolling officer called for backup. Within minutes other security officers had secured the bank and the three thieves inside.

It turns out the bank robbers were airmen who had planned the job for months. They had all applied for and taken leave. They all had their passports, leave papers, and cash and were booked on a Christmas morning flight. They had been mere moments away from escaping with the base payroll—almost a half a million in cash—when one of them happened to look out the window.

"Why did you do it?" the officers had to ask.

The nostalgic thief answered, "I wanted to see the Christmas Eve sky."

We presume he didn't see a tiny sleigh pulled by reindeer and he didn't see the wise men following a star. But he did see his future—in jail.

270. Dressed for Arrest

Sergeant Larry Bruce told *America's Dumbest Criminals* about a routine warrant he served one morning that took an unexpected twist and became a comedy of errors.

There had been a string of burglaries in the city of Brunswick, Georgia, and Bruce had been put on the case.

"I had a pretty good idea who the person was," Bruce says. "In a town of just seventeen thousand people, if you've been around for a while, you get to know what's going on and who's doing it."

When Bruce had collected all the evidence he needed, a warrant was issued for the suspect's arrest. Sergeant Bruce and another officer set out early on a February morning to serve the warrant. They were hoping to save some effort by catching the suspect while he was still in bed.

"It was exceptionally cold that morning—about twenty-eight degrees," Bruce recalls. "My partner and I walked up the crooked sidewalk to the front door of the man's mother's house. 'This shouldn't be too hard,' I remarked to my partner.

"Well, his mother answers the door and tells us that her son is already up and in the bathroom. So we explained that we needed to talk to him, and would she be kind enough to go and get him for us. Which she did. She returned a moment later with her son right behind her. He wore white jockey shorts, and his face was covered with shaving cream.

"As soon as he saw us he 'booked.' We couldn't believe it at first. The guy runs to the back of the house and out the bathroom window—in his underwear at twenty-eight degrees!"

Still shaking their heads, the officers ran to the squad car to radio for help.

"In foot pursuit of a black male . . . six-foot-two . . . about one hundred and ninety pounds . . . wearing white Fruit of the Looms and a face full of shaving cream . . . send all available units."

The dispatcher was incredulous. "We didn't copy all that. Please repeat."

Bruce repeated the bulletin. Midway through, he realized how it must sound and began to laugh. It took a minute or so to repeat the information. By then both officers were laughing.

After a few more minutes, several units had arrived in the neighborhood and an intensive search had begun. As the officers combed the neighborhood, people were coming out for their morning papers.

"Y'all looking for a crazy man runnin' around in his underwear?" one old man asked.

"Yes, we are. Have you seen him?"

"Just turned the corner to the left," he responded with a cackle. "Don't worry 'bout him. He was movin' too fast to freeze!"

The officers turned another corner. A woman in a housecoat stood pointing to a vacant house on a corner lot.

The officers converged on the house, and Bruce knocked. The door

"In foot pursuit of a black male . . . six-foot-two . . . about one hundred and ninety pounds . . . wearing white Fruit of the Looms and a face full of shaving cream . . . send all available units."

swung open. There stood the suspect, still in his undies, and still wearing the shaving cream, which by now had dried out a little. He yawned innocently, stretched, and said, "You looking for someone, Officer?"

"Yes, you!"

The man protested that he had just awakened and was shaving when the officer knocked. The fact that there was no furniture, no running water, no electricity in the house didn't really seem to bother him. Neither did the fact that everybody in town knew the house had been empty for more than a year.

The suspect, now shivering, was escorted to the closest squad car. Bruce and his partner headed around the block to their own unit.

"No, Larry," laughed the other officer as he turned up the collar of his jacket against the cold. "That wasn't hard at all."

271. Mirror Image

Most wild-game poachers work at night in isolated areas. Unless they do something really stupid, odds are they won't get caught. Deputy Sheriff Ronald Saville of Fort Benton, Montana, remembers some elk poachers who would have escaped clean but for a bit of carelessness.

Acting on a tip that someone had been shooting elk in the area, the deputy and a state game warden checked the area. This being the middle of winter, they had no trouble following the blood trail across the snow to where the poachers had gutted the animal. But other than the gory elk remains, there didn't seem to be any useful evidence—until they examined the scene more closely.

There in a snowbank, where the poachers had backed up a truck to load the elk carcass, the officers found an imprint of a license plate. It took only a moment to obtain a registration. The dumb poachers were astonished when met by a law enforcement welcoming committee.

272. Bushted

An officer in Cudahy, Wisconsin, was in hot pursuit, on foot, of a suspected burglar. After a two-block chase, he found the man crouched in some shrubbery in front of a house.

"What are you doing in there?" the officer asked him.

"Oh, hi. I locked myself out of the house and I'm looking for the spare key I keep out here in the bushes," the man told him.

"That's strange," the officer said. "Why would you do that?"

"In case I lock myself out, I told you."

"Oh, I *know* why you'd hide an extra key," the amused officer responded. "I just want to know why you would hide it at *my* house!"

As with real estate, the *key* to this story is location, location, location.

273. Married, with Problems

(England)

A string of post office robberies in 1994 and 1995 had British police stymied. A lone gunman would appear in a town's post office, demand and get his cash, then disappear without a trace. Within two years the fleet-footed gunman had made off with more than fifty thousand pounds.

What police didn't know at the time was that the lone gunman was not actually alone. True to the old saying, "Behind every successful man, there's a woman," the robberies were the handiwork of the husband-and-wife team of Bob and Betty Houlihan. Bob did the front-line work—carrying the gun, threatening violence, and carrying the loot to the car. Pedal-to-the-Metal Betty drove the getaway car. Together, they were the most successful crime team in the United Kingdom—until one fateful day in September 1995.

It happened at a small post office on the outskirts of London. As usual, Betty pulled up and parked. Bob jumped out and headed off for another day at the (post) office. He pulled his gun, threatened to shoot everyone, and demanded money. The postal clerk gathered up all the cash and shoved it across the counter. Everything worked like the usual clockwork. Crime was so easy it was almost becoming boring to him.

Then Bob walked out to hop into the car and noticed something different. Betty was not in the car. The engine wasn't running. Looking off to the side, Bob finally saw his wife looking very perturbed.

"Let's go, Betty," Bob snapped.

"Can't, Bob. Sorry." She made no move to leave.

"Let's go, Betty. *Now*!"

"Don't start with me," she said. "I just stepped out to walk Timmy, and I locked the keys in the car." Bob looked down at the couple's Jack Russell terrier. Timmy just barked and wagged his tail. And that's when the police apprehended them. The dog catcher came for Timmy, and Betty and Bobby argued all the way to the jail.

274. All Aboard!

When Nashville police officers Andy Wright and Jeff Cherry observed a possible drug buy in a known high-drug-sales area, they approached the man who had made the buy. But when they began to question him, the criminal struck Officer Cherry in the face and took off running. The chase was on.

For nearly half a mile, the officers pursued the suspect on foot. Then he ran down an embankment and over some railroad tracks into a rail yard, crossing just in front of a long freight train, Cherry said.

Officers Wright and Cherry came to a sudden halt as a train barreled down between the officers and the suspect. Says Cherry, "The train separated us from him, but we knew he couldn't run up the other side because more police were coming from that direction."

The two officers knelt down and watched the unbelievable scene that unfolded.

"Looking under the train, we could see the suspect standing there. We watched him closely because we might lose him if he simply ran next to the train," Cherry said.

Instead, standing perfectly still, this genius reached out and tried to grab the handrail on the train, which was moving at about forty miles per hour. It immediately knocked him to the ground and bounced him about ten feet down the tracks.

"We couldn't believe he did that. It's amazing that his arm wasn't yanked off," Cherry says.

The rocket scientist staggered to his feet and tried to jump on the train again. From a standing start, he just sort of threw his body up against the moving train. It knocked him down once more, only more violently this time. This time he didn't get up. His second attempt to jump the train had left him unconscious.

"We waited another couple of minutes for the train to pass while the suspect just lay there. After the last car went by, we scooped him up and took him to the hospital. They kept him overnight for observation, and he was booked on the following day."

The bad guy now knows the difference between a rail yard and a prison yard. Let's hope he also studies basic physics while he's in the joint.

We couldn't believe he did that. It's amazing that his arm wasn't yanked off.

275. I Need a Drink

Only in New York. This story is about a guy in Buffalo who had the resolve of a prize-fighter, the patience of a saint, and the brain of an opossum.

John Fly decided to break into a Woolworth's department store. His entrance of choice was one of the ventilation shafts running above the ceiling. That was his first mistake. More than one hapless burglar has met his fate from slipping down a shaft and becoming wedged with his arms pinned overhead, eventually suffocating. So don't try this at home. His second mistake was his choice of shafts. The one he selected was directly above the lunch counter grill. This guy was lucky, though. He didn't get wedged in, he got boxed in. After getting a late start the night before, by the time he got to the bottom of the vent and was preparing to exit into the store, Woolworth's had opened for the day.

Now you'd just about have to give it up at that point, unless you wanted to spend all day over a 350-degree grill. In an exhaust vent. I know this is hard to believe, but that's just what the man decided to do. Just sweat it out. For eight hours.

It wasn't until they were about to close the kitchen down for the night that the wilted Fly gave himself away. It happened as the cook was walking past the grill. Fly reached out a grease-soaked hand from the vent and begged, "Can I get a glass of water?" The startled cook almost went in to cardiac arrest. The manager immediately called the police. The medium-rare robber was extricated and arrested.

One of the officers stated that the man "had a coat of grease on him about an inch-and-a-half thick."

A very slick criminal.

276. Once Bitten, Twice Bitten

Sergeant Doug Baldwin in Pensacola, Florida, was dispatched to assist in a high-speed car chase. He responded immediately and soon was hot on the tail of the speeding vehicle.

Suddenly, the suspect's car veered off to the side of the road. The driver's door sprang open, and the driver bolted from the car. By the time

Baldwin could get out of his own car and follow on foot the suspect had disappeared.

A search of the fugitive's car uncovered a quantity of drugs. Now he was wanted for possession, speeding, and resisting arrest. But he was nowhere to be found. An extensive canvass of the area proved fruitless. After hours of searching, the officers were ready to call off the search, but Sergeant Baldwin decided to again check the area.

Looking behind an auto mechanic's shop, Baldwin heard something. It sounded like a man whispering "ouch" and quietly cursing. Officer Baldwin traced the sound to a car up on blocks. He bent down, looked underneath the car, and saw a bare-chested man twitching wildly on the ground.

The officer called to the squirming man, who identified himself as the suspect. "You're under arrest," Baldwin said.

"Okay, but hurry up!" the man pleaded. "You've got to get me away from all these mosquitoes; they're about to bite me to death!"

Sergeant Baldwin dragged the man from under the car and saw that his skin was as bumpy as a rhinoceros's hide from mosquito bites. He handcuffed the suspect and was leading him out of the fenced compound when, from out of nowhere, two security dogs appeared and jumped the bad guy. They bit him several times before Sergeant Baldwin could run them off.

Between the mosquitoes and the dogs, the man had about one hundred bite marks on his body. It was a bad case of "overbite"—and a stellar example of taking a bite out of crime!

277. Of Mice and Ex-Boyfriends

Neil Sedaka said it best years ago in his rock 'n' roll ballad "Breaking Up Is Hard to Do." Some people make it as hard as they can, and who knows how better than your beloved? Your beloved knows your dreams and your insecurities, your pet peeves and your greatest fears.

Tom H. in Massachusetts had fallen out of love. He wanted to let Sally know that she was a great person, but for whatever reason, "they" were just not meant to be. Tom let her down gently. Sally, on the other hand, wanted to hurt Tom real bad, and she knew exactly how to do it, even if it meant taking the law—and some rodents—into her own hands.

Tom was six-foot-four and two hundred pounds, and he worked out. Sally was maybe a hundred and ten pounds and all of five-foot-three. What could this diminutive demon do to this hulking bully?

You see, Tom had confided his greatest fear to Sally a while back and, unfortunately for him, Sally remembered. She went to Tom's apartment and displayed two mice in a tiny cage. Then, with Tom shaking and screaming, she released the mice under the covers of Tom's bed and left.

Police answered Tom's call for help. When they got there, Tom was on top of his refrigerator squealing like a small child.

Touché, Sally.

Tom had confided his greatest fear to Sally a while back and, unfortunately for him, Sally remembered.

278. Door-to-Door Salesman

We're all familiar with the old phrase "seeing double." Leave it up to one of America's dumbest criminals to come up with a new term, "seeing triple."

Our story begins in Utica, New York, where a lone policeman responded to a burglary call at a local car dealership. As the officer got out of his patrol car, he saw what appeared to be a flashlight shining on the inside of the building. Cautiously making his way to the wall, he peered in through the small window of a side door. Inside he saw the perpetrator looking right back at him.

As their eyes met, the man inside suddenly bolted to another door in an effort to escape. The officer quickly ran to the same door. They met again. Not ready to capitulate just yet, the man opted for the third and final door, arriving just in time to face the same officer. Realizing the futility of it all, the man threw his arms into the air in disgust and blurted, "I give up, you have the place surrounded!" And with that, the officer placed the out-of-work salesman under arrest.

Outnumbered? Nah. Outsmarted.

279. The Three Un-Wise Men

(Syria)

Justice can be swift in the villages of Syria. The great deterrent to crime is much like our Old West. The fact is, if you're caught red-handed, you stand a very good chance of losing that hand or having your neck stretched, depending on the mood of the local populace.

And just like our Old West, there are always young men willing to take the chance rather than work for a living.

Gamal, Mustafa, and Hassan were out for themselves and themselves only. They were the first generation of Syrians to have grown up exposed to western television and movies. The three amigos could quote the old Hollywood westerns by heart. They were now the "Younger Brothers," a modern-day reincarnation of three of the blood-thirstiest, meanest, bank-robbingest bad guys the West had ever seen. Or so they thought.

The three rifles were easy to get: Almost everyone in the countryside hunts, and those who don't are armed anyway. They made their getaway from their parents' house at night without a note or a word. Silently, they left the village, two on foot and the third on a burro. They traveled for an hour before they set up their hideout. It was a desert region and the boys had a tent up in no time.

Gamal had the master plan. They were going to rob the "stage," a bank armored car, at 8:00 A.M. They had their bandannas ready, guns, and plenty of ammo. By morning, they would be legends.

Hassan was assigned sentry duty first. At night in the desert, you think you can see much farther than you actually can. In the blue light of a star-filled sky, the desert can play tricks on the eye. Hassan was on edge. When a lizard darted across the desert twenty feet away, the trigger-happy youth instinctively popped off a round. Hassan stared in disbelief. He had destroyed the lizard.

Gamal and Mustafa bolted out of the tent with their rifles ready.

"Nothing but a lizard," Hassan drawled slowly in his best Clint East-wood as he pointed at what used to be a lizard. With the cool disdain of a hired gun, Hassan stuck his rifle in the sand, barrel down. Mustafa and Gamal grunted and went back to sleep.

Hassan's confidence was pumped now that he had tasted bloodshed. He scanned the horizon, hoping for another chance to fire the gun. Then there it was. *Was it a man's silhouette or just a cloud's moon shadow?* Was Hassan seeing things? Finally, the shape came over a rise fifty feet from Hassan. It was a man, a big man.

Hassan leapt to his feet. Like Chuck Connors on *The Rifleman,* he whipped his gun out of the sand, swung it up to his shoulder, and fired at the silhouette. The gun gave a muffled blast, spitting sand and a bullet about fifteen feet. The silhouette rushed up as Hassan screamed. The next thing he knew, his gun was wrenched from his hands and the man was now cuffing Hassan on the ears just the way his father did when he was being punished.

Yikes, this *was* his father, but the punishment was just beginning. Hassan's dad disarmed the Younger Brothers single-handedly.

280. Safety First

As a police officer in Baltimore, Maryland, during the sixties, Frank Walmer ran into his share of dumb criminals, including one who had a penchant for robbing mom-and-pop grocery stores. His weapon of choice was a sawed-off shotgun.

"It looked like an oversized handgun, but it was an old-fashioned twelve-gauge with a hammer," Walmer remembers. "There was nothing left of the stock except the pistol grip, and the barrel was no more than six inches long. It didn't even have a trigger guard. This guy hadn't shot anyone yet, but he was getting bolder with each robbery. We figured it was just a matter of time before someone got hurt."

It happened at the very next robbery. Picking out a small grocery store on the west side of town, he came charging through the door, like Jesse James, waving his sawed-off shotgun and making everyone lie on the floor. He scooped up the few dollars in the register, then backed out the door, sweeping the shotgun back and forth and glaring menacingly at the terrified elderly owner and his equally frightened wife. Pausing in the door for dramatic effect, he aimed the shotgun at the trembling man and said, "Old man, I'm leaving now. And you better not call the cops for ten minutes, or I'll come back and kill you."

Wide-eyed with terror, the man nodded.

"You understand what I'm talking about?" the robber shouted.

"Yes," the owner managed to croak.

"Yes, what?" the bad guy said, cocking the hammer.

"Yes, sir," the man squeaked.

The robber smiled. "That's better. Now don't move, and no one will get hurt." With that, he jammed the shotgun into his belt, catching the trigger on his pants and causing the weapon to discharge.

"Me and one of the sergeants got there at the same time," Walmer says. "We found the guy lying on the ground, moaning. The sergeant examined the wound, and the guy asked him if he was going to die. The sergeant shook his head and said, 'No, you're not going to die. But when you get out of prison, you might want to try for a job with the Vienna Boys Choir.'"

**He came charging through the door, like Jesse James,
waving his sawed-off shotgun.**

281. *Yo Quiero* Jail Time

It was a Friday lunch hour in Milwaukee when a man entered a Taco Bell and took a place in line. It was the lunch rush, so about thirty or forty people had gathered behind the man by the time he finally reached the counter. That's when he pulled a gun and announced, "This is a holdup."

Behind him, he heard metal sliding against leather and voices saying, "No, it's not." He slowly turned, only to face twenty-three weapons drawn, aimed at his head and chest.

It so happens this Taco Bell was located about a block from the Milwaukee Police Academy, where a conference for officers from around the state had just taken a lunch break.

DUMB CRIMINAL QUIZ NO. 626

How well do you know the dumb criminal mind?

A woman in New Orleans was arrested shortly after robbing a small store. Was she caught because . . .

a) She slipped on a dropped fried pie and knocked herself out?

b) While there, she filled out a raffle ticket for a new car?

c) She returned later to buy groceries with the cash?

The correct answer is (b). Doesn't she know that losers never win?

---

282. Two-Bit Thief

Rhode Island police were sure they had the right man when the suspect charged with a string of vending-machine robberies paid his four-hundred-dollar bail entirely in quarters.

283. Dear Dumb Diary

Hendersonville, Tennessee, is a peaceful town on a beautiful lake. In fact, it is unique because of its lakefront shoreline. Hendersonville has the most shoreline of any city in the USA, oceanfront and Great Lakefronts included. It is known for its low crime rate, so when a couple of houses were broken into, the Hendersonville police considered the events a real crime wave. With a little bit of luck and a lot of dumb, the crime wave came crashing down.

Sergeant Joe Calybon captured a young man in the act of leaving a home he had just broken into. He was carrying stolen property and his prints were all over the house in question, but nothing connected him to the other break-ins in the area. The police had nothing further to charge the young man with—until they searched his car.

There on the front seat of the young man's car was a diary. Sergeant Calybon opened the diary to May 12 and he couldn't believe his eyes. There in the diary, in the young man's own handwriting, was the following entry:

> *Dear Diary,*
> *Tonight at 3:35 A.M., I knocked over the house at 311 Elm Street and got away with a TV and a stereo! I wore gloves so there won't be any prints and no clues for the stupid cops to find. Ha ha!*

Sergeant Calybon found the book so riveting, he just couldn't put it down. In fact, that night he solved thirty crimes just by reading the entry for the day of every reported break-in. The "steal and tell" diary that the criminal had penned got him five to ten in the pen but, unfortunately, no book deal.

284. ...Now Weaving on Runway 31

Here's a classic example of what happens when an understanding cop meets an honest drunk driver.

In the military as a law enforcement officer for the air force at Norton Air Force Base in California, Rex Brocki was on duty one night when he spotted a civilian car driving on the base. It didn't take Sherlock Holmes to realize the male driver was quite intoxicated. Why else would someone be driving his car at night down the runway, where C-141 cargo planes landed?

Behind the weaving suspect's car, the officer called in the tag number for "wants and warrants." That done, Officer Brocki "lit him up" with his blue lights. The man drifted toward the right side of the runway, then slowly weaved back left to the yellow line. He weaved all the way to the right again, then drifted back to the yellow line, and weaved over to the right once more. Finally, he just stopped dead on the runway.

Brocki exited his vehicle and approached the discombobulated driver, who had already exited his car. Having heard it all before, the officer wondered what lame excuse the driver was about to lay on him. Before the officer could speak, however, the bewildered drunk raised his palms and slurred in earnest, "Officer, I saw your lights, I wanted to pull over. I just couldn't find the curb!"

The veteran officer, who had heard it all, found the man's honesty quite refreshing. So instead of a ride to jail, the man was given a safe ride home.

It's "plane" to see that honesty is the best policy.

285. The United Nations of Crime

(Canada)

Philip J. Cyr works as a security officer at an amusement park in Toronto. He recalls with a few chuckles the day a man with an East Indian accent tried to gain admission to the park using another man's season's pass. The photo on the pass bore no resemblance at all to the man who was presenting it, so Cyr asked him if the pass really did belong to him. The man responded in French that he spoke no English, only French.

That posed no problem for Cyr, who is bilingual in French and English. Cyr repeated his question in impeccable French. The visitor looked at Cyr, stunned. Then, his bluff called, he managed a laugh. "Did I say French?" he said, now speaking Spanish. "I meant Spanish. I only speak Spanish."

Go figure.

Okay, so here's a man who said, in French, that he spoke only French and then said, in Spanish, that he spoke only Spanish. The look on his face quickly changed from humor to horror when Cyr asked him the same question for a third time, this time in Spanish. It seems that Cyr had also taken two years of high school Spanish.

Now the guy was so angry with Cyr that he began to curse—in English. Cyr told the poor guy that he was being too hard on himself.

"Your English is quite good, really."

The look the frustrated visitor gave him would have communicated clearly in *any* language.

286. Watch That First Step

Working security at the Carter Center in Atlanta, Georgia, is a lot like working any other security job, except for having an ex-president of the United States as your boss. Protective Operations Director Jeff Dingle is used to handling the routine problems common to any big city operation. Every now and then, however, something truly unusual will happen. Like the case of the missing rosebushes.

The rose garden at the Carter Center is pleasing to the eye, but the plants are not inexpensive. So Jeff was understandably concerned when a groundskeeper told him that five of the plants had been stolen the previous night. The next day, five more disappeared, and five more the day after that. Because the thefts were obviously occurring after normal business hours, Dingle decided to set up surveillance on the rose garden in hopes of catching the thief.

Well aware that stakeouts can be mind numbingly boring, Jeff was mentally prepared for hours of tedious monotony. For the early hours he decided he could get a good view of the garden by simply sitting on a nearby bench like any other tourist. The center closes at five o'clock in the afternoon, and by that time Dingle was on his bench hoping against hope that the rosebush thief might put in an early appearance.

He didn't have to wait long. At two minutes after five, one of the local crackheads, carrying a small shovel, came around the corner and headed straight for the roses. Within a few minutes he had dug up three plants while the protective operations director watched in amazement.

Realizing he needed to take action, Dingle walked over to the man, identified himself, and asked him what he was doing. The guy threw down the shovel, assured Dingle he wasn't doing a thing, and then turned and ran. Dingle pursued him while calling for assistance on his radio.

Now picture a building built into the side of a hill, with a back roofline only two feet off the ground. The suspect jumped up onto this low-slung roof and headed for the other side with Dingle still in pursuit. Unfortunately for this dumb rose thief, the other end of the roof is twenty-eight feet off the ground, a fact he discovered only when he reached it. He skidded to a stop and looked back to see several security people closing in.

Frantically looking around for an escape route, the thief looked to one side and saw a grassy area leading down to a small lake. Convinced that freedom lay in that direction, he did the dumbest possible thing. He jumped.

Big mistake. The grassy area and lake were some distance away. And directly below the point where he jumped was a concrete sidewalk, which is what the rose thief hit, breaking both legs.

The ensuing excitement, with police cars and an ambulance and lots of uniforms, attracted quite a crowd. As the unfortunate suspect was being loaded into the ambulance, one of the late arrivals asked what the guy had done. Told that the man had stolen a rosebush, he shook his head in amazement.

"I always heard they was tough in Atlanta," he said. "But I didn't know they was that tough!"

Within a few minutes he had dug up three plants while the protective operations director watched in amazement.

287. Dogged Determination

Sgt. Doug Baldwin of Pensacola's (Florida) finest was working narcotics one hot summer day when he observed a man in a blue Camaro making a drug buy. While other officers closed in on the dealer, Baldwin chased the customer. The customer, unable to lose the officer in his Camaro, jumped from his car and scampered away on foot with Baldwin in pursuit.

Baldwin watched as the man scaled a tall chain-link fence and crept under a car parked within the fenced compound. He kept on watching as the man, shirtless in the heat, began to squirm and fidget under the car. *Ants,* Baldwin said to himself. *Might as well let him lie there a minute.*

Baldwin then heard the sound he had been waiting for—the low, menacing growl of two Dobermans. The fugitive hadn't noticed—even though he used it for a foothold—the large red sign on the fence: Guard Dogs on Duty.

288. Taxi Cabin

Patrol Commander Steve Bowers of the sheriff's department in Boise, Idaho, had the pleasure of arresting this dumb guy shortly after it appeared he'd gotten away.

It was early on a Saturday evening when the police station received a call. A woman living in a remote area had been robbed by her old boyfriend. He'd broken into her mountain cabin home, then robbed and threatened her. Commander Bowers responded to the call.

When Bowers arrived at the scene, the woman verified the facts and gave him the man's name and address. She told him the ex-boyfriend had left on foot not more than twenty minutes earlier.

Bowers called for assistance. With the help of two officers, Bowers began a sweep of the area. When an hour's search turned up nothing, Bowers decided, for the safety of all concerned, to call off the manhunt for the night. The mountain terrain was rugged and darkness was setting in.

As the law officers discussed resuming the search the next day, a call came in from dispatch.

"Is the person you're looking for named Zeke Kane?" the dispatcher inquired.

"Yes, it is," Bowers responded.

"Well, I just received a call from the dispatcher of a taxi service, who said that a 'Zeke Kane' had just called for a cab at the J&L Tavern, and he had told them to make it fast because 'the cops are after me!' "

Officer Bowers smiled. "Tell them to cancel the taxi. I'll be picking up Mr. Kane at the J&L myself."

With another officer along as support, Bowers went to the location and found the suspect hiding in the bushes, waiting for his taxi. He was charged with the crime, no charge for the ride.

289. Bloodhound Blues

During the two years that Dan Leger worked undercover down South as a narcotics officer, he had more than his share of dumb criminal encounters. And he was constantly amazed at the "cop folklore" circulated among criminals—the widespread misinformation about the law and police procedure. He tells this story about his all-time favorite dope:

"I was working undercover narcotics, deep cover. I looked like the nastiest of the nasties. I infiltrated the independent bikers and tapped into some large distribution systems. Over the course of a few months I made several buys from a fairly large supplier. We got to be pretty good acquaintances."

One night Leger and the dealer were sitting around talking, and the dealer got going on the subject of how undercover cops work. Leger could hardly keep a straight face as he listened to the man's ignorance.

"I can always spot a cop," he bragged, "the way their eyes move around a room and the questions they ask."

Then he went on to relate an old hippie myth that originated in Berkeley or someplace similar. The gist of it was that years ago a city council somewhere decreed that undercover officers had to identify themselves as police officers if they were asked a direct question three times.

"Sort of defeats the purpose of going undercover, you know?" Leger laughs. "Now, if that were the law everywhere, you wouldn't have any undercover officers, because they would all be dead now. But this guy has heard this story, and he lets me in on the secret: 'This is the trick the cops don't want you to know. If you ask an undercover cop three times if they're a cop and they don't tell you, then it's entrapment, and the case gets thrown out.'

"It's really hard to look impressed when inside you're laughing your ass off, but I nod my head like I'm committing his every word to memory.

"Then he did it. He really pissed me off. He said, 'I can smell a cop a mile away.' I was sitting about two feet away from him at the time."

Leger had to bite his tongue to keep from saying something right then, but he knew he'd have the last laugh in the near future. And sure enough, about three weeks later he took that dealer down with a rock-solid case.

"I relished the moment," Leger remembers. "I whipped out my badge and got right up in his face and said, 'Guess what? I'm the Man, and you are under arrest.' His face got as pale as a cadaver, and then I just couldn't resist rubbing it in.

"I was an inch from his nose.

"How do I smell from here?"

290. Adios, Amigos

(Mexico)

In a small town outside of Mexico City, three would-be bank robbers devised a master plan. One of the men had gathered some information about the inner workings of the bank; he even had a floor plan with an underground map of the area. The plan was to burrow beneath the street, tunnel under the bank, and, with cutting tools, torches, sledge hammers, and picks, break into the bank vault from the tunnel below. It *seemed* like a pretty good plan.

After working several nights, they finally reached the underground flooring of what they believed to be the bank. With victory close at hand, they began drilling, hammering, and cutting with an acetylene torch. Things were going faster than they had hoped and it wasn't long before entry through the floor seemed certain. But there was about to be a problem.

Unbeknownst to our three amigos, their map had been reversed. Either they drew it up backward or they had held it upside down, for just as the torch was cutting through the last of the flooring, they heard sizzling and smelled smoke. The torch had ignited the first of thousands of cases of fireworks stored in a warehouse. The inevitable explosion leveled the building and damaged several others in the area. The bank on the opposite corner suffered only minor damage.

The robbers survived and were captured, tried, and convicted. Maybe they would have been better off with a compass.

The torch had ignited the first of thousands of cases of fireworks stored in a warehouse.

291. A One-Shot Deal

This is the story of a would-be robber who had one shot at robbing a bar . . . and he took it.

When Bobby D. Landis entered Clark Ross's tavern outside of Chicago, Illinois, he meant business. The 4-10 shotgun he carried was loaded and he was about to prove it. "Everybody down!" he shouted as he fired a blast into the ceiling. "This a robbery!" The place grew instantly silent. No one moved. "I said everybody get on the ground!" Only hard stares. Bobby didn't get it. If someone walked into his bar and fired a shotgun into the roof, he'd get down. What was the matter with these people?

It wasn't so much what was wrong with the people, it was more of what was wrong with Bobby D. Landis. Of all the taverns he could have picked to hold up, Ross's was probably the worst choice. The clientele that frequented this establishment was a hearty lot. All were members of a club—a hunters' club. It's a federal offense to carry a loaded weapon into a tavern, so naturally none of the men were armed. But they knew their weapons. And they knew something else. The 4-10 shotgun Landis was carrying was a break-down single shot. Meaning it held only one shell. The first blast that he fired was also his last.

Bobby D. *came to* in the ambulance. "Is it half-time yet?" he slowly moaned to the medic.

"No . . . the game is pretty much over," the medic replied dryly. "You lost."

Indeed he had lost. Three teeth, hearing in one ear, and his freedom. He was convicted of attempted armed robbery and sentenced to two years in the state prison.

292. A Buddy Story about Mac and Pepe

Mac was a professional break-in artist who specialized in suburban residences such as, say, Dermont Hill, Illinois. He was a fastidiously neat and nonviolent person, who happened to prefer taking other people's belongings to actually working and earning money himself.

This was to be his most memorable job. The house was clear. No one was at home. Mac entered without the slightest delay through a partially locked sliding glass door. Then he met Pepe, a Chihuahua weighing in at about nine pounds. Pepe was a fairly laid-back pooch, so it only took Mac a minute or two to make friends and go about his business.

The consummate professional, Mac checked the family calendar in the kitchen. Much to Mac's delight, the family was on vacation for four days!

Mac and Pepe lived it up, enjoying the hot tub with iced drinks, bathing, and watching television. Heck, Mac even ordered pizza and forged a family check. On the morning of the third day, Mac was showering and heard something. Dripping wet, he stepped out into the hallway. That's when Mac dropped the soap. At that moment, Pepe began barking loudly and startled Mac. Mac slipped on the soap and down the hardwood hallway floor he slid until he stopped abruptly, his head wedged between two posts on the railing of the stairway.

Mac squirmed and pushed, but to no avail. There he was, naked, damp, and very stuck. Of course, Pepe couldn't resist tormenting his new captive in creative and unsanitary ways. For almost forty-eight hours, Mac took Pepe's abuse until the family returned. They stopped laughing long enough to call the police.

293. The No-Tell Motel Telltale Tale

(Australia)

A young man entered the lobby of a motel in Brisbane. He seemed nervous and ill-at-ease, until he saw the clerk behind the counter. She was a fetching young woman. When she smiled, he melted.

"May I help you, sir?" Her voice was even lovelier than her deep blue eyes, in which he was obviously lost.

"Sir?"

"Oh, uh, yes. How much are your rooms?"

She politely gave him a rate card and explained what was available for the evening.

"Oh, no. I have a friend coming in about a week. It's for him. Would you go out with me?" He had forgotten why he had come to the motel in the first place. She declined his sudden offer but, undeterred, he wrote down his name and number and told her to call if she changed her mind.

About a week later the same lovely young woman was on duty when a man in a ski mask burst into the lobby and demanded all the money in a deep, gruff voice. She frantically gathered up all the money and shoved it across the counter.

The bad guy was staring at her as he took the money. In a much higher, much more pleasant voice, he said "Thank you," and ran out. The voice seemed familiar. It reminded the clerk of the would-be suitor who had come by the week before, so she gave the police the name and phone number she had been given.

The police went to check him out. There he was, with all the money and a piece of paper on which he had written down the clerk's name and the motel's phone number. Case closed.

294. A Red-Hot Robbery

In St. Louis, Missouri, two men entered a convenience store with the intention of robbing it. They made their intention known to the clerk—but they had no weapons. The clerk told them that if they didn't leave the store he would call the police.

Frightened that their robbery wasn't working out like the ones on television, the two crooks made a run for it. But one of the robber wannabes decided he was going to steal *something*—so he grabbed a hot dog off the rotisserie and quickly shoved the whole thing in his mouth.

A few steps outside the convenience store, the hot-dog thief collapsed—he was choking on the frankfurter. Faced with this beautiful case of poetic justice—it takes a weenie to stop a weenie—the other man did the only honorable thing a dumb criminal can do. He ran like hell, leaving his partner gasping in the parking lot.

He grabbed a hot dog off the rotisserie and quickly
shoved the whole thing in his mouth.

295. O, Please

Las Vegas, Nevada, policeman Sam Hilliard and his partner were on routine red-eye patrol at about three o'clock one morning when they were flagged down by a concerned citizen about a disturbance that was keeping him—and the whole neighborhood—awake. It seems that farther down the street there was a strange man throwing rocks at the neighborhood church and cursing loudly.

After hearing the concerned citizen's story, the officer who was driving stepped on the gas and headed to the church, where he and his partner found a man fitting the citizen's description of the suspect. The officers pulled up alongside the man and asked, "Were you the one throwing rocks at the church?"

"Yes, I was. So what?"

"So why were you doing that?"

"I'm mad at the church!"

"Why are you mad at the church?"

The man launched into a brief explanation having something to do with the church not having a picture of Jesus Christ dying on the cross. And that apparently had made the man angry enough to cast stones.

By this time, the officers had managed to get a good whiff of the rock thrower. It was clear he had been drinking—a lot. The officers weren't about to get into a religious discussion with a drunk, but they felt compelled to exit their cruiser and investigate more closely. After all, this was a public place, and there had been a disturbance.

"We began patting the man down," one of the cops remembers. "Reaching into a large inside jacket pocket, we pulled out this big letter *O*. Of course, we asked him what it was."

"That's my *O*," he replied.

"Your *O*?"

"Yeah, that's my souvenir from the church."

The two officers looked up at the front of the church. Sure enough, the word *Catholic* in the church's main sign was missing its *O*. Told that the *O* rightfully belonged to the church, the man reluctantly consented to giving it back to the officers. They thanked him and told him to be on his way, but not to do any driving.

"After the man left, we returned the big *O* to its place and were in the process of writing the resident priest a note explaining what had happened when this car comes slowly rolling up."

Guess who!

The officers didn't know what to expect. Maybe the guy now had a gun on him. Maybe he had revenge on his mind. No matter. The two officers quickly drew their weapons and ordered the man to stop the car and get out.

"I want my *O*!" the man ranted and raved. "Give me my *O*! It's my *O*!"

It eventually dawned on the officers that the man wasn't armed. But he was still drunk. So they had little resistance when it came to making the arrest.

"Enough was enough," our Vegas friends told *America's Dumbest Criminals*. "We tried to give him a break the first time, figuring that his anger was between him and God. But when he became a drunk driver, that was between him and us.

"And, *'O'* yeah, we arrested him for D.U.I."

296. The Dumb Criminal Foreign Exchange Service

(Canada)

Dumb crime is like American Express for some folks: They never leave home without it. That was certainly true for two American lads who went north to see the beautiful scenery of British Columbia, Canada.

The Canadian viewing audience met two down-on-their-luck Yanks on the evening news, when the local television station interviewed them live. They related a sad tale of being robbed—more than eight hundred dollars in American money, and about one hundred bucks Canadian. They had been beaten, they said, when they tried to resist their attacker, and they sported very real bruises and black eyes to show for it. Before the next commercial had aired, hundreds of dollars in donations poured in from big-hearted Canadians with pity on two poor tourists from Minnesota.

Then came a live call from a man who claimed to be the "brute" who had beaten up Beavis and Butthead. His version was a little different. According to our caller, he purchased from the pair some drugs that turned out to be bogus. When he confronted them to demand his money back, they tried to knock him down and flee. That's when the scuffle ensued. Now the news anchor returns live to the remote crew, still with the numb-nuts. They, of course, deny the "crazy story concocted by the caller."

Within an hour, the Royal Canadian Mounted Police had linked the men to two break-ins and one robbery through their fingerprints and stolen items on their persons. They both had arrest records for arson, robbery, and petty theft. No matter, they continued to act the part of the Indignant Americans Abroad, complaining all the way to the border and their trial in Minnesota.

Stubborn stooges, eh?

297. Go Ahead, You Can Cry for Me, Argentina

(Argentina)

The teller at a major Argentina bank had been robbed on two occasions in her thirteen years there.

All sorts of things fly through the mind at moments like that. Your life flashes before your eyes. Thoughts of loved ones, unfinished business, even your own funeral are not unusual in a victim's account of a crime. But this robbery was different.

Theresa was once again being held at gunpoint, but she was not afraid. The only thing that she could think, the one thought that filled her mind was *This is my boss!*

Maybe it was the suit the robber wore, just like the one that Mr. Rodriguez had worn to work that morning. Perhaps it was the fact that the robber had called Theresa by her first name yet she wore a nametag that read "Mrs. Garcia." Or maybe, just maybe, it was the fact that the robber stuttered when he demanded the money, just like Mr. Rodriguez always did when he got nervous or stressed out. And true, Mr. Rodriguez had been acting very strangely when he left for lunch just ten minutes earlier.

Theresa did not have to speak or confront her boss though. The security guard Mr. Rodriguez himself had hired brought him down with a thud.

It seems Mr. Rodriguez was embezzling and, in his desperation, he thought he could make a withdrawal at lunch and a deposit in the afternoon at his own bank branch!

298. The Long Windshield of the Law

Veteran officer Johnny Cooley of Birmingham, Alabama, had been patrolling the same stretch of interstate highway for twenty-four years. He had seen it all on this one small portion of superslab. As with a lot of the officers we've interviewed, though, no stories sprang immediately to his mind. So we took a little ride with him.

As he drove us down the otherwise unremarkable stretch of highway, memories and stories started flooding back with each mile marker we passed. When we passed the one marked "38," he suddenly started to laugh . . . and we mean belly laughs, the kind that bring tears to your eyes. This is the story he told of the bust at mile marker 38.

The officer was actually off duty and was just headed home in the right-hand lane of a four-lane highway. His radar gun was off, he was off the clock, and as far as he was concerned he was just another guy driving home from work. He was, however, the only guy on the highway driving a police cruiser home.

Out of the corner of his eye, he noticed a car swerving erratically and then speeding up in the left lane. The officer watched as the car kept accelerating, veering in and out of lanes, narrowly missing several cars. The four men in the car, obviously, had either done something wrong or they were intoxicated . . . or both. So the officer called in the incident on his radio and fell in behind the speeding car with his lights lit and the siren screaming.

The guys in the car sped up. They shot in between cars, veered out onto the shoulder, and darted back up onto the road, trying to lose the trailing cop. Eventually, the officer noticed that the two men in the back-seat were tossing something out the windows. An object hit the police

An object hit the police cruiser's windshield as
other items flew past the squad car.

cruiser's windshield as other items flew past the squad car. Then, suddenly, the fleeing car pulled over, right by mile marker 38.

The officer cautiously approached the car and asked the occupants to step out. The four men complied willingly, coyly acting as though they had no idea why the officer had stopped them.

"What was that stuff you guys were throwing out the window?"

The officer knew it had to be drugs, but there were no drugs in the car, and none of the men had drugs on his person.

"Aw, that was just a cigarette pack," one lousy liar said while grinning really big. "I'm sorry. I guess you got me for littering." The other passengers laughed.

As his backup arrived, the officer took the four men's licenses back to his squad car to run a check for prior arrests or any outstanding warrants. That's when he noticed the object lodged on the windshield wiper of his squad car. Reaching over, he plucked off an overstuffed bag of marijuana.

The dopers had scored a direct hit, but it was the officer who hit the jackpot. He had collared four of the biggest dealers in the city. No one was laughing now—except for the officer, of course.

299. Nice Shootin'

Here's an interesting little police tidbit that we discovered in our research.

In 1922, Detective Sergeant Fred Tabscot of the Chicago Police Department was involved in a freak shooting incident. Detective Tabscot fired his weapon at an armed convict who was shooting at his partner. Tabscot's first round went directly into the barrel of the shooter's gun causing it to jam, thus saving his partner, and possibly himself.

Not exactly a barrel of fun for the convict.

300. Originality Counts

According to Charlotte, North Carolina, patrolman T. C. Owen, a man trying to explain the presence of his fingerprints at several different crime scenes insisted that "someone has been going around town, using my fingerprints."

DUMB CRIMINAL QUIZ NO. 457.2

How well do you know the dumb criminal mind?

A dumb crook tried to rob a gas station, but the attendants didn't cooperate. When neither attendant would hand over the money, did the criminal . . .

a) start crying and run away?

b) challenge the attendants to an arm-wrestling contest for the money?

c) threaten to call the police?

d) hold his breath until he passed out?

If your answer was (c), then you're getting the idea. A would-be bandit in Oklahoma grew so upset that the gas station attendants refused to give him the money that he threatened to call the police. When the attendants still refused, the man made good on his threat. Needless to say, he was half-gassed himself at the time.

301. A Three-Time Loser

Wayne Wilson was working the evening shift for the Peoria, Arizona, Police Department, when he took a call about a robbery in progress at a parked vehicle in a residential neighborhood.

Wilson rolled on it, and he was at the scene in less than two minutes. A young man had been robbed while getting into his car. Luckily, his dad saw the whole thing and called the police. The robber left on foot, headed east.

Moments later, a second squad car pulled up, the suspect in custody. He was fully clothed except for shoes. He was walking in his stocking feet when the officers picked him up. The sock-footed suspect denied any knowledge of the robbery, even though the victim's wallet and watch were in his pants pocket.

One of the backup officers found the thief's getaway car parked two blocks away. In the car were a pair of shoes that fit the thief perfectly. Still, this guy denied any involvement.

Wilson booked him, but within a few hours the suspect made bail and walked out a free man. The very next night, Wilson got a burglary alarm call at a house in that same neighborhood. When he was still a block away, he spotted his shoeless friend from the previous evening walking down the street, stereo in hand. Wilson grabbed him and took him along to the house that had been robbed three doors down the street. Again, the suspect denied any knowledge of a robbery, the whole time clutching a stolen stereo.

The family returned home just as Wilson and the suspect pulled into their driveway. They identified the stereo as theirs, and they pointed out a yellow piece of paper on the garage floor. Wilson picked it up and chuckled as he read aloud the thief's booking report from the evening before. He had dropped it in the house he was robbing.

The court made pretty quick work of the open-and-shut case, and Clueless Shoeless Joe was put away for five to ten. But Wilson advises us that two years later, the same guy was free for all of two days before Wilson arrested him again, this time at the scene of the crime, and, again, with the goods on him and a ready-made denial.

302. Junior Meets the Sandman

Officer Steve Turner of the Metropolitan Nashville Police Department had little trouble apprehending this tired, dumb criminal.

As homeowner Loretta Davin placed the last suitcase in the trunk of her car, she had no idea she was being watched. Twenty-six-year-old Fred "Junior" Williams, a small-time house burglar with a keen eye for opportunity, had been observing Davin for twenty minutes or so. Junior knew she was about to leave, and from the amount of luggage she was taking, he knew she would probably be gone for at least a couple days. Junior smiled as the car pulled out of the driveway, turned the corner at the end of the street, and disappeared.

Breaking in through a side door unnoticed was easy for our burglar. That's what he did for a living. And with the homeowner safely out of the way, this promised to be a stress-free operation.

Ah, life is good, thought Junior as he shook a pillow from its case. He then began a leisurely stroll through the house, filling his pillowcase with whatever he decided to take. There was some jewelry, some cash hidden under the mattress, the VCR—yes, life was good. This job was a piece of cake.

Hmmm . . . piece of cake. That sounded pretty good to Junior. He hadn't had lunch, and by now he had worked up quite an appetite rifling through the house. He decided to see what the kitchen had to offer.

Well, all right! The lady of the house hadn't bothered to clean out the fridge before she left. Junior found some nice chicken salad and a loaf of bread, a few carrot sticks, some potato chips, and some chocolate milk. *Hey, may as well put it on a tray, kick back, and catch a little TV.*

So that's just what Junior did. He carried the tray to the nightstand next to the bed, climbed in, clicked on the tube, and ate his lunch. But after all that hard work and that good meal, the bed was just too comfortable. The sandman came a-callin' on Junior, and soon he was out like a light.

Meanwhile, Loretta Davin had arrived at her office and learned that her business trip had been postponed. After being gone only three hours instead of three days, she returned home to find her side door broken open. Gripped with fear, she phoned the police from her car phone.

Turner was one of the first officers to arrive on the scene. Here's how he described it:

"As we entered the home, it was obvious that a burglary had occurred. Drawers were pulled out, closet doors stood wide open, and the place looked as if it had been ransacked. With weapons drawn, we cleared each room. As we got near the bedroom, I could hear voices, so we approached very cautiously. The television was still on. And there, all sprawled out, lay Junior, sleeping like he was in his own bed. The tray was there on the nightstand with some food still left on it, and the pillowcase of loot was sitting next to it.

"What a picture! We had had dealings with Junior before, so we all knew who he was. So we just kind of quietly encircled the bed and yelled, on cue, 'Junior! Wake up!' He did, and the look on his face was hysterical. We arrested him and took him to jail for breaking and entering, burglary, and sleeping on the job!"

Junior's short nap turned into a long stretch.

303. Ash Kicker

(England)

Howard Rutledge was in shock. He had returned home that morning to his Tudor-style house in Staffordshire to find a fleet of fire trucks and several policemen poking through the charred rubble of what used to be his house. The fire had consumed everything. Fortunately, he had just renewed his homeowner's insurance policy.

As he stared in stunned disbelief, a policeman approached him.

"Morning, sir." the officer said softly. "This must be your house."

"Was my house," Rutledge replied. "I was out of town. Any idea how the fire started?"

"Not at this time, although it appears to have begun in the kitchen. I'll need some information from you, sir. Meanwhile, go ahead if you'd care to look about for a bit."

Rutledge began systematically sifting through the debris. While walking through the still-smoldering ashes, he spotted what he'd been looking for. A smile came to his face. All was not lost. Though thoroughly blackened, the fire-proof valuables box had survived the raging fire. Had the contents? He glanced left and right. With the toe of his shoe he slowly lifted the corner of the box from the ashes. He bent down and took a key from his pocket. Another glance around and he quickly unlocked it. Bingo! The several thousand pounds had survived intact, as well as some personal papers and the eight ounces of pure heroin still in its asbestos sleeves. He was still smiling when he heard the constable clear his throat.

"Ahem."

"Yes?" Rutledge squeaked, slamming the lid shut.

"Forgive the pun, sir, but if that's what I think it is, your ash is mine!"

It was, and it was, and he was sentenced to fifteen years in prison.

The fire-proof valuables box had survived the raging fire.

326

304. This Law Stinks

There are some wacky old laws still on the books and here's one of 'em.

Any person caught stealing citrus fruit in Yuma, Arizona, can still be given the legal punishment for that crime. A dose of castor oil!

305. Even Cowboys Get the Blues

Working undercover narcotics in long hair and a mustache, Officer Chuck Warner of Craig, Colorado, was grabbing a cold drink at a local convenience store one night, when he was approached by a man he described as a "dirty-looking cowboy." He asked Warner which way he was headed; he needed a ride. With some time to kill, Warner agreed to give him a lift.

The man introduced himself as "Cowboy Bob," throwing his gear into the unmarked car. Bob was quite a talker. In no time, he was telling his life story. Then the conversation shifted to the police. Bob began to talk about the local cops and how dumb they all were. He patted his shirt pocket. "Yep," he sighed. "Twenty-seven years of smokin' dope and never busted."

In the middle of another babble, Bob suddenly grew quiet. Several moments of silence passed before Officer Warner looked up. Cowboy Bob's gaze was fixed on the center console. He was staring at the police radio . . . and the handcuffs . . . and the pepper spray. His eyes began drifting slowly around the squad car while his head remained frozen in place. They came to rest on the shotgun.

Cowboy Bob then deftly lifted the corner of the small satchel he'd tossed onto the dashboard as he got in. He'd discovered the blue and red dash light under the bag. His voice cracked, "Chuck, whatcha do for a living?" he stammered.

Officer Warner smiled and said, "Bob, you can't be that dumb."

"Oh, yes, I can," he gulped.

Well Cowboy "Boob" was right. The dope in the shirt (Bob) was taken down to the police station, along with the dope in his pocket. It'll be a while before Cowboy Bob's back in the saddle.

306. Arrest Report Fettucine

(Australia)

A police officer in Sydney had picked up a man on a warrant for several burglaries. After bringing the man back to the station for booking and questioning, she took the suspect into the interrogation room, under video surveillance, to give him the bad news:

"We've got several eyewitnesses who place you at the scene of the crimes and enough evidence to convict you three times over. It's all right here in black and white, so why don't you just confess, and maybe the magistrate will go easy on you."

"No way. I'm innocent, I tell ya."

The suspect was using Dumb Criminal Strategy Number 1: Deny, deny, deny.

There was a knock at the door, and the officer answered it. In the few seconds that her back was turned, the suspect grabbed the arrest report and shoved it into his mouth, chewing voraciously.

When the officer sat back down at the table, she looked for her notes. They weren't on the table. They weren't in her chair. They weren't under the table.

"What have you done with my notes?"

"Muffin." He was trying to say "nothing," but his mother had never taught him not to talk with his mouth full.

The video replay provided a laugh for the entire department. Our dumb criminal didn't realize that cops the world over do all their paperwork at least in triplicate. The evidence he thought he was eating was nothing but a healthy snack—low cholesterol, high fiber, and very high comedy.

307. A Blonde with a Conscience

Officer Wayne Strain out of Springfield, Missouri, remembers being out patrolling one quiet Friday night, when a pizza delivery guy flagged him down. Strain assumed the young man had been robbed, but it wasn't quite that simple.

The pizza guy explained that, on the previous Friday, they had received a call for a delivery to a nearby high-rise apartment building. When the delivery boy knocked at the apartment, he was told in no uncertain terms that no one there had ordered a pizza. Returning to his vehicle, he found three other pizzas missing.

Strain couldn't understand why the kid flagged him down to report a week-old pizza theft, but the kid went on. His pizza joint had just received another order to the same apartment building, from a woman with the same voice. Strain went along with the junior pizza sleuth and staked out his car while he delivered.

Seconds after the delivery guy went into the lobby, a beautiful blonde appeared out of the bushes and jumped into the pizza car. She grabbed a couple of large pizzas and headed around the corner. Strain happened to be behind that very corner. When he confronted the blonde, she dropped the pizzas at Wayne's feet and came clean.

"I didn't steal any pizza last Friday. I swear to God. I didn't steal any pizza last Friday night."

When he confronted the blonde, she dropped the pizzas at Wayne's feet and came clean.

308. Never Go to Court Without It

(Colombia)

The young man faced the judge's bench with head hung low. He had come to Cartagena to face trial for possession of a controlled substance—an ounce of marijuana. Because it was a first offense, however, the judge was lenient and gave him a suspended sentence.

The young man sighed with relief . . . until the judge added that he would serve thirty days in jail just to see what happened to convicted drug users. The young man was led away. Thirty minutes later he was back again to explain the two ounces of cocaine jailers had found taped under his arm. His plan to make a delivery as soon as the judge let him off would now have to be put on indefinite hold.

309. Dog Day Afternoon

That old saying "Don't believe everything you hear" applies nicely to this story.

Pennsylvania police officer Stephen Alcorn responded to a call of two men fighting in a bar one afternoon. After he arrived at the scene, Officer Alcorn spotted the two still pushing and shoving one another in front of the tavern.

Seeing the cop, one of the men took off running across a small field adjacent to the tavern. Officer Alcorn took the access road around the field and positioned his squad car to intercept the fleeing man. The weeds were shoulder high and only the man's bobbing head was visible. The man screeched to a halt fifty feet away and ducked below the top of the overgrowth.

"Hey!" Alcorn yelled to him, "you're not goin' to get away, so why don't you just come on out?"

"Forget you!" the man yelled back.

Officer Alcorn shook his head as he reached inside his pocket and pulled out his keys. He began to shake them vigorously. "C'mon, boy!" he said. "Let's get him!"

The man's head quickly popped up over the weeds.

"If you don't come out right now, buddy, I'm sending the K-9 unit in," Alcorn said, still rattling the keys.

As another squad car pulled up next to Officer Alcorn's, the man saw the futility of his situation. "All right! All right!" he shouted back. "I'm comin' out. Just keep that dog away from me."

The man walked out of the field and Officer Alcorn placed him under arrest without incident. In the police car, he turned to the cop and said, "Hey, where's that dog?"

Doggone, that was a great idea.

310. Nothing to Fear but Fear Itself

It was about ten at night when Deputy Sheriff Bill Cromie of Oswego County, New York, was dispatched to a traffic accident in the small town of Constantia, New York. Arriving on the scene, he found that a car had crashed into some gasoline pumps and that the intoxicated driver had fled the scene on foot. The rescue squad had foamed the whole area down to prevent a fire, and things seemed to be under control.

Cromie asked if anyone had any idea which direction the missing driver had run. One of the firefighters pointed toward a ravine next to the road. "He ran down there," he said. "He's been crashing around in the woods for the last hour. You can still hear him."

Sure enough, the sounds of something large and clumsy barreling through the foliage, could be plainly heard. The ravine was pitch dark, and Cromie proceeded cautiously down the steep slope, heading toward the sound of snapping branches. As he got closer he could also hear heavy breathing.

He turned on his flashlight. There, illuminated by the beam, was one pitiful human being. Filthy, scraped and scratched, his clothing in tatters and utterly exhausted, the still-drunk driver blinked in the glare.

"Sheriff's Department," Cromie announced. "Are you the driver of that car back there?"

The man slid to the ground, panting heavily, and raised his trembling hands. "I give up," he said. "I was driving, and I thought I could get away through the woods." He shook his head wearily. "You must be Superman."

Cromie asked him what he meant. "Man, you been chasing me for forty-five minutes, and you aren't even winded. Hell, you ain't even messed up the crease in your pants. How did you do it?"

Cromie laughed and told the man that he had only just arrived on the scene and that no one had been chasing him. The drunk let this information sink in for a few minutes, then looked up. "You mean I been chasing myself?"

"I'm afraid so."

The guy struggled to his feet. "Well, if I'm that damn stupid, you might as well put me in jail." Cromie was happy to oblige.

311. How to Collar a Crook from Your Recliner

You'd think that in Hawaii, lovebirds would coo blissfully all day. But as officer Ron Parker of Wailuku can tell you, there is sometimes trouble in paradise.

One night Officer Parker and his partner responded to a domestic violence call in their sector. As they drove to the residence, they passed a man dressed only in shorts and carrying a large duffel bag.

Moments later, the man's wife described him to the officers, right down to his shorts. Parker left his partner to take the woman's statement and then went to pick up the fleeing hubby. Five blocks away, Parker pulled over behind him, popped on his lights, and gave a little bleep from his siren.

The guy ran for it. Well, he began trotting at least. Parker patiently pursued the slow-jogging perpetrator by holding steady at seven miles an hour. After about two miles of fairly serious roadwork, the sweaty hubby collapsed under the weight of his duffel bag and crumpled to the pavement, huffing and puffing. Parker pulled alongside, rolled down the window and asked politely, "Would you like to get in the back?"

The man gathered his belongings and stepped into the squad car. Parker had just executed a chase and capture without even leaving his squad car. Book 'em, Dano!

As they drove to the residence, they passed a man dressed
only in shorts and carrying a large duffel bag.

312. Luck of the Draw

With Oregon State Lottery ticket in hand, Alice Krumm stood staring at the winning numbers posted on the cash register. So close . . . but not quite. The ticket she had just bought was only one digit away from the twenty-dollar winning number. For once in her life, Alice wanted to be a winner instead of a near-miss.

Alice struggled with her greed for a long minute before finally giving in. Creeping around behind the baked beans and canned goods, she altered her lottery ticket with a ballpoint pen to win the twenty dollars, then returned to the counter to collect her ill-gotten prize.

But she should have worked a little harder on her forgery. The clerk spotted it immediately and called the police. The dishonest lottery player was arrested on the spot and charged with fraud.

Then the arresting officer made an interesting discovery. He found the real number under her bad forgery. His revelation made her feel even dumber.

Had she looked farther up the chart of winning numbers, she would have discovered that her original ticket number had also been a winner— for five thousand dollars!

313. The Civic-Minded Cocaine Cooker

It was October 1993 in a Georgia town when Tyrell Church was in the kitchen cooking up his specialty . . . cocaine. He had been doing that for a good thirty years, but he had never seen any that cooked up like this batch. Something was wrong.

"I had never seen powder cocaine that turned red when you cooked it up," Church explained. So, being concerned for his own welfare as well as that of the public at large, Tyrell Church did what any fool would do. He took the suspicious concoction to the Georgia Bureau of Investigation crime lab for analysis.

The lab ran four separate tests. The substance proved to be cocaine after all. And Church was promptly arrested and charged with possession of the same. He opted to serve as his own lawyer in what to him seemed a ridiculous trial.

"Had I known I was going to be arrested," he argued, "I wouldn't have taken it over to the lab."

So why did Church take his cocaine to the lab?

"If kids get hold of something like this," he said, "it might hurt them or poison them. I took it over there to have it tested to see if it had been cut or mixed with any dangerous substances."

The civic-minded cooker went on to say that if something had been wrong with the cocaine, he could have warned the public.

Church insisted that he had often had his cocaine tested in New York, where he once lived.

"What's the sense in having a crime lab," he asked, bewildered, "if a person can't take anything over there?"

He also requested that the substance be retested, a request which the judge denied.

"I'm not a habitual user," the cooker complained in his final statement. "I use cocaine for my arthritis. It's a waste of the taxpayers' time for this kind of case to come to court. The grand jury shouldn't have even bothered."

"I do not think a violation of the cocaine law is a waste of time," the district attorney countered.

The jury couldn't have agreed more. It took just seven minutes for them to return a guilty verdict.

314. "My Life Is Over"

Officer Gordon Martines of the Las Vegas (Nevada) Police Department was running radar one afternoon when he clocked a car at fifty miles per hour in a thirty-five zone. After Martines pulled the car over, the driver got out and walked back to the officer waving his hands in frustration. "My life is over!" the man sighed.

Martines responded, "Well, you were only doing fifteen over the limit. I wouldn't consider that life threatening at this time. May I see your driver's license, please?"

"It's been suspended," the man said.

"Then may I see your vehicle registration?"

"The car is stolen."

"All right, then. Do the license plates belong to the car?"

"The tags are stolen."

"Well, let me see if I've got this straight," Martines said, writing the ticket. "You're speeding on a revoked driver's license, the car is stolen, the tags are stolen, and you have no registration or insurance. I'm going to have to agree with you. Your life *is* over."

315. The Big-Bag Theory

(Thailand)

Ang Lieu Khang was a busboy at Bangkok's Garden of Ecstasy restaurant which catered to the wealthiest clientele. On a good night, the manager might deposit the equivalent of ten thousand dollars in the night depository of the bank only two blocks away. At closing, the manager would transfer the money in a plain brown paper bag. Khang had watched the manager leave many times, and each time he thought to himself how easy it would be to rob his boss.

One night the chef was in a particularly foul mood and he took it all out on Khang. This was nothing new, but this night he humiliated the young man in front of his coworkers. Something inside Khang snapped. He finished his shift without a word, and the next night he was waiting in the shadows of the alley for his revenge.

Like clockwork, the manager carried his brown paper bag full of the night's revenues out the back door of the restaurant, only to suddenly spin around to start yelling at the cook, who screamed right back at him from the kitchen.

Khang saw his moment and shot out of the shadows. In the cover of darkness, he snatched the bag out of the air and was gone in a split second. The manager never heard him or saw him. The grab was perfectly executed and so was Khang's getaway.

Twelve blocks away in another alley, Khang stopped to catch his breath and count the take. He panted as he opened the brown paper sack. Then he fainted dead away: no money, all fish heads. The manager had actually been doing Khang's job for him, taking out the garbage.

The grab was perfectly executed and so was Khang's getaway.

316. It's in the Bag

Retired Tennessee State Trooper Paul Cook shared this story with us about a guy who did more drinkin' than thinkin'.

While driving in Williamson County, Trooper Cook watched as the new Mercedes in front of him crossed the yellow line *again* then gently drifted toward the shoulder. Twice was enough for the experienced officer. He could read the signs of a driver who'd probably had too much to drink. He turned on his lights and siren and pulled the car over.

Cook could smell alcohol the moment the driver rolled down the window. "May I see your driver's license and proof of insurance please?" Cook asked the plastered driver. The numb man sat behind the wheel blinking like he'd just been teleported from another planet. "Sir, may I see your license and proof of insurance?" Cook repeated. The man shook his head to clear it. It was slowly dawning on him what was taking place.

"Yeah . . . I uh . . . we didn't . . . I mean okay, sure . . . my license is in my bag here," he mumbled.

"Will you take it out of the bag for me please, sir?" the trooper asked. While the driver fumbled with the zipper, the trooper asked him how much he'd had to drink that night.

"I didn't count 'em," the man slurred, "but it was a bunch! Hey, can you help me here? I can't seem to get this thing open?" Trooper Cook unzipped the small black shaving kit and peered inside. A zip-tight plastic bag was all that was there. Cook pulled it out.

"This doesn't look like your driver's license to me," he said. "This looks like a bag of marijuana." The driver sobered up quickly now, but was still blinking.

"Uh oh . . . I think I handed you the wrong bag. Let's start all over and I'll uh . . ." He was cut off in mid-sentence.

"Step out of the car for me sir. I'm placing you under arrest for possession of marijuana and driving under the influence."

"I can't believe I just did that . . . how dumb can you get?"

Dumb enough to get in this book.

317. The Accent Is on You

(Spain)

Back in 1967, on the Spanish island of Allegoro, only one small store sold newspapers—the island weekly and a few other papers that arrived via a boat from the mainland. This scarcity of news was not a problem for most island residents, who weren't that interested in mainland goings-on. But a big, blond Russian who had somehow ended up on Allegoro was very interested in the state of politics in Eastern Europe. The English-language *International Herald Tribune* was the only paper in Allegoro he could read. So every week after his arrival on Allegoro he would trek to the tiny shop for his paper.

It wasn't long before the Russian began to run out of money. There were not many odd jobs on the island, and the Russian's trade (he had been a lumberjack in Russia) was not in demand. He begged the fishermen for work, but he knew nothing about the sea and was prone to seasickness besides. Everyone wondered what he would do.

And then, one balmy afternoon, the island store was robbed. The shopkeeper's young daughter was working there alone when a masked gunman came in and demanded all the money. She gave it over, and the man fled.

It was by far the biggest crime in Allegoro history. It was also the easiest to solve. For not only had the robber demanded the money in the unmistakable Russian accent of a visiting seasick lumberjack; he had also demanded a copy of the *International Herald Tribune*. Not to mention that he was the only Russian on the island, the only Eastern European, the only man at least six feet, five inches tall, and the only blond male.

They found him with all of the money, still reading the paper.

318. Truth and Consequences

Some criminals will go to any length to prove their innocence, even if it proves them guilty.

John Jenkins, an Akron, Ohio, police officer, and his partner made a late-night traffic stop in a known drug area. A search of the vehicle turned up two well-used "crack" pipes, and the driver and his passenger were arrested.

Both men vehemently denied the pipes were theirs. The passenger's pipe was found on the floor board on his side of the car, technically, "within his control."

"I'm tellin' you the truth, man, this is not my pipe!" he insisted.

"Well," Jenkins responded, "it was on your side of the car."

"But I swear to you it's not mine," he argued. With that, he removed his left shoe and pulled a pipe from it. "*This* is my crack pipe!"

319. All's Well That Ends

One rainy night at the state penitentiary in Michigan City, Indiana, three hardened convicts escaped through a dark, muddy field. They had been convicted of everything from armed robbery to murder. Now they were armed and dangerous and had nothing to lose.

They crept up on a dark, still house. The garage door was unlocked, and they walked right into the kitchen. Creeping from bedroom to bedroom, they bound and gagged all four members of the family. One of the criminals rifled through all the jewelry boxes while another found the car keys. The third got the man's wallet for the credit cards. Then they were off.

Back at the prison, a random bed check revealed the convicts' escape. Soon, helicopters, dogs, and numerous state, county, and city units began combing the area. Once the family managed to free themselves and call the authorities, the police had a car description and a tag number.

Within moments a state trooper spotted the stolen family station wagon moving at a high rate of speed on the interstate. He gave chase, and the escapees made a run for it, veering across the grassy median in an attempt to lose the trooper.

"We didn't know whether to turn the dogs loose on him, read him his rights, or just give him a good swift kick."

As the fleeing car bounced up onto the other side of the highway, the driver lost control. The car rolled three times, and the convict in the backseat was thrown clear into the high grass. Unharmed, he lost no time disappearing into a nearby cornfield.

Two miles away at Ollie Hardison's farm, the silent dawn was shattered by the thundering wash of police choppers overhead and the baying of bloodhounds closing in on a scent. Ollie had several hog sheds out behind his barn that were pretty well rusted out and falling down. He thought he had heard something out there just a moment before, but now he couldn't hear anything for all the commotion.

One of the arresting officers, Larry Hawkins (not the Larry Hawkins mentioned earlier in this book), will never forget the scene that followed.

The fleeing convict had cut through the fields off the interstate, running at top speed through corn nine feet high. When he came upon the dilapidated hog sheds, he tried to get into one. It was too small. But when he heard the choppers and dogs, the desperate man dropped to all fours and backed into the stinking hog shed.

Unfortunately for him, as he backed in, he also backed out. It seems the back of the shed was rusted out to form a perfect picture frame for the convict's posterior, which was totally exposed. As the police encircled the shed, the convict's rear was positioned in a most peculiar way for arrest.

"He really thought he was totally hidden. He looked like an ostrich with his head in the sand. He held perfectly still and we just sort of stared at this big rear end sticking out of that shed. We just had to laugh. We didn't know whether to turn the dogs loose on him, read him his rights, or just give him a good swift kick."

Good sense and professionalism prevailed. The officers and Ollie Hardison were the only ones to get a kick out of the situation. And they did—no ifs, ands, or butts.

320. Whose Pants Are They?

Officer Robert Johnson of the Metropolitan Nashville Police Department gave us a story that put a unique spin on the title of our book, and took the inanity to yet another level.

It seems Officer Johnson was answering a fairly routine call from a tavern where the bartender had noticed a man concealing a pistol. While it is a common call to get, it can also be a very dangerous call to answer.

Officer Johnson went into the bar as inconspicuously as possible and immediately approached the bartender. They talked like two old friends meeting for the first time in a long time, while the bartender carefully pointed out the guy with the gun. The officer then went to the restroom and called for backup.

Just as friendly as he could be, Johnson approached the man with his hand outstretched. The man shook hands as the officer introduced himself, then Johnson leaned forward and whispered in the guy's ear, "Can I ask you a few questions outside? I don't want to draw attention to us, okay?" Johnson was so friendly and the request so simple that the guy said, "Sure." Johnson greeted a couple of other patrons and then left.

Outside, the man and his female companion waited by the officer's patrol car. Officer Johnson continued with his "public relations" happy face while he explained the situation to the man.

"Hey, I hate to bother you, but we got a call from someone who thought that you were carrying a pistol. Do you have a gun with you this evening?"

"No, sir. I don't know why anyone would think that." The man was very sincere and seemed shocked at the thought of packing a piece.

"I understand, sir. But I've got to file a report and that requires me to search you. So if you'll just let me pat you down, we'll be done and you can get back to partying. Could you place your hands on the hood of the car and spread your feet? This will just take a minute." Maybe Johnson should have said "a couple of minutes" because this guy was large, maybe 315 pounds, a lot to pat down.

The guy complied with no resistance, and guess what? Officer Johnson felt the unmistakable bulge of a metal firearm in the guy's front pants pocket. He carefully removed it from the guy's pocket and held it up by one finger through the trigger guard.

"Uh, what's this, sir?" The guy looked dumbfounded, aghast.

"Well, it's . . . uh . . . a gun, but I've never seen it before!" So much for "Mr. Nice Guy."

"I just pulled it out of your pocket. It was in your pants, sir." Johnson had played out this scene hundreds of times, so he was well prepared for the inevitable next line.

"But these aren't my pants, officer!" Johnson couldn't help but think, *Here we go again.* Couldn't this guy be a little more creative? What about *Aliens abducted me and dressed me so the gun must be theirs*? Johnson had to give the guy enough rope to go ahead and finish his own hanging, so he asked, "Whose pants are they?"

The guy's eyes grew wide. He was quite literally a deer caught in the headlights of the law. Then he chose to make an even bigger mistake. He implicated his date. "They're her pants!"

Johnson looked at the guy's date. She was about five feet, three inches tall, and must've weighed all of ninety-five pounds. Then he looked back at the suspect. The gun-toting liar was about six feet tall and hefty. The woman was now staring at her feeble-minded date with what appeared to be homicidal intent.

"*Her* pants? She could fit in one leg of those pants. Those couldn't be her pants." Johnson was starting to grin. This was one of the most absurd lies anyone had ever told him. But this guy was not giving up on his story.

"She used to be much larger." The guy had just invited a fate worse than arrest and incarceration. The woman blurted out "What?" just before her fingernails dug into her date's face. Officer Johnson's backup arrived just in time to help him pry the not-so-loving couple apart. At this point, the male suspect was pleading for his own arrest, anything to avoid his date's savage attack.